W9-CDP-179

Hockey, Heroes, and Me

Hockey, Heroes, and Me

Red Fisher

M&S

Canadian Cataloguing in Publication Data

Fisher, Red, 1926-
Red Fisher : hockey, heroes and me

Includes index.
ISBN 0-7710-3147-5

1. Fisher, Red, 1926-   . 2. Montreal Canadiens (Hockey
team).   3. Sports journalism – Canada.   4. Sportswriters – Canada –
Biography.   I. Title.

GV742.42.F5A3 1994   070.4'49796962'092   C94-931518-4

The publishers acknowledge the support of the Canada Council and the
Ontario Arts Council for their publishing program.

Typesetting by M&S, Toronto
Designed by Kong
All interior photographs courtesy the private collection of Red Fisher.

The support of the Government of Ontario through the Ministry of
Culture, Tourism and Recreation is acknowledged.

Printed and bound in Canada

McClelland & Stewart Inc.
The Canadian Publishers
481 University Avenue
Toronto, Ontario
M5G 2E9

1 2 3 4 5   98 97 96 95 94

For Tillie, Cheryl, and Ian.
They know why.

Contents

Foreword

by Ken Dryden

"I wonder what Red thinks."

It would happen two or three times a year. When things were going badly for the team or me. When after a game, sleepless and alone, staring into the darkness of my office, I could find no answers. I did it with no one else. In a few hours, when the *Star* or later the *Gazette* was at our front door, I would know.

I didn't always agree with him, and when I didn't I would get angrier than I did with anyone else. I wanted so much for him to be wrong, and knew he probably wasn't.

Red was the good critic. The voice outside ourselves everyone needs and rarely has. Smart, tough, a voice that has no other agendas. He was (and remains) a star in Montreal. Everyone knew him. He did colour on the radio games (my wife, Lynda, who knows such things, always thought that through the distance and crackle, he was speaking only to her. *Bad night tonight, Lynda. Better be ready!*). Prior to Don Cherry's "Coach's Corner," Red did "The Fisher Report" on *Hockey Night in Canada*. He would outlast all the great stars he wrote about, but he never made himself bigger than his story. He had too much respect for them and for his craft. If he wrote something, he believed it. His readers could count on it, and so could I.

He loved hockey passionately, but he had a life as well. He had seen and done many things, and he brought that life to the stories he wrote. He never treated hockey as life itself, yet it was never *only* a game. It wasn't *only* anything. Since it mattered to people, that should be respected. Since it mattered to him, he would do his job right. At the same time, he didn't treat the great players he wrote about as "gods." They were people of exceptional skill, he knew, but in the final instance, still people. After my best games, to Red I was never quite as good as I seemed to others. After my worst, never quite as bad.

He had also this love to be clever. To be right. Once in reviewing Jack Ludwig's book, *Hockey Night in Moscow*, about the 1972 Summit Series, in a generally very favourable review, he couldn't resist commenting on the book's typos, including one on the dust jacket where the *t* had been left out of Max Bentley's name. "That's Bentley, Frank," Red chortled, unfortunately forgetting that Ludwig's first name was Jack. I thought this was the funniest, most perfect thing I'd ever read and couldn't wait to tell Red so. He was not amused. I'm not sure he is yet. A few frosty weeks followed.

He was as competitive as the players he wrote about. He loved to get "scoops," and would be upset if I had some news – "retiring" in 1973, coming back a year later, retiring for good in 1979 – and didn't tell him first. But he didn't depend on scoops as so much of his competition did. Like the teams he covered, he had a need to be good every day. Spectacular was nice, a bonus. But spectacular without day-to-day solid was flash, and Montreal readers, he knew, had been trained to detect the difference. In the hothouse world of the city's media, where "the competition is killing me" could be and was used to justify writing almost anything, Red kept his soul.

I am often asked what made the Canadiens so good. An ownership which sought profits but whose goal seemed only to win the Stanley Cup certainly helped. So did having the best managers who hired the best scouts to find the best players to be prepared by the best coaches. But supporting all that was something else, what I call a "conspiracy of expectations." In the Forum, on the streets, in the corner *snac* and *épicerie*, in Montreal, hockey *matters*. Long before last night's game has been reported by the morning paper, more eloquently than any coach's words at practice, the message comes to you. In smiles that make life a blessing. Or no smiles. It's why the Canadiens win so often, and the Kings don't.

Red is part of that difference. For nearly forty years, game after game, season after season, he has kept his readers informed. For many of those years, when TV games came only on Saturday nights, he was their eyes and minds. He knows what's good and what isn't and says so. His readers have come to know too. Unwilling to put up with less, together they get the best.

It is fifteen years since I left Montreal, fifteen years since I've read Red's byline regularly. I miss it. And still, after fifteen years, "I wonder what Red thinks." Again, happily, I'll have the chance to find out.

– Toronto, May 1994

Introduction

I've never seen myself as a writer of books. Books were something other people wrote. People like Ken Dryden, for example. *The Game*, published in 1983, is merely the best book I've ever read on hockey. People with lots of patience and time wrote books, but for me, the rhythms and demands of a daily deadline were what mattered.

So why now – after forty years behind first a typewriter, and now a computer keyboard?

Is it because there are stories, memories, anecdotes, and people who deserve a more permanent forum than a newspaper or a magazine can provide? Partly.

Is it ego? Partly.

Obviously, this book didn't suddenly happen. I've thought about it, and then forgot about it. The memories lingered, however.

"When are you writing the book?" friends and acquaintances have asked me now and then over the years. Almost always, the answer would be: "I don't have the time." The reality, though, is that I didn't want to find the time. I was having too much fun – and still do – being involved in the grind of a daily newspaper. Workaholics are funny that way.

A lot of people have been responsible for this book, starting with the hockey players and other athletes I've known and admired over the past four decades – which is as long as it gets in my business. Frankly, I don't know of any reporter who's been on a beat for forty years – first with the *Montreal Star* and then the *Gazette* – particularly one which involves so much travelling. I'm sure there a few out there, but where? And are they having as much fun as I've had?

The Montreal Canadiens and the Stanley Cups I've seen them win have been responsible for a lot of the fun. It's always easier to work and travel with a winner, and being with the team for seventeen of the twenty-four Stanley Cups they've won in their noble history, represents a lot of winning.

The names – many of them in the Hockey Hall of Fame – don't get better than these: Maurice and Henri Richard, Jean Béliveau, and Guy Lafleur. There's Bob Gainey, Ken Dryden, and Doug Harvey. Dickie Moore and Yvan Cournoyer. Was there ever a better Big Three on the ice than Serge Savard, Larry Robinson, and Guy Lapointe – or a trio more fun to be with off it? Glen Sather is a special friend, and so are Doug Risebrough and Tom Johnson. I wonder if enough of them realize how large a part they've played in my life. I hope they do.

Jacques Plante was important to me thirty years ago, just as Patrick Roy is now. But there are so many others who never wore the Canadiens' sweater who have had that same impact. Bobby Orr and Wayne Gretzky, Gordie Howe and Phil Esposito are among them. So are Stan Mikita and Bobby Hull. There are others, too numerous to mention.

Hockey is good for the soul, and most off-ice personnel I have known have been good for hockey. It's true I've had disagreements with some of them some of the time – if only because that's the nature of sportswriting and of fiercely competitive people dedicated to winning. I understood what people such as Toe Blake, Sam Pollock, Frank Selke, Scotty Bowman, and others have tried to do and, I think, they understood my role most of the time. I learned much from all of them, and enjoyed most of them. I still do.

Doug Gibson, the publisher of McClelland and Stewart, is another who's responsible for this book. "It's time you wrote one," he said to me late in 1991.

"My wife agrees with you," I said, "but Ken Dryden and *The Game* spoiled it for the rest of us."

"What do you mean?" he asked. Gibson had edited Dryden's masterwork.

"That book was too good," I said.

"Maybe I should be talking to your wife," Gibson remarked with a grin. "If I can't convince you, maybe she can."

My editor, James Adams, led me through the minefields of his profession. I admit there were times when I felt he should have been assessed a delay-of-game penalty for tossing a few of my chapters over the boards, but he showed me how to get to where I wanted to go.

Another who's responsible for the book is a "faceless" New York Islanders employee who had a question for me early in the 1991-92 season.

"Still hanging around, eh?" he asked.

"I'm not hanging around," was the response. "I'm working at it."

"Oh, sorry about that," he said. He paused, then he added, "Well, then, how long do you plan to hang around?"

"Until," I said, "I get it right."

I

Toe

It was cold, the man on the car radio was saying. Snow was on the way later that December day, he said. Five to ten centimetres, maybe, so bundle up warm.

The snow that had fallen in the Montreal region several days earlier had formed soft, white pillows on the short driveway leading to the nursing home. A white, lined face peered out of a second-floor window, then quickly disappeared.

Inside, Toe Blake sat in a hallway wheelchair, his head on his chest, hands crossed and eyes closed. It was 1991. Almost two years had passed since Blake had been brought to this place, twenty-three since he had retired as coach of the Montreal Canadiens. The top of the exercise suit he wore was as grey as the weather outside. The only small splash of colour on it was the CH. The words "Montreal Canadiens," in red, were below it. The bottoms were blue. He sat there, dozing, locked in the terrible vise that is Alzheimer's yet, remarkably, still looking like the big bear of a man he always was.

"Hi, Toe," said Floyd Curry, who had played for Blake's Canadiens for the first three of an NHL-record five consecutive Stanley Cup-winning seasons in the last half of the 1950s. Hardly a week passed without a visit from Curry, who had become Blake's closest friend over the years. "Look who's here, Toe," said Curry.

Blake's eyes remained closed.

"Don't wake him, Floyd, he needs the rest," a guy said.

Curry tugged at his fedora. "Toe, we've brought you some cookies. Wake up, Toe."

A slim, black man named Andrew placed a hand on Blake's shoulder and shook him gently. "Wake up, Toe," he said. "Let's get you up. You've got visitors, Toe." Then he reached for the man who had been the very best of the NHL's coaches for thirteen uplifting seasons. He shook Blake again . . . gently. This time, Blake's eyes opened. An angry yell burst from his throat.

"That's it, Toe," said Andrew, his voice rising. "Let's get you out of the chair."

Andrew was on one side of Blake, holding and steering him into the bright, spacious dining room filled with empty tables. Curry supported him carefully on the other side. "There you go," said Andrew, easing Toe into a chair. "There, isn't that good? Look what we have for you," he said, lifting a cookie toward Blake's mouth. "Eat, Toe, it's good."

Toe Blake, winner of eight Stanley Cups during his glorious seasons behind the Canadiens' bench, stared straight ahead, apparently hearing nothing, seeing less. On the other hand, would anybody have really known what he was hearing or seeing?

Once, everybody knew what Blake stood for, how he felt, what he thought, liked, loved, and hated. What he loved was to win. Losing was what he hated.

He was rough, gruff, intimidating, wise, compassionate, unforgiving, scheming, and hard-working – all of it dedicated to winning those eight Stanley Cups as a coach, including the five in a row. Winning wasn't merely a worthwhile target for Hector Blake, born August 21, 1912, in Victoria Mines, Ontario. It was everything. It was life itself – first as a player for two seasons with the Montreal

Maroons, then thirteen with the Canadiens. Blake produced 235 goals and 292 assists, and won three Stanley Cups – the first with the Maroons, the last two with the Canadiens, where the Punch Line of Blake, Elmer Lach, and Maurice Richard was hockey's finest.

Left-winger Frank Mahovlich, an eighteen-season veteran of the NHL, was one of Blake's greatest admirers, even though he never played for him. He felt Blake was responsible for fifty per cent of what was needed to win.

"I've always felt that a good coach is the one who wins," Blake agreed. "But fifty per cent? If that had been the case with me, my teams would have won a lot more games."

Goaltender Gump Worsley was once asked what made Blake special as a coach. "There are twenty guys in that dressing room," replied Worsley, "and it's seldom you find even two of them alike. Toe knew each individual – the ones who worked from the needles, the ones who needed another approach. Between periods, he never blasted an individual. He'd say some guys aren't pulling their weight. The guys who weren't knew who he was talking about and you'd see the heads drop. But he'd never embarrass anyone in front of everyone. His ability to handle players – I guess that's what made him great."

Was Toe thinking about Gump or Frank this day, as he sat at the table, a plate of cookies in front of him? Once, he was full of life and laughs and mischief and blessed with a thirst for victory. His eyes snapped and crackled with the joy of competition. Now, at seventy-nine, his hair was white and his cheeks sunken. On this day, though, there was colour in them.

"He looks good," said Curry quietly. "That's the best I've seen him lately. I was here a couple of weeks ago and he really looked terrible. I couldn't believe that was Toe."

Blake sat at the table, staring. He didn't open his mouth until Andrew gently brought a cookie up to it.

"It's good, Toe," he said.

"Eat, Toe, it's good," said Curry, now sixty-nine, who has devoted the last few years to taking care of the man who took such good care of Curry, the player. "Why wouldn't I?" asked Curry. "Toe was such a good guy."

Toe reached for a second cookie, then a third and fourth. On and on.

"He wants something to drink now," said Andrew. He lifted a small glass of cranberry juice to Blake's mouth.

"Have a sip, Toe," he said. "Wash it down."

Toe drew on the juice.

"*Merci,*" he said.

Andrew looked through his gold-rimmed glasses and smiled. So did Curry.

"His appetite is fantastic," said Andrew. "He won't refuse food. He'll finish all of this," he said, with a wave of his hand at the cookie plate. "Most of the time, this is what he likes to do – eat. You haven't seen anything yet."

He placed an arm around Blake's shoulder.

"C'mon, eat . . . there you are, Toe," said Andrew.

"Does he watch hockey games on television?" Curry asked.

"Does he know what he's watching?" a guy asked.

"I would say yes, to a certain degree," said Andrew. "My belief is he knows. My own opinion is he knows."

Curry left to make a telephone call to his wife. Toe, who always wore a fedora during his years behind the Canadiens' bench, reached for the brown one Curry had left on the table. In his left hand, he held what was left of the plate of cookies. With the other, he pulled the fedora toward him. Then he ran his fingers over it – lovingly, almost – again and again.

"He seems to like your hat," Curry was told when he returned to the table. "It's almost as if he remembers what a fedora meant to him."

Curry blinked hard. "It's a damned shame, isn't it?" he said. "Look at his hands. He still has hands like a bear. Geez, he was strong. Look, he's finished the cookies."

Blake stared at the empty plate. Then he lifted it with both hands, tilted it toward him, and let the crumbs fall into his open mouth.

"Good, eh, Toe?" said Curry. "Very good. Remember me, Toe?"

Everybody remembers Toe. Everybody, that is, who developed a passion for hockey in the 1930s, the '40s, the '50s, and the '60s. As a coach, he was simply the very best. It's true that he had the National Hockey League's best talent during the five consecutive seasons, starting in 1955-56, that his teams won Stanley Cups. What made him the best was the way, somehow, he made the best teams better.

Indeed, getting the most out of the best was what Blake did best, which is what coaches in any sport are all about. Vince Lombardi is best remembered because he got the most out of his Green Bay Packers football teams. Well, Lombardi was football's Blake.

Blake's players respected, yet feared him. He was supremely loyal to them, and they to him. He had an uncanny talent of knowing when to raise and lower the volume. He produced winners, because he had no time to waste on losers. The only thing he hated more than losing was the unexpected.

It is a Friday morning in January 1960. The Canadiens are my beat at the *Montreal Star*. No, make that my life. A snowstorm, whipped into a white cloud by gale-force winds, has blown in. Getting to the Montreal Forum is a major problem.

"*C'est froid, n'est-ce-pas?*" grumbles the usher, who always seems to find it cold in the Forum lobby. "I hate it when it's cold."

"Yeah, it's a bitch out there," he's told. "Anybody around, yet?"

Bobby Malouf is there.

"What brings you here, Bobby?" a guy asks.

"You won't believe it," says Malouf.

"Try me," I say.

Ten years or so earlier, Bobby Malouf had played some junior hockey. Tough kid, but not very good at hockey. What he was very good at, though, was fighting. He did a lot of boxing among the amateurs. Won a lot, too. That, though, was years before. Now, Bobby was a salesman. Doing well, too. A pretty happy guy.

"So try me," Malouf was told. "What don't you believe?"

"I just left Frank Selke's office," said Malouf.

Frank Selke was in his fourteenth season as the Canadiens' general manager. He was a little man, no more than five-foot-six, with grey spikes for hair. He was a giant among hockey people, though: tough and with an eye for talent unmatched anywhere in the game. He won his first Stanley Cup in Montreal in 1953. His Canadiens went to the Stanley Cup final the next two seasons, but now the dynasty was in full flower: four consecutive Stanley Cups and working on a fifth.

"Anyway," says Bobby, "I get this call from Mr. Selke a few days ago. 'Come up to my office on Friday morning,' he says. 'I'd like a few words with you.' 'What about, Mr. Selke?' 'I'll let you know when you get here.'

"I guess I was in his office for about an hour," said Malouf. "I tell you, you're not gonna believe it. I don't."

"I'm listening."

Malouf recounted the conversation. "I'm told you played some hockey a few years ago," Selke said.

"About ten years ago."

"I hear you did some fighting, too."

"Some."

"Are you afraid of Fern Flaman?" asked hockey's most powerful and successful general manager. Flaman was a tough All-Star defenceman and captain of the Boston Bruins.

"No."

"Are you afraid of Leo Labine?" Labine was a hard-nosed forward with the Bruins.

"No."

"Jack Bionda?" Another tough defenceman.

"Lookit, Mr. Selke," said Malouf, "why should I be afraid of any of these guys? Why are you asking all these questions? What's on your mind?"

"I'm getting sick and tired of my team going into Boston and getting roughed up."

"So?"

"I want you to come out and skate with my team on Monday morning," said Selke. "If you do all right, I want you to play the next time we go into Boston."

"Are you kidding me?" Malouf asked.

"I'm not kidding."

"Listen, Mr. Selke," said Malouf, "I'm not afraid of any of these Boston guys. I'm not afraid of anybody. I'll go into the alley with anybody you want, but hell, I haven't skated for years. I mean, you're talking about fighting on skates . . . in the National Hockey League, for Chrissakes!"

"Come out on Monday," insisted Selke. "Skate with the players."

"You can't be serious," said Malouf.

"What have you got to lose?" asked Selke.

"Look, Mr. Selke," said Malouf, "I still can't believe you're serious about this. Why don't we do this, though? I'm leaving town for a week. I'm a salesman, see? I'll be back next Friday. I'll call you when I get back. If you're still serious, if you still want me to come out with your team, okay, I'll do it. I'll practise with your team, okay?"

"I'd rather have you on the ice on Monday," said Selke, "but okay, call me next Friday."

"You've got to be kidding," I said to Malouf after he finished his story. "You're going to practise with the Rocket, with Henri, with Béliveau and Moore. Do you have any idea what's going to happen to you when they see you out there, when word gets around why you're there?"

"I know, I know," grunted Malouf. "I told you, you wouldn't believe it."

"Promise me one thing."

"What?"

"When you get back from your trip, call me."

"Promise," he said. "See ya."

The Canadiens were in Boston two days later. The Bruins were not the powerhouse that they became in the Orr–Esposito era, but they could be an ornery bunch. Toe Blake was drumming his fingers on the hotel suite's coffee table, his mind locked into the game awaiting him only hours away.

"Big game," he was told.

"They're all big games," he grunted.

"Piece of cake," he was told.

"Very funny," he said.

"Toe?"

"Yeah?"

"Is the old man serious?"

"Who?"

"Mr. Selke."

"About what?"

"You know what."

"Lookit, I ain't got time for games," said Blake. "What are you talking about?"

"Bobby Malouf."

"Who?"

"Bobby Malouf."

Blake's jaw dropped. His eyes widened. The colour rose in his cheeks. He seemed to have trouble getting the words out. Finally he said: "Who told you about that?"

"C'mon, Toe, what's the difference who told me about it? Is the old man serious? He can't be, can he?"

Blake stared back wordlessly.

"You mean he's serious?"

Blake brought his hands up to his temple, leaned forward in his easy chair and lowered his head between his knees. He stared at the floor for several moments. Finally he whispered: "What are you going to do about it?"

"I promised Malouf I wouldn't do anything about it until he came back from a sales trip next Friday," I replied. "But I've been thinking about it a lot. Right now, I think I'll write something about it for tomorrow's paper."

"Jesus," said Blake. Then he lowered his head again, rocking slowly back and forth in his chair.

"Tomorrow?"

"Yeah."

Blake reached for the telephone on the coffee table. He called Canadiens vice-president Ken Reardon's room.

Reardon had played with Blake in the 1940s. He was a tough, unflinching defenceman who was to go on to the Hockey Hall of Fame. His father-in-law, Senator Donat Raymond, had owned the Canadiens for some years. Raymond eventually convinced Reardon that the place for him was in the Canadiens' front office.

"Get in here," Blake snapped at Reardon. "Right away!"

A couple of minutes later, a smiling Reardon bounced into the room.

"Hi, Toe. Hi, Red. What's up?"

"He knows," said Blake, barely above a whisper.

"Knows what?" chirped Reardon. Then he grinned broadly.

"Bobby Malouf," said Blake.

Reardon stopped smiling. His face whitened. Then he lowered himself gently into a soft chair beside Blake. Both had their hands to their temples. Both rocked slowly in their seats. Finally, Reardon looked up. "What are you going to do about it?" he asked.

"He says he's going to write something about it in tomorrow's paper," said Blake.

"Jesus," said Reardon.

Both lowered their heads again, staring soundlessly at the carpet. Reardon was the first to look up. "I want you to believe this," he said quietly. "I've talked myself blue in the face for the last couple of days. I mean, I don't know what's gotten into the old man. Maybe he isn't feeling well, or something, but I'm gonna talk to him again when we get back to Montreal tomorrow.

"Look, if this thing gets out now, it'll kill our team," Reardon continued. "Can you imagine what the Rocket is going to do when he finds out that some old-time amateur fighter is being brought in to protect him against the Bruins? What do you think Henri would do? Doug Harvey? Moore? Any one of 'em, for Chrissakes!"

"I don't think they'd appreciate it," Reardon was told.

"I'm gonna talk to Mr. Selke," said Reardon. "I'm gonna give it one more shot tomorrow. I promise you this: if I can't make him change his mind, I'll call you. You can do whatever you want with it after that."

"Gimme a break," I said. "This is a big story."

"Give me one," said Reardon. "You'll kill us."

"I'll think about it," I said.

That night, Reardon left his press-box seat at least a half-dozen times – always with the same question: "What are you gonna do?"

"I'm still thinking about it," he was told.

Maybe the story should have been written for the next day's paper. It wasn't. My favourite four-letter word has always been "fair." Mr. Selke had brought much to hockey. So had Blake and Reardon. Did Mr. Selke deserve to open a newspaper and read about Malouf before at least having the opportunity of explaining his side of it? Was one needed after the confirmations from Blake and Reardon?

Early the next morning, Reardon talked with Selke. Once again, he pointed out as strongly as he could what would happen to the Canadiens, as a team, if Selke insisted on bringing Malouf to the practice. He may even have mentioned that the story would be out even before the practice. Maybe not.

"Okay, let's forget about it," Selke agreed.

The story wasn't written.

Years later, July 1985, in fact, many of us gathered for Mr. Selke's funeral. It had been a difficult day for everyone, including Reardon, who some years earlier had left the Canadiens' organization after Sam Pollock had been named to replace Selke as general manager. It was a job Reardon had coveted, but Canadiens owner David Molson chose Pollock instead. Not a bad choice.

Reardon appeared lost in his thoughts after the graveside services. We walked for a while together without a word being exchanged. Finally, though, he straightened and breathed in deeply. Then a small smile started working at the corners of his mouth. He mumbled a couple of words.

"What's that you said?" he was asked.

His face broke into a broad grin.

"Bobby Malouf," he said.

Toe Blake was a complex man, which doesn't make him unique among coaches.

I remember one evening when Toe and I had been playing gin rummy for no more than an hour in my hotel room in Toronto. As usual, he was winning the low-stakes game, so watching him fling his cards on the table in disgust was something of a surprise.

"That's it," he snapped. "I'm leaving."

"What's the rush? We've only just started. It's early. Anyway, you can't just walk out of here after taking my money."

"Those guys have been fooling around," he said. "I'm going to check their rooms."

"What do you mean, fooling around? Hell, Toe, you've got a win and a tie in your two road games. What's wrong with that? Anyway, you've never done a room check before. It doesn't make much sense to start now."

"I'm checking their rooms," he insisted. Then he left.

"What about my money?"

"You'll have a chance to get it back tomorrow," he grunted.

Five minutes later, there was a soft knock on the door. Blake stood there, wearing a weak smile.

"That was a fast room check," he was told.

"Aw," he said, "I checked the first room, and both players were there. I think I woke them up. I was so damned embarrassed I decided not to check any of the other rooms. Get the cards. I need more of your money."

Ah yes, money . . .

Sports departments now spend a substantial percentage of their budgets sending reporters on the road. Today, for example, the Canadiens are accompanied on the road by twenty media people during the regular season, and more during the playoffs. It wasn't always that way, however. When I joined the *Montreal Star* in March 1954, reporters, with few exceptions, went on the road with the Canadiens only during the playoffs. What's more, the Canadiens paid for the transportation and hotels. They even provided the beat writers with a ten-dollar per diem. Hard, cold cash. Nobody questioned the practice – not the people who owned the newspapers, not the sports editors, not the team owners, not even the coaches and players. The few among us who did travel consistently didn't give the set-up a second thought. If our newspapers thought it was all right, it was fine with us. Case closed.

The Canadiens were in Detroit on this night in 1963, and, as usual, there were a few reporters in the dressing room before the game. Blake was deep in conversation with two Detroit reporters. I stayed off to one side waiting for the reporters to finish with Blake.

After several minutes, Blake turned and noticed me waiting there. He reached into his pocket for a wad of money. "Is this what you're waiting for?" he asked, peeling off a ten-dollar bill.

Both Detroit reporters laughed uncomfortably.

"Here," said Blake. "Take it."

"Stick it," I snapped, and stormed out of the dressing room.

Blake was nonplussed for a moment, then he stammered: "Hey, wait a minute, I was only kidding . . ."

Of course, he was kidding. What he was really doing was getting a laugh from the Detroit reporters at my expense, but this one wasn't even remotely amusing. I was still fuming the next day when I stormed into sports editor Harold Atkins's office. I explained what had happened the night before. "That's the last time I'm going on the road," I told Atkins, "unless this newspaper pays its own way."

"I'll have to check it out with the publisher," Atkins sighed.

John McConnell was stunned when the story was repeated to him. "Do you mean the Canadiens have been paying our expenses all this time?" he asked. "I had no idea we weren't paying our way," McConnell said. "Make certain we pay our way from now on."

Blake was properly embarrassed over the incident – after thinking about it. His problem was that he often had a problem determining the fine line between amusement and humiliation. For instance, he didn't find anything funny in a story I once wrote – even though that was the idea when I wrote it. This was in December 1965.

"Toe there?" I asked the Forum's secretary.

"One moment," she said. She was heard talking to Blake.

"Who's calling?" she asked.

"Red Fisher," she was told.

The message was passed along. A voice sounding suspiciously like Blake's could be heard replying.

"He just left," she said.

"Thank you."

The story in the next day's newspaper detailed that brief conversation. It also mentioned that if Blake had been available, he would have been asked the following series of questions, but since he wasn't there, these are the answers he would have given if he had been there. Great material, folks. Trust me. What I didn't know was the reason he didn't have time to talk to me on the telephone: he was driving his wife to an appointment with her doctor. She hadn't been feeling well for a while and Toe was worried.

The next night, while his team warmed up before the game, he charged into the press room, which was located down the hall from the Canadiens' dressing room. His face was beet-red with anger.

About thirty people watched him stride to where I was sitting, shouting profanities along the way.

He stopped in front of me, clenching and unclenching his fists. "I should biff you one," he yelled. A Toe Blake about to lose control was not a comforting sight in those days. It never has been. The situation needed a strong and, I hoped, brave response.

I rose, adjusted my horn-rimmed glasses, and said: "Go ahead, you son of a bitch, I can use the money." Then I sat down – quickly.

Now he was so angry his lips moved but no sounds came out. His fists, however, continued to clench and unclench. Finally, he blurted: "You're so goddamn cheap, you probably *would* sue!" Then he turned, tore open the door and slammed it behind him.

Whew!

The next day, broadcaster Doug Smith started his sports report: "Toe Blake lost his cool again last night . . ."

These things happen in this business now and then. Blake wasn't really angry about the story. Mostly, it was a case of feeling a lot of concern, as he should have, for his wife and best friend, Betty. He lost his cool, as Smith pointed out, which wasn't the first time a coach had lashed out at a hockey writer. Nobody died.

His mistake, though, was to strike out at a friend in front of a roomful of people. For more than a decade, we had spent a lot of time together on the road. Hardly a day went by when Blake, *Montréal-Matin* hockey writer Jacques Beauchamp, and I didn't have dinner together. If either Beauchamp or I reached for the bill, except on Christmas Day, each ran the risk of having our wrists snapped. Then, there were the card games in Blake's suite on trains and in hotels. Sure, occasionally, our voices would be raised in a disagreement, but this time was different. "I should biff you one," he had threatened.

We stopped talking that night in 1965. Days passed. Then weeks.

Betty Blake telephoned one day: "Why don't you talk to Toe?" she asked.

"He tried to humiliate me in front of a roomful of people," I said. "I'll talk to him when he apologizes."

"You know how stubborn he is," she said. "He won't apologize."

"I'm just as stubborn as he is," she was told.

Mrs. Blake tried to act the role of the peacemaker several times during the weeks and months which followed. So did mutual friends.

"No problem," I would tell them. "He knows my number. He knows where he can find me."

The months came and went. The Canadiens lost the first two games of their Stanley Cup final to the Detroit Red Wings, then won the next four, giving Blake his seventh Cup in eleven seasons, a record which is likely to stand forever. Still, not a word passed between us. It was embarrassing. Childish, too. We would be the only two individuals on an elevator, and neither would say a word. Not a look was exchanged. Nothing. It wasn't easy. In almost every way it was a terribly difficult and sad situation. Try going through more than one half of a season and the entire playoffs without once interviewing the coach of the team you are being paid to cover. The people who saved me were the players, who were aware of the situation. They kept me fully informed of what was going on in the Canadiens' family. So did my colleague, Beauchamp, who knew everything there was to know about the Canadiens.

Eight months after Blake had blown his cool, my wife, Tillie, and son, Ian, were injured when a cab they were in was involved in a collision. Ian had suffered cuts and bruises. My wife's shoulder was broken.

Early the next morning, the telephone rang in my home.

"It's Toe."

"Yes, Toe."

"How's your wife and kid? I just found out they were in an accident yesterday."

"They'll be fine, Toe. My wife has a pin in her shoulder, but she'll be up and around in a few days."

"That's good," he said. "Uh . . ."

"I'll tell my wife you called."

"Give her my best," said Blake.

"Toe?"

"What?"

"It was nice of you to call."

I haven't gone back to see Toe since that day in late December in 1991. Why? I've convinced myself that that visit was too painful. I sat with him for nearly two hours, and he didn't look at me once. His "*merci*" to Andrew was the only word he spoke. Too painful? Does that make sense? Was that reason enough not to go back? Probably not.

Blake missed coaching terribly after leading the Canadiens to his eighth Stanley Cup as a coach in 1968. He mourned long and hard after his wife lost a five-year battle with cancer. He joined the Canadiens' front office and had a desk there for years, but he never really liked the idea of sitting behind one. The onset of Alzheimer's was painfully slow, but people noticed. His friends, starting with Floyd Curry, feared for him and looked after him – looked after him as much as a proud man would allow. Eventually, Toe needed the constant care only a nursing home could provide.

He was one of a kind, particularly during the hockey season when every practice was a joy and every game an adventure. Now, the leaves turn red and yellow and die, the snow falls and I see him again and again the way I once knew him and I tell myself that's the only way I want to remember him. It's the only way he would want to be remembered.

Does that make sense? I think so.

2

Off and Running

My seventh-grade teacher, Miss Hecht, probably had better things in mind for me, but I guess she forgot to mention them.

If she had, she would have discovered that a sportswriter is what I've always wanted to be, although there's nothing in my background, real or imagined, that started me thinking that way. Why would any ten-year-old even think about what he wanted to do when he grew up?

In the 1930s, the newspaper business was alive and thriving in Montreal. Even in a predominantly French-speaking city, there were three daily English-language newspapers, each one publishing editions at various times of the day. The *Gazette* produced what it called a bulldog or early edition by 9:30 p.m., but the baseball or hockey scores and stories had to wait until the morning edition. It came off the presses after all the games had ended and was delivered to homes before most people left for work. I was part of a small army of boys who shook themselves awake before dawn to deliver the paper – for a little while, at least.

The *Herald*, a tabloid, followed the *Gazette*'s morning edition to the news-stands. The afternoon *Montreal Star*, which owned the *Herald*, was far and away the largest and most profitable newspaper in the city. It also owned the Montreal *Standard*, which was published only on Saturdays – after the three dailies had hit the streets. There were no Sunday papers.

Why sportswriting instead of the law or medicine or any other noble profession I suspect Miss Hecht would have wanted for teacher's pet?

Maybe it's Al Parsley's fault. He covered the Triple A baseball Montreal Royals and the Quebec Senior Hockey League Royals for the *Herald*. Maybe it's because his photo on top of his daily column made him look so much at peace with himself. Maybe it's because he seemed to be enjoying what he was doing. Or perhaps it was because his byline over baseball stories from spring training camps in Florida and cities all over the United States seemed "the right thing to do." He would write about mingling with sports people at Montreal watering-holes, and that seemed right, too, because too many things seemed wrong when I was growing up not far from St. Lawrence Boulevard, which Montreal people have always referred to as The Main.

Even then, The Main had a ghetto-like look. Lots of stores and restaurants, reeking with sharp and spicy smells. Its jewel was Moishe's Steakhouse – and still is. In those days, the area was home to a large Jewish population, and when they left for more affluent neighbourhoods and the suburbs, they were replaced by Portuguese and Italian immigrants.

My father, Sam, had come to Montreal from Russia after stopping over in Glasgow for several years. It was there he met and married my mother. For years, my parents, three sisters, and I lived in the back of a store where my father repaired and sold second-hand shoes. Nobody went without food, but there wasn't much money for anything else, other than a few pennies for a weekly visit to the nearby Mount Royal Arena, where Butch Shapiro, a hunk from Plattsburgh, New York, was a headliner on wrestling cards. So was Tiger Flowers, whose head-butt left bad guys lost in the fogs of concussion. It wasn't easy to find the admission each week, but it was a small price to pay for the privilege of watching good triumph over evil. Sometimes, good guy Jack Miller lost to a Sam Chuck, but not often. That was good.

The Canadiens? The closest I came to them was through the pages of the *Herald* and, once in a while, the *Star*. *Herald* sports editor Elmer Ferguson brought me there with his word pictures and occasional commentary on radio. So did the *Star*'s Baz O'Meara. The *Gazette*'s Dink Carroll was another hero – all to become colleagues of mine a long way down the road. With Parsley and the *Star*'s Lloyd McGowan, it was baseball and senior hockey. Their lives seemed filled with excitement. Who wouldn't want to be part of it – and get paid for it? I knew for certain it beat the hell out of living in the back of a shoe store.

Aberdeen Elementary School, across the street from St. Louis Square in east-end Montreal, was where Miss Hecht, Miss Flanz, and Miss Friedman brightened my days. So did Mr. Bacon, the principal. But his successor, Mr. Ferguson, often took the joy out of it. Once in a while, before the start of the school day, he would bring his son, Maynard, to the gymnasium where he would limp through the national anthem on his trumpet. That was about as good as it got with Mr. Ferguson who, as it turned out, knew something the rest of us didn't while we listened to Maynard struggle with the national anthem. He went on to become a world-class trumpet player.

School was no problem, I was at the top of my class through the first six grades, but then the stormclouds gathered. Leo Breitman was waiting. Somehow, Leo and I had never landed in the same class until grade seven, where the prize at the end of the school year was a scholarship covering the two-dollar (or was it three-dollar?) monthly fees for high school.

Leo was a brain. He had breezed through the first six grades. No pressure, eh? Now, for the first time, there was a scholarship to be won. Trouble is, only one of us could win. There was one scholarship for the leading boy, another for the leading girl.

Leo had an idea. "Don't you live on Mount Royal Avenue?" he asked.

"Yep. 324 Mount Royal East. Back of a shoe store."

"That's a lot closer to Mount Royal School than it is to Aberdeen," he said.

"So?"

"So why don't you transfer there? That way, you win there, I win here. No problem."

"I've got a better idea," I said. "Why don't you transfer there? I win here, you win there."

"My parents won't let me," said Leo.

"I guess it's you and me then," I said.

Leo and I were only a few points apart at the end of the school year. Our competition was so close, our teachers were instructed to ask each of us the same questions in oral examinations. Leo was sent out of the room while I was being asked the questions. Then, he'd be called in and asked the same questions. We'd take turns on who would be questioned first. Each exam was a playoff game. The Stanley Cup was the scholarship covering the monthly high-school fee.

Some years later, the Montreal Protestant School Board voted to abolish the fee, but until they did, kids who wanted a high-school education had to ante up. No fees, no high school.

Anyway, I should have listened to Leo when I had the chance, because I finished a close second to him. I cried many tears when the final results were announced. Where, I sobbed, would the monthly fee come from?

I found out at the end of my first month at Baron Byng High School. "You don't owe us anything," I was told. "We were sent a cheque covering your fees for the school year. A Miss Hecht sent it."

I've never forgotten Miss Hecht, my Aberdeen School hygiene teacher. I've never forgotten my two years at Baron Byng, or the four at Montreal Technical School.

"You have to learn a trade," my mother explained. "There won't be any money for college." And so I majored in electronics at Montreal Tech. I still have my silver medal for finishing a close second.

My mother, as it turned out, was wrong. There was, in fact, a little money for at least one year at Sir George Williams College. Some of it came from the monthly cheques she received from the government after my father joined the army early in the Second World War. Patriotic fervour wasn't a factor in his decision. Escaping his creditors was. More important, we needed the money. The rest came from the few dollars she earned working in a dress factory on The Main. When the money ran out, so did my college education, but it was a year well spent.

The college student newspaper, the *Georgian*, was looking for a sports editor. Actually, what it was really looking for was a sports staff of one with a lot of free time on his hands. A guy has to start somewhere, right? Montreal Tech taught me how to fix a radio but sportswriting remained a world to conquer. Parsley made me do it. Butch Shapiro and Tiger Flowers head-butted me in that direction. Then Hugh McCormick reeled me in at the *Monitor*, a weekly newspaper he owned in Notre Dame de Grace in west-end Montreal. McCormick had carried a notice in his weekly seeking students to report on college sports events. I telephoned his office.

"We're looking for a story every week," he said. "Think you can do it?"

"I know I can do it," I said.

"Fine. You're hired," he said.

"How much do you pay?" I asked.

"Nothing."

"I'll take it," I said.

I finished the school year at Sir George, but now there was no money. I landed in the public relations department at Northern Electric (it's now grown into Northern Telecom) where I wrote and edited the *Northern News*, the company publication. Andy O'Brien, the *Standard's* sports editor, telephoned several months later. The NDG Maple Leafs junior football team was in the playoffs, and O'Brien was looking for someone to cover the game. The year was 1947.

"Phone our office with the details, and we'll write it from here," said O'Brien.

"Why can't I write it?"

"No time," he said. "The game won't be over until 4:30 or so. By the time you get to our office, we'll be too close to our deadline. You won't have enough time to write the story."

"I can do it," I said.

"Are you sure?"

"Positive, Mr. O'Brien."

O'Brien wasn't happy with the story. He skimmed quickly over the two typewritten sheets, arched an eyebrow at me, and tossed the story into the wastepaper basket beside his desk.

"Still got your notes?" he asked gruffly. "Bring 'em over."

He sat down at his typewriter, slipped a fresh sheet into the machine, glanced at the first page of notes and started to type rapidly. Then, a second sheet. Finally, he said: "See, that's how it's done." Then he slipped the first sheet back into the typewriter and wrote across the top: "By Red Fisher."

Have you any idea what something like that does to a seventeen-year-old? When Andy tossed my story into the basket, part of me went with it. When he typed my name across the top of the story he had written with my notes, the sun shone again. It burst into full glory about six months later when he offered me a regular, albeit part-time job. Monday through Friday, I'd be chasing stories to fill the pages of the *Northern News*. On Saturdays, the *Standard* owned me. Five years later, when it was decided to put that splendid newspaper to rest, the *Star* moved in to fill the void.

A.J. West, a feared and crusty old bird, was the *Star*'s managing editor. He invited me to his office. "I guess you know the *Standard* is going out of business. We're coming out with a late edition in its place on Saturdays. Interested?"

"Of course."

"How much did they pay you over there?" he asked.

"Thirty dollars for the day."

"I'll give you fifteen dollars," he said.

"I'll take it," I said.

Two years later, in March 1954, the *Star's* sports editor, Harold Atkins, invited me to join his department full-time. Harold and I had worked together during my time at the *Standard*. We had been a pretty good team. My role at the *Star* was to be something akin to an assistant sports editor, but without the title. That would come thirteen years later. My week would run Monday through Saturday. The weekly salary would be $110.

"Sounds fine to me," I said, "but only if I can cover the Canadiens. It's what I've always wanted to do."

"I can't promise you that," said Atkins, "but I'll check it out with Mr. West. Give me a few days to think about it."

Two days later, he telephoned. "When can you start?" he asked.

The rest you know.

3

Red's Rite

The Canadiens were everything to me and my generation. They still are. I was twenty-seven when I joined the *Star* full-time, and here I was with the best beat in the sports department. The Canadiens were the Rocket and Big Jean, Boom-Boom and Doug Harvey. But one didn't win the trust or confidence of hockey's greatest franchise simply by being there. There were tests to be endured, rites of passage to experience, and woe to him who failed – or tried to avoid – them. The team's rookies had to go through them, and so did rookie reporters. No exceptions permitted.

In the mid-1950s, the Canadiens travelled by train to out-of-town games in the five other NHL cities (Detroit, Boston, Chicago, New York, and Toronto). The train's sleeping cars were where the tests were always conducted. They usually involved a bucket of ice, wet towels, warm water, and an electric shaver, the last wielded by Maurice "Rocket" Richard.

"We were looking for you on the train," Richard said to me one day. "The guys were wondering where you were."

"Looking for me? Forget it. I'm flying to the games now. Anyway, the first son of a bitch who comes close to me gets punched in the jaw."

This was a big mistake. Nobody, not *anyone*, threatened the Rocket. He was too important, too fiery, too much in control of everything he did to mess around with – even in jest. He meant too much to everyone, including me. It's why, years later, in early July 1975, playwright Rick Salutin sat with me near Banff, Alberta, talking about Richard.

The early afternoon sun was sending little shivers of light along the crest of the Bow River that summer day. A breath of wind sighed through the trees. Salutin was there because he had been commissioned to write a play about *Les Canadiens*.

"Tell me," he said, "about the Canadiens. What do they mean to the people of Quebec?" he asked.

I remember telling Salutin that if you fight but don't win the real battle against those who are perceived to be the real rulers, you try to win elsewhere in a forum where you can be successful. In other words, *Les Canadiens*.

Later, in an introduction to his play, which was first performed at the Centaur Theatre in Montreal in February 1977, and was the winner of the Chalmers Award for Best Canadian Play that year, he wrote that it was very much the same answer he got at a bar in Quebec City. "I watched a hockey game on television and marvelled at the frenzied involvement of the patrons," he wrote. "I put to my drinking partner this question: 'How come?'

"She said: 'The Canadiens – they're us. Every winter they go south and in the spring they come home conquerors!'"

"Talk to me about Maurice Richard," Salutin said.

Well, I said, if the Canadiens were the conquerors, Richard was their general – and more. He brought to them a tradition of winning which reached remarkable heights from the 1955-56 season through 1959-60, the years when they won five consecutive Stanley Cups. No team had done it before, and none since. It may have been the best team of magical talents ever assembled, but what made it truly special was that its leader was Rocket Richard. He exemplified what winning was all about – to the people, as well as to a team.

Former Canadiens goaltender Ken Dryden, who assisted on Salutin's award-winning play, once noted that at a press conference in 1976 to promote Jean-Marie Pellerin's book, *Maurice Richard, l'idole d'un peuple*, Claude Charron, Quebec Minister for Youth, Sport and Recreation at the time, commented: "I have the impression that Maurice Richard was one of the original men responsible for giving a special meaning to Québécois life and to have encouraged the élan of the Quebec people."

"I was just a hockey player," Richard protested at the same press conference. "Just a hockey player."

Of course, he was much more than "just a hockey player." It wasn't just that he was a winner during his eighteen seasons with the Canadiens, it was the way he won. He could lift a team, a province, and at times even a country into a frenzy of winning. He pushed himself to the brink, and when he and the team won, "his people" imagined themselves winners as well – even if it was for only a little while. When he was Number One, they were too. When he lost, they lost. It's why "his people" erupted into what will always be remembered as the Richard Riot on March 17, 1955 (see chapter 11). The reason? After clubbing Hal Laycoe of the Boston Bruins with his stick, Richard had been suspended by National Hockey League president Clarence Campbell for the last few games of the regular season and for the entire playoffs.

With Richard, the eyes had it. They were coal-black, wet, and shining with the intensity he brought to every game. No wonder he lit up every arena in which he performed. It was the menace implicit in him each time he swooped in on an opposing goaltender, often with another player clinging to his back. It was in his arms and in the barrel of his chest which threatened to burst his sweater at any moment. It was in the tight line of his mouth, and in the snarl it formed when he was challenged.

A few days after my brief meeting with Richard, the telephone rang at my home. Dickie Moore, the Canadiens' star left-winger, was on the line. He and I went back to his days with the Junior Canadiens. I'd written a long feature-photo essay on him for the *Standard* and we had become close friends.

"Are you coming to the practice tomorrow morning?" he asked.

"I don't think so. It's my day off."

"If I were you, I'd be here," he said.

"Why?"

"I hear there's a big story coming down. I can't say what it is, but, well . . . it's up to you."

Toe Blake was sitting in his small room beside the main dressing room when I arrived the next morning. There was a chair on each side of a long table. He looked up.

"Whoa! Wait a minute! I wouldn't come in here today," he said darkly.

"Why not?"

"I wouldn't, that's all."

"Anything happening here today I should know about?" he was asked.

"Not a thing," he said.

I told him I heard that a big story was breaking, but Blake denied it. Undeterred, I said I would hang around the room for a little while.

"Suit yourself," Blake said with a shrug. A few minutes later he announced he was going upstairs to his office.

I sat and stared at the floor for the next few minutes, wondering about the telephone call the night before. Moore wouldn't have called unless he knew about something. After all, we went back together a long time. He wouldn't have dragged me out on this sub-zero day unless it was important, would he?

I was still staring at the floor, chin in hand, wondering, when the first set of legs appeared. Then a second and a third. Several more sets of legs and oh! oh! I looked up hurriedly to see at least a dozen wildly grinning faces staring at me. Jesus!

I had barely brought back my right hand when the first pair of hands grabbed me. Then another set of hands locked around my ankles. Somebody else – it could have been Moore – grabbed my shoulders. One . . . two . . . three . . . seconds later I was on my back on the long table. The overcoat came off first. Then the suit, shirt, shoes, socks, and underwear. The entire sneak attack took no more than fifteen seconds. I was naked now, shivering, my arms and legs tied to the four legs of the table. Somebody filled my rubbers with ice shavings and planted them firmly on my feet. The shivering increased. Happy whoops from the players filled the room.

When I opened my mouth to protest, warm water was poured down my throat. Wet towels, wielded like truncheons, slapped across my legs, stomach, and chest.

"You bastards, I'll . . . ," and more warm water! More slaps of the wet towels. More laughter. *Slap! Slap!* More warm water, and, then, a deathly silence. Not a sound. What now?

A door opened and in walked a man with a white mask covering the lower part of his face, a white surgeon's cap on his head. He wore a white doctor's coat. In his right hand, a bulky, black electric shaver. The eyes: coal-black, glittering.

The Rocket leaned over and fixed me with his best stare.

"Gonna punch me in the jaw, eh, you son of a bitch?"

The shaver coughed to life. *V-r-o-o-o-m!* It was time for major surgery. *V-r-o-o-o-m!*

"You're flying now, eh? We're not gonna get you, eh? Welcome," he rasped, "to the family."

V-r-o-o-o-m! V-r-o-o-o-m!

This rite was all wrong. This wasn't supposed to be happening in the temple of hockey. But wrong or right, it lasted a long time, at least six or seven minutes, minutes that seemed as if they would never end. Finally, laughing loudly, the players filed back into the main dressing room. I was left bound to the table.

Fifteen minutes later, Red Burnett, a visiting hockey writer from Toronto, opened the door to the small room. He took one look at the bound, shivering heap of pale, utterly naked flesh on the table, let out a shriek and went racing up to Blake's office on the second floor.

"Come and see what those bastards did to Red Fisher," he roared.

"Get out of here," snapped Blake, "or you're next."

Burnett left quickly.

Ten minutes later, Moore and Doug Harvey untied me and helped me into my ruined clothes. Goaltender Jacques Plante had an announcement. "Now that you're one of us," he said, "we want you to know we take care of our own. We've taken up a collection to get you a new suit. Eighteen cents," he giggled. More laughter from the players. "I put in the first five."

Once in a while, when some of the old-time players get together, my initiation is mentioned. Moore still laughs about it. So does Geoffrion. I used to laugh about it, but no longer.

"Bah, it took eighteen of you to do the job," I once told Moore and Geoffrion. "Anyway, the only thing that really upset me about the whole thing was the warm water you guys poured down my throat every time I opened my mouth to yell."

"*Tabernac!*" said Geoffrion. "You don't really think that was warm water, do you?"

4

Slats

You might think that someone who's covered the Montreal Canadiens for forty years would have a Canadien as his best friend in hockey. Not me, though. That "honour" goes to Glen Sather (a.k.a. "Slats").

Sather is the sum of many things. He coached the Edmonton Oilers to four Stanley Cups, and was the general manager for a fifth. He has been the team's president since it entered the National Hockey League for the 1979-80 season.

He is combative, arrogant, heavy-handed, smart, amusing, compassionate, wealthy, a winner, a good family man – and heartily disliked, even hated, by some people who don't know him. Sather played for six teams during his nine seasons in the NHL. At best, he was a journeyman left-winger – with an 80–113–193 record in 658 games. Small numbers. Big heart. Bigger brain.

The first time I met Sather was prior to the start of the 1974-75 season, after the Canadiens had acquired him from the St. Louis Blues. He had been, in every way, a fringe player with four other teams by that time. Unsurprisingly, hardly anybody understood why Canadiens general manager Sam Pollock would be even remotely interested in adding him to a team that was showing every sign of developing into a dynasty. There Sather was, though, ready to give everything he had, just as he had done with the Blues, Pittsburgh, the New York Rangers, and Boston.

What everyone learned quickly about Sather is what Pollock knew all along: his heart was many times the size of his talent. What they also learned is that he kept the other players loose: he was a fun guy. He never met a lighthearted moment he didn't like. At the same time, he came to work every night.

During his tenure with the Canadiens, Sather was surrounded by giant talents such as Larry Robinson, Ken Dryden, Guy Lafleur, Steve Shutt, Jacques Lemaire, Guy Lapointe, and Serge Savard. The team's coach was Scotty Bowman, in his time by far the best in the business. Yet Sather never felt overwhelmed by any of them.

Sather's greatest talent was that nobody enjoyed playing against him. They didn't like the way he played the game. His arrogance unsettled them. Of course, at season's end, Sather had accumulated yet another undistinguished set of numbers. Still, this hadn't kept the Canadiens from finishing first in their division. True, they fell out of the playoffs, but almost everyone was convinced that greatness was only a season away, two at the outside, provided this group could be kept together.

Sather shared the optimism and the vision that he'd be there for a piece of the glory.

"This team is gonna win a bunch of Stanley Cups," he told me.

"Don't worry about it," I replied. "I don't think you'll be around to enjoy it. You're history after this season."

"I'll be back," he said.

A few weeks later, he was on the telephone. "See, I told you I'm coming back," he said.

"What makes you say that?"

"I just got off the phone with Scotty," he said. "He promised me I'd be with the team in training camp."

"That clinches it. You won't be back."

"How come?"

"If Scotty promised you'll be back, it means you won't."

"We'll see," he snapped.

A few weeks later, Sather was traded to the Minnesota North Stars.

Sather is special. Unique, maybe. No one in hockey has been as successful as quickly. Few individuals in hockey have been as successful off the ice. One reason is that he has always surrounded himself with the best people he can find. "I'm a great organizer," he says. "That's my strength." Another reason: he's always looking for an edge, and almost always gets it.

One day, in 1979, he announced to me that he had purchased a restaurant about twenty miles east of Banff in the Alberta Rockies.

"So?" I said.

"It was once owned by the Canadian Pacific Railway."

"Uh-huh."

"What I'd like you to do is go down to the CPR museum in Montreal and see if they have anything in their files about the restaurant. If they do, get a copy of whatever they have and mail it to me. The customers might like to see something like that on the wall. A little bit of history, you know."

I said I would help him, but the service wouldn't come free. There was a painting Sather had in his Edmonton home of an Indian, his chin raised, pride shining from his eyes. I've always had a fondness for Indian paintings. Michael Lonechild's works have found a place in my home. Allan Sapp is another favourite. I wanted Sather's painting for my collection.

The museum had several items in its files about the restaurant. Sketches, too. A few days later, the material was on its way to Sather's residence in Banff.

"I just got that stuff in the mail," he told me a few days later. "It's great. Exactly what I wanted."

"Fine. My wife spent a whole day tracking it down. Now you know what you've got to do."

"I'll put the Indian painting on the train this afternoon," he said.

Several weeks passed. No sign of the painting.

"What's happened to the painting?" I asked him on the telephone.

"I can't understand why it hasn't arrived. Maybe it's sitting in the warehouse at the station."

More weeks passed. Still no sign of the painting.

"I've put a tracer on it," he explained.

"You sure?"

"Trust me."

Three months later: "You'll be getting it any day now," he promised.

"I hear you're going out west," I said to Canadiens scout Ron Caron one day. "Edmonton, maybe?"

"It's on my schedule," said Caron.

"Do me a favour," I said. "Call Sather. Somewhere around 2:00 a.m., preferably. Tell him Fisher wants to know what's happened to his Indian painting."

"At two o'clock in the morning?"

"At two. I owe him one."

"You've got it," grinned Caron.

He telephoned several days later from Edmonton. "I called him. He wasn't happy."

"What about the painting?"

"He told me he put it on the train yesterday. You can expect it any day."

The Edmonton Oilers, who were in the World Hockey Association at the time, were about to enter the NHL. Sather was the team's coach and general manager. Leo LeClerc, a television talk-show host, telephoned from Edmonton.

"The Oilers will be in the NHL next season," said LeClerc.

"So?"

"We'd like you to come out here for a show with Sather in July.

You know, talk about the Oilers joining the league, talk about Sather . . . stuff like that."

A month or so later, Sather and I sat side by side on high stools in the television studio. After the preliminary introductions, LeClerc started to ask a question.

"Before I answer that question," I said, "let me tell you a little bit about the guy sitting next to me."

"By all means," said LeClerc. "Tell us about coach Sather."

"More than a year ago, this man promised to send me an Indian painting for services rendered. So far, I haven't seen it. I've called him about it at least five times. Each time I've been told it's on the way. I've had friends of mine call him. 'It's on the way,' he's told them. Now, after all this time, after all the phone calls, still no painting.

"What I want to tell all of you out there," I said, pointing a finger at the eye of the camera, "is that if you people want someone like this guy to coach your team in the best league in the world, all I can say, folks, is that I feel sorry for you!"

LeClerc was bent over with laughter. Sather's face was beet-red. His lips moved, but for the first time in his life, he was left speechless.

"We'll be back with Red and Glen after this message," sputtered LeClerc.

"I'm gonna get you for that," hissed Sather during the commercial break.

"What for? Did I say something wrong?"

Sather brought his fist back and landed a punch high on my shoulder.

"Sore loser," I muttered from the floor.

A couple of months earlier, Sather had asked for yet another favour. The NHL's Expansion Draft was coming up and Sather wanted me to look at the list of available players and indicate what players, if any, I liked. "There doesn't seem to be much talent there," he said.

Sather was right. There wasn't much talent available.

"I'd have to say the best of the bunch is this one," I said.

"Lee Fogolin?"

"A good steady defenceman. Comes to play every night. Tough kid. A leader."

"You sure?"

"He's the first one I'd take if I were you."

Defenceman Fogolin was the first player Sather selected. He went on to become team captain for three seasons and an important factor in the Oilers' Stanley Cup victories of 1983-84 and 1984-85.

"I can't pay you for this," Sather said after the draft.

"Did I ask for money?"

"Tell you what I'm gonna do, though," he said. "When we win the Stanley Cup, I'll send you a ring."

"What a nice thought," I said. "But it won't happen in my lifetime, chum."

Five years later, there's bedlam in Northlands Coliseum, because only moments before, the Oilers won their first Stanley Cup – a five-game series with the New York Islanders.

Sather leans over and yells into my ear. "What's your ring size?"

"Huh?"

"Your ring size. I promised you a ring."

"Forget it," he was told. "I forgot about it a long time ago."

"If you don't give me your ring size, I'll have my secretary call your wife and get it from her."

"Forget it."

The ring was waiting for me when the Canadiens visited Edmonton early the following season.

"You didn't have to do this, you know," I told Sather.

"Sure I did. I promised. You didn't think I'd remember the ring. You didn't think you'd ever get the Indian painting, either. Now you've got both."

Two years after our appearance on Edmonton television, Sather was in Montreal for the NHL's June meetings.

"Hot, isn't it?" I said.

"It's cool in my suite. Why don't you come up?"

There were about twenty-five people in the suite. Naturally, the first few minutes were spent with me telling most of them about how Sather had welshed on the Indian painting deal.

Sather came out of his bedroom. "What's going on?" he asked.

"I'm telling everybody about the Indian painting you've owed me for three years."

Sather thrust a parcel at me. "Here," he snapped. "I'm sick and tired of your bitching about the Indian painting. Here it is. Take it."

"What's this?"

"It's your goddamned Indian painting. Open it."

The package contained an sixteen-by-twenty colour photograph of former New York Rangers defenceman, and full-blooded Indian, Jim Neilson. It showed Neilson, who happened to be in the suite at the time, standing atop a ladder painting the outside of his home. He was wearing an Indian headdress.

"What kind of a joke is this?" I asked Sather.

"You wanted an Indian painting," crowed Sather. "Neilson's an Indian. He's painting. What you're looking at right now is an Indian painting."

Few people I know work harder than Sather, but he also knows when it's time to turn down the volume. Riding horses in his beloved Banff is a favourite leisure activity. Chasing Arctic char at Tree River in the Northwest Territories is another passion. So is hunting.

"A bunch of us are going up to the Northwest Territories for five days," he said. "Interested?"

"I don't fish. Never have."

"I'll show you how. You'll love it," he said.

Well, Tree River above the tree line proved to be fine. Great Bear Lake, with its three-foot waves and enormous stock of trout, was even better – particularly after I landed my first-ever fish. Nine pounds, seven ounces. A monster, by my calculation.

"Tell you what I want you to do, Slats," I said. "Take this one back to Edmonton. Get it stuffed and mounted. I'll pick it up when the Canadiens are in Edmonton early next season. Okay?"

"No problem," he said.

A week or so before the Canadiens were due to head west, I telephoned Sather to ask how the taxidermy was proceeding. "How's my fish?"

"It was delicious," he said.

"What do you mean it was delicious?"

"When I brought the fish to the taxidermist, he said the friggin' fish's lower jaw was broken. He wanted $250 to repair it. Stuffing and mounting would be another $750. I didn't figure you'd want to spend a thousand dollars for one fish."

"Damn it, Sather, it was my first fish! I'd have paid twice that."

"Sorry about that," he said.

After the Edmonton–Canadiens game, a few of us went to dinner. Oilers owner Peter Pocklington and his wife, Eva, were there. So were Glen and his wife, Ann. Doug Risebrough, who had not yet gone to the Calgary Flames and was still playing with the Canadiens, also was there.

"Can you believe this guy would do that to me?" I asked. "I catch my first fish – a beauty. I ask him to have it stuffed and mounted, and what does he do? He eats it."

"That's a pretty sad story," said Pocklington.

"Don't you know Glen by now?" asked Ann Sather.

"Yeah," agreed Risebrough.

Sather had left the table halfway through the Tale of the Trout. A few minutes later, he returned, grinning. He held a three-foot-wide board in his hands. A stuffed fish was mounted on it. Below it, a brass plate, engraved: "Caught by Red Fisher, Great Bear Lake, August 4, 1981, 9 lbs., 7 oz."

"Here's your fish," he growled. The stuffed fish was about eight inches long.

"This isn't my fish," I snapped.

"Sure it is."

"My fish was at least two feet long. Weighed, like it says right here, nine pounds, seven ounces."

"When you stuff and mount a fish, it shrinks," said Sather.

By this time, owner Pocklington was convulsed with laughter. Risebrough was giggling hysterically.

"Oh, Glen," sighed Mrs. Sather.

"What have you done?" asked Eva Pocklington.

"Ann, I've gotta tell you something about your husband: he's losing it," I said.

Sather turned quickly on his heel and left. A few minutes later, he was back . . . grinning. This time, he had the genuine article. "Only kidding," he laughed.

Another time, Sather invited me to go goose-hunting with him in a farmer's field a hundred miles southeast of Edmonton.

"I've never fired a gun in my life," I told him.

"Hell, there's nothing to it. We'll drive up to his place tomorrow afternoon, spend the night at this farm owned by Johnny Golka, and go after the geese the next morning."

There was a bite to the fall Alberta air. Black, angry-looking clouds followed us throughout the drive out of Edmonton.

"You'll like Johnny," Sather promised. "We played junior hockey together. Good guy. Got a pretty good thing going for him."

We arrived at the Golka farm around four in the afternoon. Thirty minutes later, we piled into the Golka pickup for the twenty-minute drive to the farm where the geese had been landing every morning. Rain started to fall by the time we arrived.

"There's gonna be six of us here tomorrow," said Golka, "so we'll need a pretty big trench."

"A trench?" I asked.

"Tomorrow, see, we pile into this trench so that the geese don't spot us when they're landing in the field," explained Sather. "It shouldn't take more than a couple of hours to dig it out."

"What about the rain?"

"There's nothing we can do about it. Let's start digging."

"I thought you said this was gonna be fun."

"Dig," he snapped.

Three hours later, the job was done. The rain wasn't.

"Let's get you back to the farm," said Golka. "We'll have something to eat, then hit the sack. We've got to be up at five."

"At five?"

"We've got to be here before the geese arrive."

"I told you it would fun," said Sather.

It rained all night. The rain was falling even harder the next morning. Now and then, a soft rumble of thunder was heard in the inky blackness.

"Boy, oh boy, Sather, this is fun. I'm really enjoying this," I said. "Think of it, I've been missing this fun all my life."

"Stop your bitching," snapped Sather.

The overnight rain had left about ten inches of water in the trench. There was mud everywhere.

Golka breathed in heavily. "Good thing the water isn't higher," he grunted. "Wouldn't do any of us any good."

"How long do we wait here?" I asked. "The water is starting to get into my boots already."

"No more'n an hour, I guess," said Golka. "That's not long."

"It is to me," I said.

The first white-grey streaks of dawn started to appear about one hour later. Thirty minutes after that, a soft *honk, honk* was heard in the distance.

"Oh, oh, they're comin'," said Golka.

"Since they are," I said, "don't you think it's about time somebody showed me how to load and fire this thing?"

"Oh, right," said Golka. "Glen told me this is your first time. Here, let me show you: the bullets go in here, you close it . . . like this, stick the barrel, good and solid, into your shoulder, and when you think you've got him lined up, just squeeze the trigger. A nice, little squeeze. No more. Okay, now everybody down in the trench. We don't want to scare 'em off."

"Here he comes," said Sather.

"The first one is mine, guys," I whispered loudly.

"You want it, you've got it," said Sather loudly. Then he raised his shotgun and, *boom!*, the sound of the morning's first shot echoed and re-echoed around the field.

A few seconds later: *thwack!* Something landed on my head.

"Will you look at that," said Golka, pointing to the ground on my left. A dead goose lay there.

"What the hell was that?" I sputtered. "What hit me on the head?"

"The goose, I guess," said Golka.

At the opposite end of the trench, Sather was hooting.

"I've gotta tell you something," he said. "Winning the Stanley Cup was tough. Winning the Canada Cup was even tougher. But this . . . this . . . shooting a goose out of the sky in such a way that it would land on your head is the toughest thing I've ever done!"

He denies it to this day, but Sather had, of course, set up the whole thing. The flying goose was real. So was the one which lay dead on the ground beside me. What Sather had done was have the guy in the trench beside me swat me over the head with a dead goose a second or two after he had fired at the high flyer. It may still be flying.

As you can see, Glen Sather always has been willing to skate a long way for a laugh. He'll go to astonishing lengths for one – but only if you happen to be his friend. He loves laughing with people he cares for – but his friends also have learned from time to time that in the business of hockey, friends is friends, and business is business.

Let me relate an incident that happened in June 1988, mere weeks after Sather's Oilers dynasty had won its fourth Stanley Cup in five years. It happened at the NHL's annual congress in Montreal.

Bob McCammon, who was the coach of the Vancouver Canucks at the time, came up to me and said, "Have you heard?"

"Heard what?"

"Gretzky."

"What about him?"

Wayne Gretzky had scored 149 points the previous season, which wasn't unusual for the game's greatest player. For the first time in nine years, though, he hadn't led the NHL point-getters. Pittsburgh's Mario Lemieux had – with 168 points. Gretzky, however, had led the Oilers to the Stanley Cup. He had also won the Conn Smythe Trophy as the most valuable player in the playoffs. That was a whole lot better than leading the league in scoring. Better than anything.

"The Oilers are trying to deal him," said McCammon.

"Yeah, Bob, sure they are."

"I'm not kidding," said McCammon. "Pocklington has offered him to the Los Angeles Kings. He's offered him to us. Fifteen million U.S. and five first-round draft choices if the Kings want him. He wants twenty-two million Canadian from us."

I told McCammon to can the humour. "You're making me nervous."

"I'm telling you, it's going down. I don't know where he's going, but Gretzky's going." Then McCammon laughed loudly.

Jay Greenberg, a bright and entertaining hockey writer who was with *Sports Illustrated* at the time, had joined us in time to catch the end of our conversation.

"Any chance of that happening?" he asked, after McCammon had left. "Is it worth checking out with Sather?"

"Bob gets a kick out of throwing around stuff like that," Greenberg was told. "If the Oilers deal Gretzky, Pocklington gets lynched. I don't think I'd even want to ask Sather the question."

"Got a minute?" I asked Edmonton's then assistant coach, John Muckler, later in the day.

"Shoot."

"Peter isn't thinking of dealing Wayne, is he?"

"Wayne?"

"Gretzky."

"If Gretzky goes, I'm right behind him," he laughed. "Are you kidding?"

"Just asking," I said.

I hustled up to Sather's hotel suite where he was examining Stanley Cup rings. After four Stanley Cups in five seasons, it was getting more and more difficult to find a ring that was different. "Which one do you like best?" he asked.

"All of 'em."

"Get serious," he said. "I've got to give the guy an answer pretty soon."

"I've got a question you won't think is serious. I don't even want to ask the question, but heck, since I'm here, I might as well ask."

"What's the question?"

"Gretzky. What's this I hear about the Oilers trying to deal Gretzky?"

Sather didn't lift his head from the rings. "Ridiculous. Where'd you hear that?"

"Let's just say I heard it."

"Ridiculous. Now, about the ring . . ."

A couple of days later, over breakfast, Canadiens president Ronald Corey mentioned Gretzky. "The marketing people had a meeting yesterday," he said. "A few of them mentioned a big trade. You won't believe this . . ."

"Gretzky," I said.

"Check it out."

"I already have. I asked Sather about it. He laughed at me."

"There were a lot of marketing people talking about it," said Corey. "Maybe you'd better check it out some more."

The hockey people had left for their homes the day before. Sather was at his office in Edmonton.

"The Gretzky thing won't go away," I told him. "His name came up again today."

"Tell you what," said Sather. "If you don't believe me, why don't you call Peter?"

"I didn't say I didn't believe you. I just find it curious that a bunch of marketing people were talking about him being for sale. But okay, I'll call Peter. Might as well hear what he's got to say," I said.

A few minutes later I was speaking with Pocklington. "What's this I hear about you wanting to move Gretzky?"

"Ridiculous," he said. "I kinda like the idea of having a dynasty. Anyway, something like this isn't new. I guess we get three, maybe four offers for Gretzky every year."

"I'm not talking about people asking you for Gretzky," I said. "I'm talking about the Edmonton Oilers offering him to Los Angeles for fifteen million and five first-round draft choices."

"Ridiculous."

"Twenty-two million Canadian and five first-rounders if Vancouver wants him."

"Ridiculous."

"You sure?"

"Trust me."

I have often wondered why I didn't go ahead with the story for my newspaper, the *Gazette*. One reason is that I have made it a hard rule never to deal in rumours. I find them distasteful, and often harmful. Of course, in this business, they grow like wildflowers. The easy thing is to reach for the bouquet now and then and pick one. Once in a long while, a rose without the thorns is found. The Gretzky story would have been a rare orchid. But I wondered then, was it true?

The end of the hockey meetings marked the start of my summer-long holidays, but in the final analysis, the biggest reason for deciding the supposed Gretzky deal was a non-story was that my closest friend in hockey had sniffed at the idea. So had Pocklington, another friend.

Ridiculous, both had said.

What I did do on that late June day was punch a speculative story into my computer – just for fun. It started: "Is The Great Gretzky about to become a King? Edmonton owner Peter Pocklington calls the idea 'ridiculous,' but the *Gazette* has learned . . ." The story ended at about 650 words, then the computer was put away for the summer.

Weeks passed without any mention of Gretzky, other than the hoopla surrounding his royal wedding in Edmonton to actress Janet Jones. That, too, was forgotten after a couple days. Holiday time. Portugal.

Hockey was the last thing on my mind August 9, when the telephone rang in my hotel room at 9:55 p.m. Two days earlier, my wife and I had settled in on the Algarve, where the days are long, hot, and dry, and the beaches stretch as far as the eye can see.

Dick Irvin, the Canadiens' radio and TV man, was on the line. "Don't get excited, nobody died," he said, "but as we speak, there's a press conference about to start in Edmonton and –"

"Wayne Gretzky," I said.

"Huh?"

"Gretzky. They're trading Gretzky. Where's he going?"

"He's going to Los Angeles for fifteen million dollars U.S. –"

"– and five first-round draft choices."

"How did you know that?" asked Irvin.

"It's a long story, Dick," I said.

"Everybody is going nuts over here," he said.

"So am I, pal. So am I."

Click!

The next time I saw Sather was a little more than two months after the Gretzky trade. "Got a minute?"

"Sure do," he said. "What's on your mind?"

"The Gretzky trade."

"What about it?"

"You'll remember I asked you about it during the June meetings."

"I remember."

"I also asked Peter about it."

"He told me."

57

"What I'm saying to you now is that I don't care how you deal with the media about something like that. They've got a job to do, you've got one. If you didn't want to talk about the trade before it happened, that's your business. I understand that. What you don't do is lie to your friends."

The colour rose high in his cheeks. "I didn't lie to you," he said. "When you asked me about it, nothing was done. Nothing really happened until a couple of days before the trade was announced."

"I've got a story in my computer," I told him. "Want to see it? I wrote it in June after you and Peter told me the idea of offering Gretzky to other teams was ridiculous. The story says that you wanted fifteen million dollars U.S. and five first-round choices for Gretzky. Is that ridiculous, too?"

"What about Marty McSorley and Mike Krushelnyski?" he asked. "Did you have them in your story? That part of the deal wasn't made until the day before the trade," said Sather. (Oilers McSorley and Krushelnyski were traded to the Kings for Jimmy Carson, Martin Gélinas, and Los Angeles' first-round picks in 1989, 1991, and 1993.)

"Screw McSorley and screw Krushelnyski," I said. "They're not the story. They're no part of the story. Gretzky is the story. Fifteen million U.S. is the story. Five first-round choices is the story. Do you understand what I'm saying to you?"

"I didn't lie to you," he muttered.

"Fine, let's leave it at that. I just wanted to let you know how I feel about it."

Nothing is forever in this business. The important thing is for good and warm memories to endure. Like these:

It's late May 1985 and the Edmonton Oilers are in Philadelphia for the start of the Stanley Cup final. The year before, Edmonton had won its first Stanley Cup, winning in five games over the New York Islanders.

I had fallen ill during the Philadelphia–Quebec semi-final, and had been told by doctors to rest at home for several weeks. It was the first Stanley Cup final I had missed since covering my first one in 1956.

The Oilers were on the ice for their pre-game warmup shortly before 7:00 p.m. A couple of minutes later, Sather was on the telephone.

"Why are you calling?" I asked him.

"I hear you're not feeling well," he replied.

"I'll survive," I told him.

"Just wanted to know how you're getting along," he said.

"Don't you have a few other things to think about, like tonight's game, for example?"

"Let me worry about that," said Sather. "Right now, I want to know how you're feeling. Are you gonna pick up the series later on?"

"I'm feeling pretty good," I said. "And no, I don't plan to pick up the series. I'll watch it on television."

We chatted until the players started returning from their pre-game warmup. The Oilers lost to the Flyers, 4–1, that night. Two nights later, at precisely 7:00, he was on the telephone again. "My guys are warming up," he said. How are you doin'?"

Fifteen minutes or so later: "Gotta run, Redso, some of the guys are comin' off the ice. Gotta win this one tonight. All of us would feel pretty good going home tied, with the next three games in Edmonton."

The Oilers did, in fact, beat Philadelphia, 3–1, and went on to take a 3–1 lead in the best-of-seven final with victories in the first two games in Edmonton. On both nights, while his team was on the ice for the warmup, Sather called my home from his dressing-room office. How were things going? How was I feeling? Getting better?

He was on the telephone before game five, as well. "I'll call you after the game, because this series is over tonight," he said.

"What makes you say that?" he was asked.

"We've just heard that [Philadelphia goaltender] Pelle Lindbergh has bailed out. Bob Froese is starting the game for 'em, and our guys can hardly wait to get at him. I'm telling you, it's over."

"Listen, with the two-hour time difference, your game won't be over until nearly one o'clock, my time. And hey, if you do pull it off tonight, there'll be a whole lot of other things going on."

"I'll call you after the game." he said.

The Oilers crushed the Flyers, 8–3. A little after 1:00 a.m., the telephone rang. Sather's voice could hardly be heard above the din. "How'd you like that one?" he laughed. "Didn't I tell you it was over?"

He's still my best friend. Always will be.

5

Sam

The hard, white light played on the round face, catching the blush in his cheeks and the thin line of wetness above his upper lip. Sam Pollock dabbed at his forehead even as a few individuals at the sports celebrity dinner rose to their feet. Then, as if by lemming-like instinct, more and more followed, and soon there was no longer applause from the thousand guests sweeping through the grand ballroom of the hotel in downtown Montreal, but a noise engulfing it.

The Canadiens' general manager stood there, blinking into the lights. Just a few months earlier, in September 1978, he'd been admitted as a "builder" to the Hockey Hall of Fame. His knuckles whitened where he gripped the back of his chair. A small, embarrassed smile started to form at the corners of his mouth.

"Thank you," he whispered. "Thank you . . . please . . ."

The Canadiens' organization always has been blessed with high-quality general managers, but none were as successful as Samuel Patterson Smyth Pollock. Frank Selke was starting his tenth year in the post when I started to cover the Canadiens for the *Montreal Star.* Pollock replaced him at the start of the 1964-65 season and watched his teams win nine Stanley Cups during his fourteen seasons of leadership. Irving Grundman replaced Pollock after the 1977-78 season, and promptly won a Stanley Cup with the team he inherited. Serge Savard has filled the chair since 1983-84, and won cups in 1986 and 1993. Pollock was special, though. Even today, more than sixteen years after leaving hockey for the corporate world (he's now chairman of John Labatt Limited), his name still has a special ring in hockey circles.

"When great general managers are mentioned," the late Clarence Campbell once said, "you think of names such as Jack Adams, Lester Patrick, Art Ross, Frank Selke – and Pollock. And except for Selke, Pollock didn't have the advantage of others I mentioned. Adams, Patrick, and Ross were major-league players themselves. They were coaches in the National Hockey League. Pollock wasn't.

"What Sam always had going for him, though," said Campbell, "is that he knew what was needed to win. He was as shrewd as anyone in the judgment of players and I don't know of anyone who was more knowledgeable as to the workings of the bylaws.

"There was an element of suspicion in Sam all the time, but despite the enormous input he had into the creation of what were deemed to be improvements, I'm not aware of a single situation where he designed it for his own benefit. He was very resourceful in the ways he went about some of the things, but none was off-colour, nor could you say they were the product of a scheme."

What Campbell meant was that Pollock didn't allow his personal feelings to affect the way he handled his job. He was, for example, deeply disturbed when a number of his players defected to the World Hockey Association in 1972 and '73, among them Marc Tardif and Réjean Houle. He was irate when Ken Dryden decided to retire only a few days before training camp opened in 1973 after Pollock had declined Dryden's request to renegotiate his contract. However, when the opportunity arose to get Dryden back into the fold, Pollock didn't hesitate. It was the same with Houle.

"Exactly one minute ago," Pollock told me on the telephone one day in 1976, "I signed Réjean Houle to a contract."

"You what? Is that the same guy that had you screaming when he jumped to the Quebec Nordiques? What made you change your mind?"

"He can help our team," said Pollock. "Is that a good enough reason?"

That's what made Pollock so good at what he did: he always seemed to have the right answers. He was a private person who made a career out of keeping things to himself. He did, however, have all the answers. Even his opponents knew that.

When, in 1971, the late Stafford Smythe, who owned the Toronto Maple Leafs in partnership with Harold Ballard, was facing a prison sentence on charges of defrauding Maple Leaf Gardens of hundreds of thousands of dollars, he told me he'd have "a lot of time to think" behind bars.

"So?" I said.

"Well, when I come out," observed Smythe, "I'll have all the answers. Pollock won't be able to put over a thing on me."

Smythe died before he went to jail, in October 1971, but the reality is that nobody in hockey ever truly had as many answers as Pollock. If he didn't, he pursued them relentlessly and, somehow, always found them.

The Dryden situation, for example, dismayed him – if only because it was unlike any he had ever encountered. In Pollock's time, players didn't challenge constituted authority. If a general manager instructed a player to jump, the only acceptable response was: "How high?" That's the way it had worked for years, and that's the way it was supposed to work forever.

Dryden, of course, was different. This was one goaltender who danced to his own tune. When he walked out before the start of the 1973 training camp, his decision left Pollock in a rage.

"Why don't you talk to Dryden?" Pollock was asked one day. "How are you supposed to settle this thing if you don't talk?"

"He's got a contract," said Pollock. "He hasn't honoured the contract, so we may go to court. If he wants to talk to me, he knows where I am. If I approached him, I could damage our case. I can't do that."

The temptation to write Dryden off was great, even though Dryden had led the Canadiens to a Stanley Cup in 1972-73 against Chicago. However, Pollock was a businessman. As the 1973-74 season wore on, it was clear that there was a weakness in the nets, which is why the Canadiens were eliminated in the first round of the playoffs. At the same time, Pollock knew that Dryden had kept in touch with developments within the organization through regular telephone calls to me. Similarly, Pollock delivered several "unofficial" messages to Dryden through me. In other words, each knew exactly where the other stood. However, what Pollock and Dryden needed was a reason to get together. This finally happened several weeks before the start of the 1974-75 training camp.

"You know, I've never given Dryden his miniature Stanley Cup for '73," Pollock said to me one day in his office at the Forum.

"So?"

"He was on the team. He's entitled to get it."

"Do you want me to deliver it the next time I'm in Toronto?"

"Uh . . . no, I think that's something I should do myself."

"What about your court case? What if it comes out that you met with Dryden? Remember, you told me you might take him to court and meeting him could damage your case."

"All I want to do is give him the cup. That's all. We're not going to talk about anything else."

"Sure, Sam."

Well, they did meet. They did settle their differences. Dryden would return for the 1974-75 season. Admittedly, Dryden and Pollock would have resolved their differences even without the small role I played in getting them together. However, I had earned first rights to the story, hadn't I, because friends is friends and business is business.

"Have you talked to Dryden lately?" a friend asked.

"Not for a while."

"Give him a call."

Dryden wasn't home. He telephoned about 11:00 that night. "I've been trying to think of a number of reasons why I shouldn't return your call," he sighed, "but I had to do it."

"You're coming back, aren't you?"

"The Forum will announce it at a noon press conference tomorrow. I'll be in Pollock's office at 10:30."

The story was in the *Montreal Star*'s morning edition, which landed on the streets at a little after 10:00. I was in Pollock's office at 9:30, so he had no idea the story was in the paper.

"When is the big guy coming in?" Pollock was asked.

"When is who coming in?" he asked.

"Dryden," I said. "Ken Dryden."

Pollock stared wordlessly at the ceiling.

I left.

Pollock was different, starting with the element of suspicion he carried with him. He never trusted anyone completely. That quality irritated a lot of people in his employ, but it and they served him well. He was in control, and one of the reasons was that he had to know about everything that was going on.

Pollock, who was born on December 15, 1925, was always several steps ahead of everybody. He always had to get the last word. I knew him when he was a teenager, and even then he was developing a mystique for winning. He was only seventeen, for example, when he managed a fastball team comprised largely of Canadiens players. Goaltender Bill Durnan was his pitcher, the best in Canada. Doug Harvey was his third baseman. Toe Blake and Elmer Lach were on the team, as well as Ken Reardon. They were among hockey's grandest, no-guff names, but Pollock was in charge. He put the pieces together and, more important, held them together, as he was to do with his teams when he succeeded Frank Selke in 1964.

Unlike most general managers, he didn't travel as much as he would have liked to because a fear of flying stayed with him for most of his fourteen years in the general manager's chair. But woe to the coach who wasn't on the telephone to Pollock within minutes after a road game. He had to be told everything: who played well, who played badly, why wasn't this or that done – everything.

"Sam! Sam! You've got to come out here," coach Claude Ruel would yell into the telephone near the Canadiens' dressing room after a road game. "You've got to talk to the players, Sam. They're not listening to me, Sam!"

Nobody ever knew what Pollock was really thinking. Not completely, at any rate. It was business, and Pollock's business was nobody else's business. His need to win was more important than anything else. Nothing else mattered. Nothing else was acceptable. Was Sam Pollock smarter than any of his peers? Probably. Did he work harder at his job? Definitely.

"I'm heading out your way," he said one day. "Need a lift?"

"That would be nice."

At the time, Pollock's Canadiens were well on their way to another season rooted in excellence. Pollock was feeling good about a lot of things.

"Your team's playing well these days," he was told.

"Yeah, pretty well," he said. "We could use a little help in a couple of positions, but we'll be all right."

"Everybody says you're by far the best general manager in the game, and there's no question you are, Sam, but I've got news for you . . ."

"What's that?" he grunted.

"You're the best, but some of the other general managers in the league are making you look better than you are," I said. "You're surrounded by a pack of dummies."

Pollock coloured slightly, but stared straight ahead.

Ten minutes later, after he had dropped me off, the telephone rang in my home. It was Sam. "What you said to me in the car . . . about the other general managers making me look good."

"Oh, that. I was only pulling your leg, Sam. Tryin' to be funny, Sam. I hope you didn't take me seriously."

"What about you in the newspaper business?" he snapped.

"That's exactly what I mean, Sam!"

Click!

His teams won Stanley Cups in his first two years, and they were to win seven more in the next twelve seasons. Pollock, of course, had many memorable seasons with the Canadiens, but none, he once said, was as gratifying as 1970-71.

"It came after the year we missed the playoffs, which was a very big disappointment for all of us who were connected with the club at that time. We had won the Cup in 1968-69 [Claude Ruel had succeeded Toe Blake as coach] and the second-to-last day of the season we were in third place [in the Eastern Division], but we lost out on goals on the last day of the year to finish fifth behind the Rangers.

"The next year, nobody gave us much of a chance against the Boston Bruins in the first round. The Bruins had finished first. We had finished third. They had 121 points. We had 97. They had Bobby Orr and Phil Esposito at their best. Hell, they had won the Stanley Cup the year before, and it seemed that nobody would be able to beat them."

Everybody was right to think that way. They were the Big, Bad Bruins in every sense of the word. Besides Orr and Esposito, they had Gerry Cheevers, one of hockey's best money goalies, Ken Hodge, Wayne Cashman, Johnny Bucyk, Derek Sanderson, Ed Westfall, and John McKenzie. They were, in short, a fun-loving, intimidating, and immensely talented team, the best of its time. The Canadiens weren't given even a remote chance of beating the Bruins, particularly since an unknown goaltender named Ken Dryden had drawn the starting assignment over Rogatien Vachon. Dryden had played in only six games after joining the team for the last few weeks of the season.

The Bruins won the first game, 3–1, but only after goaltender Cheevers had played splendidly. The second game also was in Boston.

When Bruins coach Tom Johnson told me he would be playing Eddie Johnston in the nets for that game, I was aghast. "Are you nuts? Didn't you see last night's game? Cheevers had to stand on his head to make the saves he did."

"I promised Eddie I'd use him in the second game," insisted Johnson. "If I don't, I'll lose him for the rest of the playoffs."

"Screw him," Johnson was told. "You've got to use your best and, last night, Cheevers was the best player on the ice."

Johnson shrugged.

The next night, with Johnston in the nets, the Bruins toyed with the Canadiens for the first half of the game. Yvan Cournoyer had opened the scoring in the first period for the Canadiens, but Orr and Ted Green scored before the period was over. McKenzie, Cashman, and Sanderson ripped shots past Dryden in the second period before Henri Richard scored. Behind the Boston bench, coach Johnson barely arched an eyebrow. After all, with a little more than one period to go the score was 5–2. No sweat.

That third period, Jean Béliveau scored one goal, then another. Jacques Lemaire tied the game. Then, John Ferguson who, along with Béliveau, was to retire at season's end, scored. Frank Mahovlich also scored. Montreal 7, Boston 5.

The Canadiens went on to take the series in seven games. They won the next series on the road in Minnesota, and headed to Chicago for the finals.

Al MacNeil was the Canadiens' coach at this time, having taken over from Claude Ruel behind the bench twenty-three games into the regular season. From there, the Canadiens enjoyed a 31–15–9 record. Then came the startling upset over Boston and the hard-fought series victory over Minnesota. Against Chicago, they lost the first two games, but won the next two in Montreal. Game five saw the Canadiens lose a game in which Henri Richard spent a lot of time on the bench. Richard sat there and burned. After the game, the Pocket Rocket went ballistic: "He's the worst coach I've ever played for," he fumed. "He's an incompetent."

Asked for reaction on the charter flight to Montreal, MacNeil snapped: "I guess I must have been a pretty good coach when we won our two games in Montreal."

Meanwhile, back in Montreal, Pollock stayed cool. "If I know Richard as well as I think I do, he'll probably score a big goal before this series is over," he said. For once, Pollock was wrong. Richard scored two big goals. The Canadiens won the next game in Montreal and returned to Chicago for game seven. They fell behind 2–0, but midway through the game, Jacques Lemaire scored with a shot from beyond centre-ice that sliced through Tony Esposito's legs. Richard, by now playing a regular shift, scored the tying goal and the winner.

Pollock was successful before the NHL expanded to twelve teams from six in 1967. He was even more successful beyond it. He has nine Stanley Cup rings because the teams he put together mirrored the quality of their general manager. Nine rings . . .

One day in the mid-1970s I informed Pollock that, having covered his team through twenty seasons and twelve Stanley Cups, I had "nothing to show for it. No rings. Nothing."

Pollock made no response. A few days later, he was on the telephone. "Who was coaching the team when you started covering the Canadiens," he asked, "Dick Irvin or Toe?"

"Actually, I joined the paper late in Dick's last year, but I didn't really start covering the team until Toe came along. Why do you ask?"

"It's got something to do with a memento I'm having made up for you," he said.

"Aw, c'mon, Sam, I hope you didn't take me seriously the other day. I was only kidding."

"No, no, I insist," he said.

"Look, Sam . . ."

"I insist," he said.

"You really don't have to do it, Sam, but thanks. It's very nice of you."

That was twenty years ago.

Maybe it got lost in the mail.

6

Scotty – and the Other Guys

Sam Pollock's eye for talent rarely failed him, and nowhere was this more evident than in his hiring of Scotty Bowman. Indeed, over the course of eight seasons Bowman became the premier coach of the Pollock era, winning five Stanley Cups, including four in a row with one of the Canadiens' truly great dynasties. He probably would have won several more with the Canadiens were it not that he decided to pack it in on June 11, 1979. At the press conference announcing his departure, he said he was leaving because he no longer felt comfortable with two people – one within, the other outside the Canadiens' organization.

Irving Grundman, the Canadiens' general manager, was the inside man. Yours truly was the outside guy. "Listen, there was no room for Irving Grundman and me on the same team," Bowman explained. "It was a power struggle that I could have won over the years if we'd started from the same point, but he had the lead. It was better for them and for me that I go. It had reached the point where I couldn't tolerate any further deterioration of my personal situation. It was a question of hockey philosophy. I was convinced I had the competence to be general manager, and I couldn't tolerate the way

71

Grundman directed the club. He said he had a lot of respect for me as coach and I had some for him as a businessman, but I have no respect for him as a hockey man and I couldn't continue in this way."

Here's where I came in: "There were all sorts of things I couldn't endure anymore. I couldn't take Red Fisher of the *Star* anymore. Fisher and Grundman were very close and I always felt Fisher was just waiting for chances to corner me. Maybe I'm exaggerating, but these are the sort of things that build up pressure to the point where a man can't continue."

Scotty's passionate goodbye – under the byline of Réjean Tremblay – appeared the next day in the French-language Montreal newspaper, *La Presse*. Tremblay's piece carried the headline: BOWMAN'S LAST SHOTS. It made for interesting reading. What it didn't mention was that only minutes after Bowman had delivered his broadside at the press conference, we had walked toward each other in a Queen Elizabeth Hotel hallway in downtown Montreal. I hadn't been at the press conference. I had no knowledge that Bowman had even scheduled one.

"Hi, Red," Scotty said, his face beaming. "How's everything?"

"Fine," I replied. "Anything happening?"

"Nothing much," he grinned, and walked on.

Strange guy. Bowman could be warm one moment, ornery the next. At times, it was for real, but often it was for show. Successful coaches are almost always good showmen, and Bowman was – and is – among the best. Almost all coaches are character actors, but only a few are actors with character.

You had to wonder about Bowman. Did he really think anyone would accept his argument that one of the reasons for his departure was that he could no longer "endure" what he perceived to be my close friendship with general manager Grundman? Was he really telling his audience – and did he honestly believe – that I had enough muscle to run a five-time Stanley Cup coach out of town? I'll say this about Scotty: he has always known how to flatter a guy.

I knew Scotty Bowman long before Pollock hired him to replace Al MacNeil as the Canadiens' coach a mere few weeks after they had won the Stanley Cup in 1971. I knew him casually when he coached junior hockey teams for a few seasons, got to know him a little better when he scouted for the Canadiens, and a lot better when he was hired as an assistant coach by the St. Louis Blues in time for the NHL's expansion to twelve teams from six in 1967-68. Eighteen games into the season, and with the Blues in last place in their division, Bowman became the team's head coach.

Coaching the Canadiens was supposedly the only job Bowman wanted – until, that is, Pollock announced he was leaving hockey after the 1977-78 season. That's when Bowman raised his sights. Coaching in the NHL is fine, but a general manager's job is better. From the start, it was obvious to everyone that Bowman and Grundman, who had been president of the Montreal Forum, were the only two candidates for the Pollock vacancy. It was also evident that Pollock's endorsement would be essential.

Jacques Courtois, a gracious, impeccably-mannered lawyer, was president of the Canadiens at the time. Shortly after Sam Pollock had announced his intention to retire, Courtois and I were head-table neighbours at a roast organized by some of Pollock's friends.

Ever the news-hound, I asked Courtois: "Who replaces Sam? Bowman?"

"Not a chance," he said quietly.

"Why not?"

"Scotty is the best coach in hockey, but he gets excited too easily," Courtois explained. "We wouldn't want to walk in one morning and discover he'd traded Guy Lafleur and Larry Robinson the night before. We don't like surprises."

"Who gets Pollock's job when he goes?" one of Bowman's friends asked a few days later. "Scotty?"

"Not a chance," I told him.

"You don't think he'll get it? Why not?" asked the friend.

73

"All I can tell you is that he doesn't have a chance," I replied.

Scotty's friend, of course, promptly rushed to Bowman with the news, but several months passed before he was told officially that Grundman would succeed Pollock as general manager. Moreover, Grundman would continue to run the Forum as well. Bowman raged over what he considered a betrayal by Pollock. He stayed on as coach for another, albeit uncomfortable, season, but when the Buffalo Sabres received permission from the Canadiens to talk to Bowman about taking over as both general manager and coach, Scotty was poised to jump.

I have often wondered what really made Scotty run. After all, he was only forty-six when he left the Canadiens, so what was the rush? He was a winner behind the bench, and if he had stayed and let the inevitable maturation of middle-age take hold, Grundman eventually would have offered him the general manager's job. Instead, Scotty went to Buffalo, where he was embraced as a saviour by the media. Eight years later, he was bitter and disillusioned. Gerry Meehan, who had played for six NHL teams, including the Sabres, was now armed with a law degree and was being groomed for better things. Soon there was no room for Bowman and Meehan in the same organization.

Sound familiar? Bowman left.

Nobody has captured the Bowman psyche as well as Ken Dryden did in his brilliant book, *The Game*. "There are autocrats and technocrats, mean SOBs and just plain folks," wrote Dryden. "What makes Bowman's style work is an understanding, *the* understanding that must exist between a coach and his team: *he* knows the most important thing to a team is to win; *we* know he does what he does to make us win. . . . Just as he will allow no player to stand above the team, he will not stand above it either. The team must believe in itself. . . . To him loyalty is doing what you can and doing it well. . . . What you have done counts only until you can't do it again."

How good was Bowman? Toe Blake was the best among the nine

coaches I've covered during my four decades with the Canadiens, but Scotty ranks a close second.

By now you know what Blake was all about — starting with his eight Stanley Cups in thirteen seasons. He wasn't stylish as the left-winger on that great line with Rocket Richard and Elmer Lach, but he was its hardest worker. Not surprisingly, he coached the way he played. Frills were for losers, in Blake's view, while winning was everything.

Bowman was a Blake disciple and the biggest lesson he learned from Toe was that the best teams don't necessarily win Stanley Cups unless their coach has the talent for getting the most out of the best. They won because Bowman, like Blake, showed them what it takes to win. Many, if not most, of Bowman's players didn't like him as a person, but they certainly liked winning. Bowman was a winner.

One of the things I liked most about him was his lack of reticence. Although a shy man, he always had something to say and almost all of it was interesting. He was very good for the people in my business, and still is now that he's coaching again at the NHL level. He knows more about what's going on with other teams in the league than most of the people running those teams. The telephone has always been an extension of his arms and ears, as he pulls in information about other players, other teams. He likes to telephone media people, too, to talk about something that had been written, heard, or seen.

Yes, he and I have had our differences, but that shouldn't be a surprise to anybody. Coaches — and some reporters — have always happily subscribed to the "us-versus-them" syndrome. Once, after he had criticized several of his Canadiens players during a rare slump, I approached the players for their views. Predictably, their position was that the Canadiens won as a team and lost as a team — and the team included the man behind the bench.

Scotty, of course, found something wrong with that. The next day, he called a press conference to declare that, contrary to what had been written in the *Montreal Star*, he was not at war with his players and they weren't at war with him. I wasn't invited to the press conference, naturally. Actually, I didn't hear about it until Al Strachan, who was covering the Canadiens for the *Gazette* at the time, telephoned to let me know what had been said.

Another fracas with Bowman occurred after I'd attended a morning skate at the Forum.

"What's wrong with Jacques Lemaire?" I asked. Lemaire was the team's best centreman.

"Upset stomach," Bowman tersely explained.

"Well, he seemed to be favouring his shoulder."

"Stomach," Bowman repeated. "He'll be all right."

A few minutes later, one of the Canadiens players said quietly to me: "Lemaire has a slightly separated shoulder. Nothing serious, but I guess it's uncomfortable."

Back at the office, I began a story with this paragraph: "Jacques Lemaire is doubtful for tonight's game with what Canadiens coach Scotty Bowman describes as an upset stomach. The pain, however, has gone all the way up to his slightly separated shoulder."

As it developed, Lemaire played that night in a game the Canadiens won. After the game, Bowman stood in the centre of the dressing room and, within earshot of all of the players and media people, started to fire from the hip.

"Lemaire played, eh, eh?"

"Excuse me?" I said.

"You wrote he wasn't playing. He played."

"I wrote that his status was doubtful because of what you called an upset stomach. He has a separated shoulder."

"He played, eh?"

"He played and you said he had a bad stomach."

"He played," Bowman persisted.

"One more thing . . ."

"Yeah?" asked Bowman.

"Go and fuck yourself."

At that, I left the dressing room, crossed Atwater Street, and walked into the Alexis Nihon Plaza. A few minutes later, a hand tapped me on the shoulder. Peter Mahovlich, the Canadiens winger, stood there, a big grin on his face.

"What was that thing in the dressing room all about?" he asked.

"Nothing much. Happens all the time."

"Not what you told him just before you left happens all the time," said Mahovlich.

"Aw, I just lost it for a few seconds. The guy got me pissed off putting on a floor-show in front of everybody."

"I've got something to say about what you said," said Mahovlich.

"I'm listening."

"On behalf of the Montreal Canadiens players, thank you very much."

Claude Ruel was only thirty when he replaced Blake, who retired after the 1967-68 season. He would be coaching superstars such as Jean Béliveau, Henri Richard, Yvan Cournoyer, Jacques Lemaire, Lorne Worsley, Jean-Claude Tremblay, and Jacques Laperrière. Until his appointment, which was a surprise to me and to others, Ruel had done some scouting and coaching at the junior level, but this was "the bigs," and what the Canadiens' management and its players had to find out was whether Ruel was big enough to handle it. No one was surprised when the Blake team Ruel inherited won a second consecutive Stanley Cup and its fourth in five years. The real test, everyone agreed, would come the following season.

I was hard on Ruel that first season. I was harder on him, perhaps unfairly, when, for the first time in twenty-two years, the team failed to make the playoffs in 1969-70. At the same time, I liked him. His loyalty to the organization was as strong as Blake's. He worked hard. He was enthusiastic. He knew the game. Unfortunately, too many of his players didn't take him seriously, primarily because he wasn't as firm with them as he should have been. The mistake Claude Ruel made with his players was that he was too chummy with them.

I remember the time the Canadiens were in Oakland for Ruel's first-ever road trip as head coach. Minutes after checking into their rooms, several of the players were having a drink at the motel bar. Ruel joined them.

"It's probably none of my business," I told him the next morning, "but you shouldn't be drinking with your players. Blake never did."

"I am not a policeman!" snapped Ruel.

"Sorry I mentioned it," I said. "It won't happen again."

Halfway through his third season, in 1970-71, Ruel was gone and his assistant, Al MacNeil, took over. MacNeil sensed that a firmer hand was needed. The talent was there, but it needed direction. It also needed stronger goaltending, and that was to come from Ken Dryden, whose heroics playing every minute of twenty playoff games – after he had played in only six regular-season games – brought the organization its seventeenth Stanley Cup. MacNeil had played the game hard as a defenceman with five NHL teams, including the Canadiens, from 1955-56 to 1967-68. He also coached hard. He went with those players he felt would win for him – and if they didn't like it, well, too bad. No special strokes for special folks, including icons such as Henri Richard. Trouble is, it cost him his job. Only a few weeks after Richard was benched for most of a play-off game in the Stanley Cup final with Chicago, MacNeil was out and Bowman in.

Bernard Geoffrion succeeded Bowman as coach in 1979. His biggest problem as a coach, of course, was that he expected too much from his players. He had so much to give during his playing days, and couldn't handle it when his players didn't give as much as he had. Geoffrion left a team that was to finish first in its division with 107 points in 1979-80 under an older, wiser Ruel who, stout and loyal company man that he was, readily agreed to take over as head coach after Geoffrion's sudden departure in December of 1979. However, when the Canadiens fell to the Minnesota North Stars in the second round of the playoffs that season, then got bumped by the upstart

Edmonton Oilers the next despite a 103-point regular season, the front-office felt it was time for another change.

Enter Bob Berry. Berry, a native Montrealer who's now behind the St. Louis Blues' bench, had been coaching the Los Angeles Kings for three seasons. His West Coast team had finished the 1980-81 season with 99 points – a 25-point improvement over the previous year. In Berry's view, at least, that was worth a long-term contract and a substantial raise. However, when neither was forthcoming, he was on the telephone: "Tell Irving Grundman I'm available," Berry told me. "I'd love to go up there."

Bob Berry: decent guy, decent coach, lousy gin player. I lost an annuity when he was fired at the end of the 1982-83 season, re-hired for the start of 1983-84 season by incoming general manager Serge Savard, then replaced by his assistant, Jacques Lemaire, midway through the season. Berry was fine during regular-season play. He led the Canadiens to a division-topping 109 points in his first season, but this was followed by the team's elimination in overtime in the fifth and deciding game of the first-round series with the Quebec Nordiques. The next season, the Canadiens slipped to 98 points. After they lost in three to the Buffalo Sabres (the Canadiens were shut out in the first two games in Montreal), Canadiens president Ronald Corey had seen enough. Irving Grundman's contract wasn't renewed and Bob Berry's status as head coach was put on hold until a new general manager was named.

Was Berry the problem in the playoffs? Perhaps. Playoff heat can be suffocating, particularly in Montreal where "us-versus-them" is in full flower in late spring. Berry's teams had failed to get beyond the first round in his three years of coaching at Los Angeles and two in Montreal. Time to go.

Berry's successor, Jacques Lemaire, hasn't talked to me since the day after he quit as coach on July 29, 1985. His idea, not mine. It had something to do with what he perceived to be a nasty column I wrote about his resignation, but since I don't recall Lemaire thanking me whenever – and it was often – I wrote something complimentary about him, let's just say that tells you something about him as a person. He's an outstanding coach, though. Hardly anybody was surprised when he was voted the NHL's best coach (Adams Trophy) for 1993-94.

Lemaire was always comfortable with authority – but only up to a point. He was fine when he fired from the hip. However, he couldn't handle the heat when it was turned in his direction, especially by the media. The team he inherited from Berry wasn't a very good one, and proved it by finishing the eighty-game schedule in fourth place with 75 points – the lowest total by a Canadiens team since 1950-51. (That year, the Canadiens earned only 65 points in a seventy-game schedule.) Indeed, the Berry team Lemaire inherited finished 19 points behind the third-place Quebec Nordiques and 29 behind the Adams Division-leading Boston Bruins. Needless to say, there was every reason to believe this team would be eliminated quickly from the playoffs. Instead, they swept the heavily favoured Bruins in three games. They needed six games to beat the Nordiques in the Adams final. Then, incredibly, they won the first two games of the conference final against the New York Islanders, by that time winners of four consecutive Stanley Cups and eager for a fifth.

The Islanders won the next four. Looking back on it, one of the reasons the Canadiens fell tantalizingly short of making it to the Stanley Cup final was that Bob Gainey, the team's best defensive forward, played against the Islanders with major shoulder injuries. A healthy Gainey might have been able to lead the Canadiens into the final where, plausibly, Lemaire would have found a way to beat the Edmonton Oilers.

One of my favourite Lemaire stories goes back to the hours before game six of that Canadiens–Islanders series. That's when he asked me if I would speak to one of his players, Perry Turnbull. Turnbull had been acquired by the Canadiens from St. Louis in late December of that season for forwards Doug Wickenheiser and Greg Paslawski, and defenceman Gilbert Delorme. Turnbull joined the Canadiens with excellent credentials, but he just didn't fit in. He struggled almost from the moment he joined the team for a game in Quebec City. His game didn't improve as the season wore on, so now he wasn't even being dressed for any of the playoff games against the Islanders.

"Why would you want me to speak to Turnbull?" I asked Lemaire.

"Gainey has two bad shoulders. Real bad," he explained. "He's got a separation in one and a dislocation in the other, but we've been keeping it quiet. Now, though, I can't see how he can play tonight. If he doesn't, I've got to dress Turnbull. I've got to get him ready to play."

"You're the coach, why don't you speak to Turnbull?" I suggested.

"Sometimes a player listens more to a guy who's been around for a long time than he does to his coach. Talk to him for me," said Lemaire.

I found Turnbull in the hotel lobby, flipping idly through the pages of a Long Island newspaper. It was time for my best motivational speech. "What's going on, Perry?" I asked.

"What do you mean what's going on?"

"Early this season, you came into Montreal with St. Louis. You got into two fights with Chris Nilan and did all right. You scored two goals and had an assist, or maybe it was a goal and two assists . . . I don't really remember. What I know for sure is that you were so far and away the best player on the ice for either team, it was no contest. Now look at you," I said. "Lemaire isn't even dressing you for the games. So what's going on, Perry?"

"Oh, Christ, Red," said Turnbull, "I was crazy that night. It'll never happen again!"

Poof! There went my motivational speech, but the only thing that was lost that night was the game by the Canadiens. Happily, Gainey had insisted on playing, so there was no need to dress Turnbull. The Islanders skated into their fifth consecutive Stanley Cup final, where they lost to Edmonton in five games, and a new dynasty was born. Turnbull, in the meantime, went to the Winnipeg Jets and retired in 1988.

Jean Perron, who replaced Lemaire behind the bench for the 1985-86 season, seemed to restore the Canadiens' fortunes in his rookie year by winning the Stanley Cup, but he wasn't regarded highly by his players. Perron had strong ideas, but he had all kinds of trouble earning his players' respect. Team discipline was lax, and Perron did little to tighten the reins, largely because he was uncomfortable with that side of the coaching game. He had inherited a good team and an excellent game plan dedicated to defence from Lemaire, and Perron made it better by not tinkering with it. The arrival of goaltender Patrick Roy made it much better. Perron was the coach, but it was Roy's remarkable 1.92 goals-against average in twenty play-off games which brought a twenty-third Stanley Cup to the Canadiens' organization.

The fact that Edmonton, Philadelphia, and Washington – teams which had finished well ahead of the Canadiens during the regular season – had been eliminated by the time the Canadiens got to the Cup final against Calgary, didn't hurt either. The Stanley Cup victory saved Perron's job. He would not have been invited back for a second year if the Canadiens hadn't gone all the way.

Pat Burns didn't win the big prize during his four seasons with the Canadiens – the longest tenure of any Montreal coach since Scotty Bowman – but unlike Perron, he was in control. NHL players feed on soft coaches. Give 'em an inch, and they'll snap off a foot, usually the coach's. Burns, an ex-cop, could play the "bad cop" to near-perfection, as he still does with his current charges, the Toronto Maple Leafs. It worked for him in his first season behind the Canadiens' bench, when he took the 115-point Canadiens to the Stanley Cup final in 1989, only to lose to Calgary. However, different players often have to be treated differently to get the most out of them. Burns's idea of solving a personnel problem was to get rid of him. Over time this black-hat act wore thin. It's why several of his players criticized him publicly after the Canadiens fell to the Boston Bruins in four games after the strike-interrupted 1991-92 season. Then, the

French-language newspaper *La Presse* had Canadiens president Ronald Corey questioning Burns's attitude and suggesting it would have to change the following season. Instead, Burns decided he needed a change of venue, not a change of attitude.

I learned about his move the morning after the Pittsburgh Penguins had taken a 2–0 lead in their Stanley Cup final with Chicago. Many of us were at the airport awaiting a flight to Chicago, where the next two games would be played. That's when *Hockey Night in Canada* analyst Harry Neale approached me. "Boy, have I got a story for you," he said. "Burns is leaving the Canadiens. He's going to Toronto. They're holding a press conference in Montreal at 1:00 p.m., and then Burns is flying to Toronto for a 5:00 p.m. conference."

"I don't believe it," I snorted. "Hell, it wasn't more than two weeks ago he was telling me how he was going to spend a lot more time at the Forum during the summer getting ready for next season."

"Check it out," Neale suggested.

I telephoned Burns at his apartment-hotel in Montreal, only to learn from the operator that Burns wasn't taking calls. "I'm leaving for Chicago in a few minutes," I told her. "Ask him to call me at my hotel in Chicago."

Burns never forgets a friend. He got my message and called. Trouble is, he didn't call until five days later.

I have known Jacques Demers, Burns's successor, for a long time. I knew him when he coached St. Louis from 1983-84 through 1985-86 and, after a messy split with the Blues, for the four years he spent behind the Detroit Red Wings' bench. His hiring by the Canadiens wasn't greeted with enthusiasm by some people, including yours truly, but it's difficult to argue with success. I didn't think he could win a Stanley Cup with the team he took over from Pat Burns. Few people did, but he and they won mostly because Patrick Roy's brilliance produced ten consecutive overtime victories in the playoffs. What that says is that teams don't need a miracle to win a Stanley Cup, but it helps.

Demers has been good for the Canadiens. He's also been good for the players, who, after four years with Burns, found Demers's "good cop" approach refreshing. Unlike Burns, Demers spends most of his waking hours trying to keep his bosses, his players, and the media happy which, in the final analysis, shouldn't be that difficult. All he has to do is win.

7

Boom-Boom

Pierre Larouche wasn't happy. The twenty-four-year-old centreman stared at the Canadiens going through their pre-game warmup for the start of the 1979-80 season and swore softly. The problem? They were in uniform on the ice, he was sitting in the broadcast booth, wearing a blue blazer and grey slacks.

"Scotty Bowman," he muttered.

"What about Bowman?"

"The guy didn't dress me for a lot of games last season. Now, here I am again. I'm sure he told Geoffrion to keep me out tonight."

In his time with the Canadiens (1950-1964), Joseph André Bernard Geoffrion was one of the NHL's truly great players. None could shoot harder. Most couldn't shoot as hard. Geoffrion was "Boom-Boom" – The Boomer.

Now, though, Geoffrion was going into the season as the team's replacement for Scotty Bowman, who had left for Buffalo two months earlier. At age forty-eight, Geoffrion was behind the bench, and Larouche – a man who, at twenty, had scored fifty goals in one season for the Pittsburgh Penguins – was in the broadcast booth feeling sorry for himself.

"Bowman," he muttered.

"Get serious," he was told. "Bowman had nothing to do with this. He's in Buffalo. Maybe if you'd worked harder in training camp, you'd be on the ice right now. Anyway, don't worry about Geoffrion."

"What do you mean, don't worry about Geoffrion?"

"He'll be gone by Christmas."

"Oh, sure," said Larouche. "That bastard, Bowman . . ."

Geoffrion always has been one of my favourite people. He was there when I started travelling with the Canadiens. In the mid-1950s, it wasn't common practice to go on the road with an NHL team. Reporters would be assigned to the playoffs, but the regular season was out. Too expensive. The Canadiens' management offered to pay a reporter's expenses, but there were few takers. Jacques Beauchamp, who was the sports editor of the French-language tabloid *Montréal-Matin*, was the first to travel with the team during the regular season. He was joined by Marcel Desjardins of *La Presse*. Toe Blake was the coach when I started travelling – by train, of course.

Geoffrion was one of the team's brightest stars. He was loud and profane and secure in his status. Of course, he had joined the team when Rocket Richard was all that mattered. As good as Geoffrion was, the Rocket remained everything to Montreal. How good was Geoffrion? He was only the second player, behind Richard, to score fifty goals in a season. In all, he scored 393 goals in 883 games with the Canadiens and the New York Rangers. He was on six Stanley Cup teams in Montreal. He was, plainly, among the very best. But was he among the very best coaches? Pierre Larouche had already made up his mind. The fact that Geoffrion was in Montreal again, at the Forum and with the Canadiens, was a minor miracle.

In 1958, Geoffrion was being checked closely during a Canadiens practice. André Pronovost, a young player, was left staggering after bodychecking Geoffrion, who continued skating. Then, a minute later, Geoffrion collapsed to the ice. At first, the players thought Geoffrion, a great kidder, was having a little fun at their expense. He thrashed around on the ice as they gathered around him.

"Get up," Pronovost laughed. "Quit fooling around."

Geoffrion, however, continued to thrash on the ice. Bill Head, who was the team's sports therapist, rushed to the fallen player. By this time, Geoffrion was breathing with extreme difficulty. His face was turning blue.

"What happened here?" Head yelled. "Let's get him out of here and over to the hospital."

Minutes later, Geoffrion was being wheeled into the Herbert Reddy Memorial Hospital across the street from the Forum. A quick diagnosis appeared to indicate a ruptured bowel. Even as he was being prepared for immediate surgery, last rites were administered. The next day, team doctor Larry Hampson reported: "Geoffrion spent a comfortable night. He went through a delicate, painful operation that probably will keep him from playing again this season."

Geoffrion left hospital in mid-February, three weeks after the surgery. Against the advice of doctors, he insisted on returning to the lineup during a playoff series against the Boston Bruins. He scored two goals in his first game and was an important contributor to the Canadiens' third consecutive Stanley Cup in 1957-58. Geoffrion spent most of his playing career with the Canadiens, but, in 1966, after a two-year hiatus, he was coaxed out of retirement to play 117 games with the New York Rangers, where he scored 22 goals and 41 assists. Then, in a stunning move, he was behind the Rangers' bench for the start of the 1968-69 season. Two months into the season, however, ulcers forced him out. Four years later, he was named the Atlanta Flames' first coach. The results were the same as in New York: Boom-Boom had to leave after less than three seasons. Too much pressure, he explained. He moved into Atlanta's broadcast booth as an analyst alongside play-by-play man Jiggs McDonald. That seemed to be that.

Except it wasn't. Training camp for the 1979-80 season was drawing closer, and the Canadiens, having lost Scotty Bowman, were still without a coach. Shortly after 1:00 a.m. on a Saturday morning, the telephone rang in my office.

Jiggs MacDonald was on the line with some news about the Boomer. "He's got it, you know."

"Got what?" I asked.

"The Canadiens' coaching job. I was with him today. He told me he's signed. They'll announce it on Tuesday."

"You feeling all right, Jiggs?"

"A little surprised, but I've never felt better."

"Geoffrion?"

"That's what he told me."

"Do you believe him?"

"I do."

"Impossible. The guy had to quit the Rangers' job because he couldn't stand the heat. He had to quit Atlanta. How long would he last in Montreal? He's pulling your chain."

"He wouldn't kid me about this," insisted McDonald.

I called general manager Irving Grundman at his country home north of Montreal. Reluctantly, needless to say, because it was now 2:00 a.m. Nobody should be called at that hour unless it's a matter of life or death.

"I'm really sorry about this," I told Grundman, "but it can't hold. I'm told Geoffrion is your coach. He told a friend of mine in Atlanta he's signed."

Grundman didn't reply for a long time. Finally, he said: "He's not signed. He's one of several people I've talked with."

"He told somebody in Atlanta he's got the job."

"I've talked to a number of people," Grundman repeated.

"Irving," I said, "you and I know he was a great player, but I've got to tell you this: if you sign him, he won't last 'til Christmas. I admired and respected him as a player, but he's tried coaching twice and couldn't handle it."

The telephone fell silent again. Then Grundman sighed. "Like I said, he's not signed. Thanks for calling."

The next day, my newspaper carried a short item announcing that

Geoffrion was one of several individuals interviewed for the coaching job, and that in all likelihood he would get the nod. That same day I called Geoffrion at his home in Atlanta to confirm his acceptance of the job. He wasn't home. A message was left to have him call back. He didn't. On Monday, the Canadiens called a press conference for the next day. Geoffrion was introduced as the coach, effective September 4, 1979. You win some, you lose some.

Of course, there were reservations in some quarters about Bernie Geoffrion getting the job. In truth, though, he was a popular choice. Nobody was – and still is – more at home with the media. He never met a camera he didn't like, which doesn't make him unique among coaches, but it helps – particularly in Montreal. He liked them and they liked him because he always had something to say. He was entertaining, if only because he never allowed the facts to intrude on a good story.

The day he was signed he looked like a winner. He had a snappy-looking suit, the Georgia sun had given his complexion a bronzed glow.

"This is the dream of my life," he gushed to the assembled media throng. Of course, this is what every coach before him and since has said on the day he's signed to a new coaching job. It was the dream of his life to get the job with the Rangers, just as it was the dream of his life to find himself behind the Atlanta bench. This time, though, the dream was a little more real, this time he had a team that had won four consecutive Stanley Cups.

"I'll do everything possible to win a fifth straight Stanley Cup with this team," he told his audience, "and with help from Toe Blake and Claude Ruel [both were in the Canadiens' front-office] I feel we can do it. I welcome their advice. Three heads are better than one. I've been trying to get back here for twelve years, and now that I'm here, I plan to finish my years here. I'm signed for three years but if they like my work I'll be here longer. I'm not afraid to face challenges. I'm afraid of nothing," he thundered. "I'll give 150 per cent. I'll need help from all the players and I'm sure I'll get it. Any questions?"

Somebody asked him about his health.

"Everywhere I go, people ask me about my health," he growled. "Let me just say this about my health once and for all: I'm sick and tired [he paused to wait for the laughter, which came quickly enough] of answering that question. My health is one thousand per cent better than when I was playing. Now don't ask me about my health any more. What about your health?" he asked the reporter who had asked the question. More laughter.

Twenty-one days later, the Canadiens were on their way to Ottawa for an exhibition game with the Chicago Blackhawks. The team bus, the players were told, would leave the Forum at 3:00 p.m. It would stop briefly at Dorval to pick up several players, and then would continue on to Ottawa at 4:00 p.m.

A couple of minutes after the appointed hour, the team bus left the Forum. The remaining players – except one – were waiting when the bus arrived at Dorval. Minutes passed, and no sign of the missing player. More minutes. Still no sign. At 4:20, defenceman Serge Savard arrived and slipped into his seat.

"I was held up on the Champlain Bridge," he mumbled by way of explanation.

Geoffrion didn't reply.

Former coach Blake, an unflinching disciplinarian during his thirteen seasons behind the Canadiens' bench, had been glancing at his watch several times while the team waited for Savard. He didn't like the idea of one player holding up a team bus for twenty minutes. He liked it even less when coach Geoffrion didn't bring it to Savard's attention. "That's the beginning of the end of Geoffrion," he grunted.

Two hours later, the bus arrived in Ottawa. Glen Cole, who was the *Gazette*'s hockey writer at the time, was waiting when the players spilled out of the bus.

"Guess what?" he said to me.

"What?"

"The *Montreal Star* stopped publishing at 4 o'clock."

"No kidding," I said. A telephone call to the *Star*'s sports department elicited no response, which was normal.

A call to my home confirmed the newspaper's passing.

"Don't be upset," my wife said. "Come home."

After their 3–2 victory over the Blackhawks, the Canadiens went on to Toronto for a Wednesday night game against the Maple Leafs. General manager Grundman and I drove back to Montreal.

"What do you do now?" my wife asked when I arrived home at 1:00 a.m.

"I'll drop into the office tomorrow. Then, we'll see. Things will work out."

The *Star*'s doors were locked that morning, but editor-in-chief Frank Walker waved me inside. "Can you stay on for another eight days?" he asked. "We'll be getting calls from our employees, so I'd like the department heads to be around."

"What happens after eight days?" he was asked.

"Everybody out," he sighed. "Can you stay on?"

"I don't see where I have much of a choice," I said. "Sure, I'll stay on."

I was shaken by the *Star*'s closure, even though it wasn't a complete surprise. The *Star* was the city's number-one English-language newspaper, by a good margin, when the employees walked out on June 14, 1978. By the time they returned to work on February 12, 1979, the battle to regain lost circulation was all uphill. Seven months later the *Star*'s doors were closing forever. A lot of tears were shed during the eight days management people stayed on.

Wakes aren't much fun. Funerals are worse. Eight days of watching a newspaper, where I had been employed for nearly twenty-six years, being prepared for burial was almost too painful. Finally, everybody out, but first . . .

The man behind the pay wicket looked at the list of names before him, frowned darkly, then checked the list again. "I don't see your name here," he said.

"Well, I've been here for the last eight days."

"I'll have to clear this with the publisher," he said.

"Do that."

A few minutes later, the clerk declared: "Mr. [Art] Wood says he didn't ask you to stay on for eight days."

"That's true, but tell him Mr. Walker did."

"Oh, fine. I'll tell him."* He returned a few minutes later: "Mr. Wood says he'll pay you for five days."

"Five days instead of eight?"

"Yes."

"Give me the five days," I said.

Three days after the *Star*'s doors closed for good, I was offered the sports editor's job at the *Gazette*, but didn't join the department until late October. Two weeks earlier, though, I'm with Pierre Larouche. It's the regular season's opening night and Geoffrion is behind the bench. Larouche is in the press box, grumbling.

"I know Bowman told Geoffrion not to dress me," he insisted. "I know that for sure. This is going to happen all season."

"What I know for sure," Larouche was told, "is that you don't know anything for sure. Anyway, don't worry about it."

"What do you mean, don't worry about it?" Larouche groused. "Of course I'm worried about it. I don't want to sit in this damned place all season."

"Geoffrion won't be here after Christmas," I repeated.

"Yeah, sure," said Larouche.

Superficially, of course, Larouche's pessimism was understandable. Under Boom-Boom, the Canadiens had won seven games in a row. But success, it seemed, was bringing with it pressures that Geoffrion couldn't handle.

"Those guys, they're gonna put me in my coffin," he barked.

"How can you say that?" he was asked. "You guys haven't lost a game in your first seven."

"I can't take it any more," he said.

Eventually, small cracks did start to show. The Canadiens' goal-tending was shaky, what with the retired Ken Dryden being replaced by his former backup, Michel Larocque. Then, the team's offence fell off. Injuries struck. Doug Risebrough had a bad knee. Bob Gainey broke a bone in his foot. By December, the team started to lose, and by the time Geoffrion decided he'd had enough, its record had fallen to 15–9–6, including losses in their last two games – 7–5 to the mediocre Colorado Rockies at the Forum on a Sunday night and, two nights later, 4–1 in a game at Long Island against the Islanders. Wednesday morning, Geoffrion wasn't at the team's practice.

"Has he quit?" asked left-winger Steve Shutt after the practice.

"What makes you think that?" he was asked.

"Well, there have been other times this season when he hasn't been on the ice, but at least he watched from the stands. Today, nobody's seen him."

"Has anybody seen the coach?" asked Larouche.

Grundman had seen Geoffrion that morning and confirmed that the coach wanted to leave. "I simply told him this wasn't the time to make a decision like that and that he should come back in the afternoon and we'd discuss it further. He's a very sensitive individual. He hates to lose, and I would expect him to hate to lose. But I've told him that once the game is lost, what you have to do twenty or twenty-five minutes later is start working on the next game. That's all that matters. You can't bring back anything."

Grundman was to learn later that day that he couldn't bring back Geoffrion, either. Geoffrion had put out as a player. When his players weren't putting out the way he felt they should, he couldn't accept it. He walked away.

Grundman and Geoffrion met again in the early afternoon. Five hours later, Grundman came out to meet the reporters who had gathered. "This thing could go well into the night," he told them. "There's no point waiting around."

One hour later, thirteen days before Christmas, Boom-Boom Geoffrion was gone.

Two years later, four days before Christmas, Pierre Larouche was on his way to Hartford.

My wife, Tillie, and I on our honeymoon in Atlantic City in 1948.

daughter, Cheryl, and son, Ian.

Above: Discussing lay-out issues at the *Montreal Star* with sports editor Harold Atkins (centre) and photo editor Art Wood (left). Wood later became managing editor and then publisher of the *Star*. *Below:* At radio station CKGM in Montreal with Frank Selke, Jr. (second from left), Danny Gallivan, and Jacques Plante.

ove: I'm wearing the bow-tie. The guy to my right is Elmer Ferguson, dean of the Montreal *rts*-writing fraternity. The guy in the middle is, of course, Maurice "Rocket" Richard. *(Jerry nati) Below:* In the dressing room with (from left) Tom Johnson, Jean-Guy Talbot, *I* Lou Fontinato.

Yours truly posing with Canadiens coach Toe Blake minutes after the team had won the first of what were to be five consecutive Stanley Cups. The date: April 10, 1956.

ve: An interview with the brilliant general manager of the Canadiens, Sam Pollock. *(Gerry idson) Below:* A rink-side chat in the Forum with Canadiens goaltenders Gump Worsley (left) Cesare Maniago in the early 1960s. *(Gerry Davidson)*

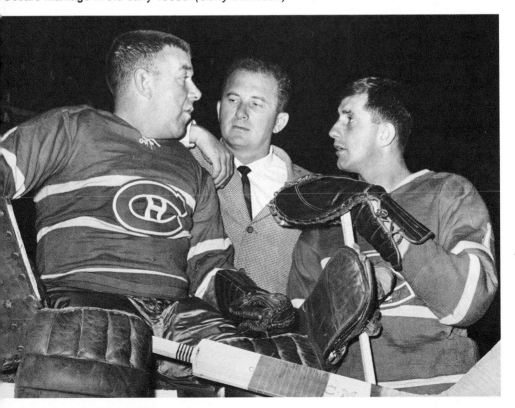

Above (left): Sugar Ray Robinson, at the piano here, remains the best boxer I've ever seen. *Above* (right): Shooting the breeze with the inimitable promoter Eddie Quinn. *Below:* Archie M(
(right) fought a memorable bout with New Brunswick's Yvon Durelle in Montreal in 1958.

author talks with Jean Béliveau. The year was 1962.

Goaltender Ken Dryden (left) and centreman Jacques Lemaire (right) were members of the gr
Canadiens teams which won Stanley Cups in the 1970s. That's me in the middle with the Mol
Cup.

8

1972

Most Americans born before or around, say, 1950 can recall where they were and what they were doing on November 22, 1963, the day President John Kennedy was assassinated. It's a touchstone experience, one of those public moments that seems to tap deeply into the collective psyche of a nation and reverberate there for a long time.

Canadians don't seem to have as many touchstone experiences as their neighbours to the south. And when they do, they seem to involve hockey. It's one of the great clichés of Canadian history that most Canadians born before or around 1960 remember where they were and what they were doing September 28, 1972, when Paul Henderson scored his last-minute goal in the final game of the first, titanic Canadian–Soviet hockey series. It's also one cliché that happens to be true.

Of course, with the collapse of the Soviet Union, it's hard these days to recall the intensity of the hockey rivalry that existed for so many years between Canada and the Soviets. It was, quite literally, the Cold War on ice. By 1972, the Soviet Nationals had won a staggering nine International Ice Hockey Federation world amateur championships in nine years, and they were the defending Olympic champions. Canada had bowed out of international competition three years earlier, arguing that its definition of "amateur" didn't match the Soviet definition. Hockey fans across this country were mightily peeved that the Soviets were being permitted supremacy in "our game" without having to battle NHL professionals. If only such a contest could occur, well, all would be right with the world.

I was at Moscow's Luzhniki Arena for that heart-stopping nation-boosting 6–5 win. But my presence in the Soviet capital that fall day actually went back to a hot afternoon early in July in Montreal in 1972, when Frank Walker, editor-in-chief of the *Montreal Star*, sauntered over to my desk.

"What," he wondered, "are we going to do about that series of yours?"

"Huh?"

"The National Hockey League and the Soviets," said Walker. "Isn't it coming up in September?"

"It is . . . and I've got an idea I want to run past you. Nobody knows much of anything about the Soviet team. Why don't we get somebody to do a lengthy piece on those people? We could carry it a few days before training camp opens."

I told Walker that our stringer (a freelance writer who does occasional articles) in Moscow could do the piece quite handily.

"I've got a better idea," said Walker. "Why don't you go over for a week or so?"

I was taken aback a bit. I didn't speak Russian. I didn't know Moscow from Johannesburg. Walker, however, was unperturbed. "I'll speak to somebody at the Soviet embassy in Ottawa," he said. "We'll get you cleared for the trip. They'll want to know who you want to see, where you want to go, so let me know as soon as possible. You can go over there for seven or eight days, talk to the players, come back and do a series. We'll get our people to sell it. We may even make a few dollars out of this."

"It's fine with me. What about our guy in Moscow?"

"Phone him. Tell him what we're doing. I'll get on to the Soviet people in Ottawa. Let's get going on this. I want you over there and back before anybody knows we're there."

A few days later, Walker said he had talked to a friend in the Soviet embassy who would arrange a visa and a ticket on an Aeroflot plane. A few days after that, everything seemed in order. Except for one thing.

"What about a hotel room in Moscow?"

"We'll get our man in Moscow to reserve one," Walker replied. "That shouldn't be a problem, either. The people over there know you're coming. You're leaving in two days – Wednesday night – by the way. Aeroflot only flies out of here on Wednesdays, and we don't want to waste an extra week. Don't tell anybody you're going. I don't want this to get around to other newspapers."

Wednesday morning, just a few hours before my flight, Walker asked if I had heard about my hotel room yet. "Not a word," I replied. "What do I do if I don't hear anything? I can't go there without a hotel room."

"Don't worry about it," said Walker.

Walker's friend from Ottawa was at the airport that night. He smiled a lot. "Everything is in order, Mr. Fisher," he said. "You will be met at the airport in Moscow by our hockey people. They are looking forward to an exchange of ideas. There are no problems."

"I've got one," I said. "I don't have a hotel room in Moscow."

"That is not a problem," he said. "Our people will meet you. They will take care of you. You will enjoy Aeroflot," he promised. "It will be very interesting. Goodbye."

In July of 1972, Aeroflot flew overnight from Montreal to Paris, a flight of seven hours. From there, it was a direct four-hour flight to Moscow, landing at 4:30 p.m. Unless, that is, the pilot had a surprise up his well-worn sleeve. In July 1972, Soviet pilots were full of surprises.

The overnight flight to Paris was uneventful. I couldn't say the same for the Paris-to-Moscow "hop." Just moments after the Aeroflot plane lifted off from Orly, a garbled message came over the public address system. "Did I hear him mention Kiev?" I asked my neighbour. "Isn't this a direct flight to Moscow?"

"Eventually," he smiled. "Yes, it does seem we'll be landing in Kiev first. There are twenty-five people on this flight whose destination is Kiev. The captain has decided he will fly to Kiev first."

"I'm supposed to be met in Moscow this afternoon," I told him. "How much of a delay will there be getting to Moscow?"

"Only six hours," he sighed. "All in good time. No problem."

When the flight from Kiev in Ukraine landed at 10:30 p.m. in Moscow, there was no welcoming committee of hockey people waiting at the airport. Rudy Hucl was there, though.

"I'm the Air Canada manager in Moscow," he said with a tight smile. "I see you had a short stay in Kiev."

"Six hours at the airport in one hundred-degree heat is a short stay? Anyway, it's a long story, Rudy," he was told. "Right now, I'm too tired to tell it, but what are you doing here?"

"I saw your name on the Aeroflot passenger list," said Hucl, a native of Winnipeg. "I figured you might need some help."

I told Hucl that some Soviet hockey officials were to have met me at the airport, then to have taken me to a hotel.

"In this country, it happens a lot," Hucl explained. "That's why I'm here. I'll drive you downtown to your hotel."

"Hotel? I hate to tell you this, but I don't have a hotel room."

"And they let you fly into the country without a hotel room?"

"I'm here and I don't have a room."

"No problem," said Hucl. "Our office is in the Metropol Hotel. I'll get you a room there."

The Metropol was a large, old, dusty hotel only a few blocks from Red Square. It had style, though, dating back to the time when many of Russia's social lions stayed there. Lee Harvey Oswald had stayed there for six months. Now I was going to, as well.

It was midnight when we reached the hotel. Moscow sweltered in the still of the night. "Biggest heat wave in thirty years," Rudy explained. "One hundred degrees every day for the last three weeks. No sweat."

"Don't they ever turn up the air conditioning?" I asked.

"Are you kidding?" he laughed. "This is Moscow. The hotel doesn't have air conditioning. We've got one in the Air Canada office, though. Drop in and visit if you're uncomfortable. Drop in any time. One more thing. Make sure you keep your passport in a safe place. Whatever you do, don't lose it. Don't leave it lying around in your room, because somebody'll grab it. Those things are worth a lot of money in this country. If somebody walks off with it or you lose it, you'll have a hell of a time getting out.

"No sweat," I said.

My room in the Metropol was huge and richly carpeted. An ice-box stood in the corner. There was a table and four chairs in the centre of the room, and a small bed behind a curtain. Nothing stirred. It was hot. Even the discoloured water coming out of the cold faucet was warm.

The next morning, breakfast was a soft-boiled egg, which was hard, black bread, and tea. The first lesson I learned in Russian customs was that if breakfast is being served from 7 to 10, 7:00 a.m. is when the food is on the table. No seconds. No reheating the tea. Take it. Leave it. No problem.

Later that morning, I was on the telephone to the Canadian embassy. "I've got a problem," I said. "Some Soviet hockey people were supposed to meet me at the airport yesterday. The plane was six hours late because we made an unscheduled stop in Kiev. Nobody was at the airport. How do I track these people down? I don't even know their names."

"Leave it with me," the embassy man said. "It might take a day or so. Oh, your old buddy is coming in next Tuesday. That's four days away."

"Old buddy?"

"Milt Dunnell."

"Really?"

"Alan Eagleson [then executive director of the NHL Players' Association] is bringing in a gang with him. Harry Sinden. John Ferguson. [Sinden and Ferguson would coach the Canadian team.] Johnny Esaw [head of CTV Sports] is coming in with a few television people. Milt is coming over for the *Toronto Star*."

Uh-oh. My game plan would have to change now that my illustrious colleague from Canada's largest-circulation newspaper was about to arrive. If Dunnell got here Tuesday, he'd have something in his newspaper on Wednesday. Thursday at the latest. I telephoned Montreal to tell the *Star* we'd have to forget about my using the trip as strictly an information-gathering exercise. I'd have to start writing my stories now.

"What have you got in mind?" asked the *Star*'s managing editor, Art Wood.

"I haven't been able to track down any of the Soviet players yet, so the next best thing, I figure, is to talk to some of the citizens on their main drag, Gorky Street. I'll find out from them if they know anything about the series and get their views on how they think their team will do. It's worth a try because, right now, that's the only thing I've got. I'll get our man in Moscow to interpret for me."

Gorky Street on a sweltering July night in 1972 was small exhaust-spewing cars careering at breakneck speed on a six-lane avenue. It was the chatter of the young, the bemused look of a tourist and the natives' stares at the tourist. Gorky was a postcard street, with new and shining buildings swallowing wall-to-wall people, but, somehow, the parade went on and on. One group would no sooner disappear when another would take its place. Where did they all come from?

Sasha Petrosyan, twenty-five, was an artist, with thin lips, a pale face, and sandy-coloured hair. "I think the chances of the Canadians are a great deal better than the Soviet team," he said. "They are substantially greater. Naturally, professionals are stronger than amateurs. The Russians are strong, as amateurs, but players like Gordie Howe and Stanislas Mikita, they are very, very strong."

Petrosyan was unaware that Gordie Howe was retired and that Stan Mikita had not been named to the team, although he was added later.

Alexandr Grinberg was there. A twenty-eight-year-old truck driver with broad shoulders, dark, slicked-down hair, and grey shirt and grey trousers, he told me that, yes, he had heard about the upcoming Canadian–Soviet series. "I think the chances of the teams are exactly the same," he said. "I am a fan of my team and I hope that our fellows will play well. I would hope that out of the eight games, our fellows would win a good three, even though I know the Canadians are a very serious team, because they have very strong players. Bobby Hull, Bobby Orr . . . they are colossal players, I know, but we have players like that too. Alexander Maltsev, Valery Kharlamov, Boris Mikhailov . . . they are very strong players. Still," he acknowledged, "I am told the professionals are something special and that is why we shall suffer."

"Bobby Hull and Bobby Orr will not play on Team Canada," Grinberg was told through my translator. (Bobby Hull was now with the Winnipeg Jets, of the World Hockey Association. Bobby Orr was recovering from major knee surgery.)

"In that case, that will be better for our chances, I think," he said.

Iosif Green, a lawyer from Baku on the Caspian Sea, walked alone on Gorky Street, his white shirt open at the collar, his blue trousers slightly baggy at the knees. He was a stocky man, with a five o'clock (Moscow time) shadow on his chin.

"I understand a little English very well," he said.

"Excellent," I told him. "How do you think the Soviet team will do against the Canadians in their series? As you know, they are playing four games in Canada and four in Moscow."

"The match will show," he said.

"True enough, but how many games will the Soviets win? How many do you expect they will win?"

Iosif, the lawyer, hesitated. Then he said: "I think I ask to Russian." He appeared a little embarrassed, then the words poured from him in his own language. "I think the games between Canada and Russia . . . well, I am a fan of the Canadians. In recent years, in games in the tournaments that took place in Prague and other cities, I think that our team had a lot of luck. Despite their good playing, they were fortunate to win. I think there were kind of predestined circumstances that allowed them to win, but against the professionals from Canada, this will not happen. I think that Canada will win the majority of the games, of course."

By this time, a small crowd had gathered around us to watch, listen, and smile. They whispered among themselves, then a tall, thin man with a hint of a beard made a comment.

"What did you say? What is it you think about the hockey series?" he was asked.

A grin crossed his face. Then he moved back rapidly three or four steps and said: "I would like to speak about chess." Soviet Boris Spassky and American Bobby Fischer were in Iceland at the time competing for the World Chess Championship.

"We are talking about hockey."

The tall, thin man laughed and retreated a few more steps, lingering there, with his head inclined to try to catch Iosif Green's last few words.

"The Canadians," said Iosif, "are too strong. As professionals, they are too strong."

The tall, thin man shook his head, laughed a sharp laugh, then turned to disappear into the deepening dusk.

Viktor Nikolayevich Kostyukov had chosen this night to walk along Gorky Street with his factory co-worker, Vyacheslav Sekgeyevich Smirnov. At first, Kostyukov didn't want to mention his name, but the word *Kanadski* put him at ease.

"We are Soviet fans," he said finally, "and naturally we cheer for our team. The series should end, 5–5."

"But there are only eight games in the series," he was told.

"In that case, it should end, 4–4," he replied.

"I don't agree," interjected his friend Vyacheslav. "I think we should win six out of the eight games. We are good. We are very good."

Kostyukov shook his head vigorously. "Inasmuch as the home of hockey is Canada, we have to let the Canadians win," he said to his friend. Vyacheslav laughed at the suggestion and Kostyukov joined in. They seemed to be enjoying Hockey Night in Moscow very much.

Kostyukov pointed to the interviewer. A lady standing nearby explained that I was "the Canadian Ozerov." Kostyukov's grin grew because, at the time, Ozerov was Russia's Danny Gallivan or Foster Hewitt. Both, maybe.

"Have either one of you heard about Bobby Orr?" Kostyukov and Smirnov were asked.

"We don't know about this man," said Kostyukov. "It has been quite a long time since Canada has been playing in the world championships."

"The team that will play the Soviets is not the same team that has played in the world championships," they were told. "Bobby Orr is a professional."

Kostyukov and Vyacheslav looked at each other quickly. Smiles started between them and in seconds they threw up their hands in mock horror. "Ah," said Kostyukov, "that is a different story."

Vyacheslav, who had said they would win six out of eight games, added: "I thought on that team there would be mainly amateurs."

"No, only professionals."

"Of course, in that case, the games will be complicated," said Vyacheslav.

"They will be complicated for our players," added Kostyukov.

"Why do you think the Soviets would now consider playing the professionals? They want to win, don't they?" they were asked.

"In any game that is worthy of the adversary," said Kostyukov, "even the loser gains. Even the loser learns a lot from it."

"But what if the Soviets were to lose all eight games? Would that not be a disgrace?"

"But that is not going to happen," said Vyacheslav.

Once in a while, not often, I think back twenty-two years to that night on Gorky Street and the people I met there – particularly now that so many Russians are playing with honour in the NHL. Who would have imagined it possible on that hot July night in 1972? Who would have thought that two decades later, there would no longer be a Soviet Union? Does Alexandr Grinberg, who would now be fifty, still drive a truck? Does Sasha, who would be forty-seven, still paint? What about Iosif, the lawyer? Does he still practise in Baku on the Caspian Sea? Do Viktor Nikolayevich and Vyacheslav Sekgeyevich still have a factory to go to each day?

All of them appeared in a front-page story in the *Montreal Star* on July 17, 1972. My long-time friend, Milt Dunnell, who arrived in Moscow the next day, was among those who read it. "I get on the plane in Toronto heading for Moscow," Dunnell would recall later. "I'm pretty excited about it, see, because since I'm the only reporter on the trip, it's like a free ride, almost. No pressure.

"We had a stopover in Montreal, and I'm still feeling pretty good about everything. Then I pass this news-stand and there's your paper with the story spread across the top of the page. It's July, and I'm reading a headline that says: DATELINE MOSCOW: THE TOPIC? HOCKEY! Right then, I stopped feeling pretty good about everything."

The next day in Moscow, the Canadian embassy informed me that it had tracked down "the Soviet hockey people." A man named Gresko was awaiting my call, I was told. A few minutes later, Alexander Alexeevich Gresko was on the line. "We have been expecting you," said the Deputy Chief of the Department of International Sports Relations of the Committee for Physical Culture and Sport Under the Council of Ministers of the U.S.S.R. "We are anxious to meet with you."

"We" included approximately twenty stern-faced men sitting around a table in a conference room alongside Gresko's office.

Alexander Gresko sat at the head of it, a tall, athletic-looking man wearing the long Elvis-style sideburns of the day which had become so popular in the West. His English was flawless.

"We would like to ask you some questions about your Canadian team," Gresko started.

"Before you do," I said, "where were you on Thursday night? I was promised by your embassy in Ottawa that I would be met at the airport."

"You came a day late," Gresko said.

"I did not arrive a day late," I said. "You were informed that I would be arriving on Thursday. Unfortunately, I was six hours late, but that was only because the Aeroflot pilot decided to stop in Kiev before coming to Moscow."

"You came a day late," said Gresko.

"Your Aeroflot airline flies to Moscow only once a week – every Wednesday night – from Montreal," I said. "I am sure you'll agree that it's impossible to leave Montreal on a Wednesday night and arrive in your country the same day. That is why I arrived on Thursday."

"You came a day late. . . ."

I realized persistence in the face of this would get me nowhere. "All right, let's say I arrived a day late. Now that I'm here, where is Kharlamov? Where are Yakushev and Maltsev? Where is your coach, Bobrov? I know your embassy has told you they are some of the people I would like to see."

"Ah, since you came a day late, Mr. Fisher, I regret to tell you that Kharlamov is in East Germany, Yakushev is at the Black Sea, Bobrov is at the Caspian Sea . . ."

"You mean I've come all this way and I won't be able to talk with your players and coach?"

"You came a day late," said Gresko.

"Mr. Gresko," I said, "I am certain you're aware that the Canadian embassy has spent almost two days trying to find you. I have come a long way and my newspaper has spent a lot of money to get me here. I came here to write about your hockey team, but since, as you say, all of the players and the coach have left the city, I must tell you this: there is an Air Canada plane leaving for Montreal tomorrow. I will be on it. My newspaper will expect something in return for all the money it has spent, and right now, all I will be able to write about is how you have screwed me up."

"Do not be so impatient, Mr. Fisher," replied Gresko. "We will talk for a little while, and then you will go back to your hotel. We will try to get these people back for you."

"The first man I want to speak with is your coach," Gresko was told.

"That would be the elusive Vsevolod Bobrov. You will telephone me tomorrow morning at 10 o'clock and we will arrange to talk with Bobrov," said Gresko.

The next morning, at 10:00, Gresko was on the line. "I have not yet heard from Mr. Bobrov," he informed me, "but I will have more information for you in half an hour."

Thirty minutes later, I called Gresko.

"You will rest a little while," he said, "and then we will have the information we need."

I continued to sit in my hotel room in the midst of the worst heat wave in Moscow in three decades. No air conditioning. And no telephone calls from the Deputy Chief of the Department of International Sports Relations of the Committee for Physical Culture and Sport Under the Council of Ministers of the U.S.S.R. For the next eight hours, I rang his office every fifteen minutes. Nobody picked up the telephone at the other end.

It wasn't all monotony, however. A journalist who worked for Sovietsky Sport paid me a visit. "As a Soviet," he said cheerfully, "I can understand that it is not always easy to discover Bobrov. As a journalist, I have sympathy for you. It is not Bobrov you are trying to reach," he smiled, "it is James Bond."

Eventually, some hockey people were produced, including coach

Bobrov. A few players, but not all. Very little of it was fun. Even trying to get something to eat in Moscow was a chore.

The dining room at the Metropol Hotel was huge. At one end a bored-looking nine-piece orchestra played on a stage. The room could seat at least eight hundred, but when I visited, there were no more than twenty-five customers – and not a maitre d' in sight. After waiting twenty minutes to be shown to a table, I took a seat at a table in one corner of the room.

A waiter approached me.

"Occupied," he grunted.

"Oh, sorry." I moved to another corner of the dining room.

"Occupied," said the waiter.

Another corner. Occupied. A fourth. Same. I sat. Thirty minutes later, a menu appeared. Forty-five minutes later, the food arrived. Good, too, but getting it had been an adventure. It helped to know the right people.

Sergei, for example. I was introduced to him three days later by my new friend, Gresko. He was short, no more than five-foot-six. He was almost as wide, though.

"When you visit with some of our people," Gresko explained, "Sergei will be with you. He will translate for you. He is a sportswriter, so he is aware of the information you will need."

"I would like to visit the arena where the games will be played," I said.

"Ah, yes," said Sergei, "I know it well. We will go there, but first, we will have lunch. Where would you like to have lunch? There is a very fine dining room at your hotel, the Metropol. We will eat there."

I told him that wasn't a good idea. "I had dinner there three nights ago. It took hours."

"We will go to the Metropol," he said.

When we arrived that noon, we were met with a lineup of at least two hundred people who wanted to get into the dining room. There wasn't an empty table in sight.

"There was nobody here a few nights ago," I said. "Now, everybody's here. We could be waiting all afternoon."

Sergei was not fazed. "Come with me," he said. He walked to the head of the line and waved over someone who looked suspiciously like the maitre d'. He flashed his open wallet, all the while talking earnestly. The maitre d' nodded his head vigorously.

"He has found a table for us," said Sergei. "The food will be very good. I promise."

We were in and out of the Metropol dining room in less than an hour. And just as Sergei "predicted," the food and the service were excellent.

As a sportswriter, Sergei proved uncommonly helpful in a lot of ways for the next few days. He seemed to have a talent for opening a lot of doors simply by displaying his wallet.

"You seem to know a lot of people," I told him one day. "Will you be covering the hockey games in Moscow?"

"I will be at the games," he said.

"And after the games, what then? What do you do after that?"

"I believe I will be going to our embassy in Iran," said Sergei.

Boy, I thought, Soviet sportswriters sure do get around.

Two weeks later, back in Canada, my wife, Tillie, and I were guests at a wedding. Perry Carman, the bandleader, and a long-time acquaintance, came over to our table. "My violinist would like to meet you," he said. "Would you mind very much if I brought him over?"

A short man approached us. "Do I look familiar to you?" asked the violinist.

"As a matter of fact, you do. Have we met before?"

"No, we haven't."

"So?"

"My name is Gresko," he said. "The man you were writing about from Moscow is my first cousin."

"Your first cousin is a son of a bitch," I said.

Violinist Gresko laughed loudly. "It's a small world."

Every once in a while I think of Alexander Gresko, if only because he was a lot more than the weighty title he carried said he was. Long after the series was over, for example, the international media reported that well before the "Series at the Summit" was conceived, Gresko had been one of ten Soviet spies tossed out of Great Britain in the early 1960s. Indeed, this was the same Alexander Gresko who, when the eight-game series was about to begin in Canada, was among a group of Soviet officials greeted in Ottawa by Prime Minister Trudeau. Alex even took photographs while he was in the PM's office. There were some red faces at RCMP headquarters later over that one, but, really, should there have been? Alexander Gresko was the kind of guy who could turn up in a lot of places: at the 1975 Pan-American Games in Mexico City, for example. Small world.

"What brings you here, Alex?" I asked.

"I have been appointed Secretary General of the Moscow Olympics," he grinned. "My superiors felt it would be a good idea to see how these Games are organized. It is a learning experience."

We spent several hours together in his hotel room talking about the '72 series and other things.

"The Canadians played with a lot of emotion," he told me. "It was a learning experience for our players. It is always good to learn," he smiled sadly. "There were some very good players on the Canadian team: Esposito, Henderson, a few others. Alan Eagleson . . . he was an emotional man," he added. "He was very hard on us."

"You were pretty hard on him," he was told, referring to the manhandling Eagleson received from Soviet soldiers in game eight of the '72 series after Eagleson protested a botched goal signal.

"He was a difficult man to convince," said Gresko.

We talked about the spy business in Great Britain.

"A mistake," he said. "There were no spies."

We talked about a lot of things that afternoon. He almost seemed sorry when I rose to leave.

"It's too bad I couldn't get to know you better in '72," I said. "Maybe we'll meet again."

"Maybe," he smiled. "Who knows?"

I was still waiting for the hotel elevator when he rushed out of his room toward me.

"Do me a favour," he said.

"What's that, Alex?"

"If you write a story, don't mention that spy crap!"

Did I say it was a small world? Sometimes, it's this small: In August 1987, one of the band members at my daughter Cheryl's wedding walks over and asks me if I remember meeting a violinist named Gresko fifteen years before.

"As a matter of fact I do," I reply. "Why do you ask?"

"He was my father."

Where, I wonder, is Alexander Alexeevich Gresko today? Is he still among the living? I haven't seen him since those few hours in Mexico City almost twenty years ago. He wasn't seen at the Moscow Olympics, either. Perhaps his past caught up with him. Amusingly, even a few people who were at his side throughout the '72 series deny they ever knew him.

"Where is Alex?" I once asked a Russian sportswriter, Vsevolod Kukushkin.

"Who?"

"Alexander Gresko. You were always with him in '72."

"I don't know that name," he said.

I met the same sportswriter several times during the 1980s, when the Soviet Union was still alive and at least semi-well. Gresko's name was mentioned and each time I received the same response. "I don't know that name."

The next time I met Kukushkin was in September 1990, when the Canadiens trained for several days in Moscow. By then, there were signs everywhere that the breakup of the Soviet Union was imminent. The people were more outgoing. They talked more. They had opinions. The iron curtain of secrecy was rising.

"Gresko," I said to Kukushkin, "what's happened to him? Nobody seems to know where he is."

Kukushkin allowed himself a small smile. "These days," he said, "who knows where a full colonel in the KGB would be?"

9

Bobby and Doug

He would walk into the room, wearing a shy, soft grin and golden spikes for hair. His neck was thick, his hands large, and his chest would strain against his T-shirt.

Bobby Orr, eighteen, burst like a golden flower on hockey at a time when so many new, young stars had come along in the mid-1960s. Jim Ryun already was the greatest middle-distance runner of his time and before it. Joe Frazier was the best of the young heavyweights. Other sports had their own new, young faces, but none had greater promise, none shone brighter than Orr. And, as it developed, this child prodigy of hockey was everything he was supposed to be. He arrived in time for the 1966-67 season, and twelve seasons later – several of them unhappily shortened by injuries – he had left his mark on the game as no player had before him.

He was, simply, the best hockey player I have ever seen. He pulled me out of my press-box seat more often than Maurice Richard and Gordie Howe, more often than Jean Béliveau and Bobby Hull, Doug Harvey, and Guy Lafleur, and more often than Wayne Gretzky and Mario Lemieux. All of the great stars before Orr and since did certain things at top speed. Some skated at top speed. Others passed at top speed. Many shot the puck at top speed. Orr was the only player who did *everything* at top speed. In the process, he lifted the game to another level. He brought offence to defence. He brought new meaning and style to his position and, by extension, the game itself. He was its golden boy.

"When Orr was playing," recalls Canadiens' Hall of Fame defenceman Serge Savard, who entered the league in the same season as Orr, "he was somewhere up there. The rest of us were down here."

Orr leads my list of all-time All-Stars I have watched during the past four decades. Doug Harvey would be his partner on defence, and Jacques Plante would be the goaltender. Plante was the best goaltender I've seen, particularly during the five consecutive seasons (1955-56 through 1959-60) the Canadiens won the Stanley Cup. Chicago's Bobby Hull is my choice on left wing, Wayne Gretzky at centre, and Detroit's Gordie Howe at right wing. Orr is the best of the lot.

Wren Blair was handling Kingston, a team owned by the Boston Bruins in the Eastern Professional Hockey League, the first time he saw twelve-year-old Bobby play. Blair's team was meeting Sault Ste. Marie and all of the Boston people were there to watch for prospects. Blair suggested to Bruins general manager Lynn Patrick that they also watch a bantam game between Gananoque and Parry Sound because the Boston organization was interested in two youngsters on the Gananoque team.

"We're at this game," recalls Blair, "and I'm watching the two kids. A funny thing happens. I see this little guy on the Parry Sound team out of the corner of my eye. It seems I'm going back to him all the time.

"I certainly felt he had everything from the first moment I saw him. I knew Lynn felt the same way. The only doubt was his size. He wasn't too big then, but the thing you had to remember about Orr was that he always played ahead of his time. He was a peewee when he played bantam. He was a midget when he played Junior A hockey. He was a junior when he joined the National Hockey League."

Shortly after Blair saw Orr, people started to wonder why Blair would take weird routes to cities where his Kingston team had to play. Somehow, it seemed, his team was always stopping in Parry Sound for the pre-game meal. Of course, what Blair was doing was dropping in to see Orr and his family. At this time, Bobby wasn't nearly old enough to play junior hockey, but in those days professional hockey people were not reluctant to go after prospects even if the youngster happened to be only twelve. The Bruins were happy to subsidize Parry Sound's entire minor-hockey program as long as Orr was available to them. First of all, though, the Bruins had to get Orr's name on a form binding him to Boston. It took two years before Blair convinced Orr and his family that his future was with the Boston organization. Then the Bruins dispatched him to their Oshawa junior team.

"I'll never forget the day I reported to Oshawa," Orr once told me. "They had a roll call when we arrived for the first day of training camp. The players had to call out their names and the position they played. There were some big guys there and when my turn came, I called my name. Position? I said defence – and everybody laughed. I guess it was kinda funny, at that. There I was with all those big guys and me in the middle of them – fourteen years old and weighing 125 pounds and claiming I'm a defenceman."

Blair wasn't concerned about Orr's size, and nobody should have been. He was never a boy. He was making the same moves at fourteen that he made in his first year in the NHL. He was a boy surrounded by men, yet in his first year in junior hockey, he was named to the second all-star team. He scored 30 goals as a defenceman at fifteen and the following year set a league record for defencemen with 34 goals. He scored 37 in his last junior year.

Emile Francis has been a coach and general manager with several NHL teams – the Rangers, St. Louis, and Hartford among them. He saw a lot of Orr during his years in junior hockey. "The kids would give him the puck and then they'd stand around and watch," he remembers. "In the pros, I figured they'd throw the puck to him and then set themselves up for a return pass. I'd look at my scoring sheet after each game against Boston, and there's Orr with six, seven, eight shots. One game, he's got twelve shots. Hell, he's a defenceman. He's not supposed to get that many shots. I figured that since he's a defenceman, maybe he should spend more time defending. But then I'd try to think how many times we'd caught him for a goal and I couldn't find it happening too often. I would see veterans panic in a tough spot and most of the time you couldn't blame them. Orr? He'd stand there as if he owned the place. He was some meal ticket."

Orr arrived in hockey at a time when the best rookies always were tested physically. More so then, than now.

"Don't back up," Orr was told. "There'll be players who resent you. When that happens, throw off your gloves and go at them. Let them know right away where you stand. There are damn few players who really want to fight. If you show them you want to fight, they'll get the message in a hurry. Get it over with, then let your hockey ability take over."

The best fighters of Orr's time when he arrived in the NHL were Ted Harris, a defenceman with the Canadiens, and Orland Kurtenbach, a centreman with the Rangers. Each outweighed Orr by twenty pounds and were several inches taller. Harris and Kurtenbach were classic fighters, stand-up guys who knew how to dish it out.

One night, during the 1966-67 season, the Bruins and the Canadiens were involved in a bench-clearing brawl. In these free-for-alls, nobody goes looking for another player. You fight whoever happens to be there.

"Wanna go?" Orr asked Harris, who had his back to the boards.

"I guess so," said Harris.

Orr's gloves were off and the punches were raining on Harris even before the Canadiens' player had finished talking. In seconds, Harris was on the ice in a sitting position, staring wide-eyed up at Orr. There may even have been a hint of a smile on his face.

"Did he really knock down Harris?" Kurtenbach asked me a few days later.

"Twice."

"The kid's got good balance," Kurtenbach laughed. "He's hard to knock off his pins."

Goaltender Eddie Johnston, who remains Orr's closest friend to this day, was with the Bruins when Orr joined the team in 1966. At the time, hockey's highest salary was something in the area of $38,000. A small fortune, really. "He'll be hockey's first $100,000 player," Johnston told me late in Orr's rookie season.

At season's end, I asked a member of the Bruins' front-office: "What would happen if Orr came to your people after his current contract runs out and asked for $100,000 a season?"

"We finished in last place this season, yet our attendance was up by 41,000 fans," he replied. "To what would you attribute the increase of 41,000?"

One of hockey's tragedies – for the fans as well as for Orr – is that knee injuries sliced several seasons from Orr's career. He played in 657 games in twelve seasons, but the reality is that fans saw him at the top of his game in only eight seasons. He was named the NHL's top defenceman (Norris Trophy) in each of those seasons.

How much did he mean to the Bruins? He led them to the Stanley Cup in 1969-70 – a mere four years after he burst upon the game. The last time a Boston team had won the Cup was twenty-nine years earlier. He led them to another two seasons later, in 1971-72.

Yet despite his star status, Orr was uncommonly shy. After a game, he would almost always hide in his team's clinic, which was off-limits to the media. He was there after the 1972 Stanley Cup finale at Madison Square Garden against the Rangers.

"Come in here," he said after the game. "I've got something for you."

"Why don't you come out here and join in the fun?" I said.

"Naw. I like it better in here," he said. "Come!"

He handed me an autographed photograph. "Thanks for everything," he said. "And oh, I guess I should tell you I'm having surgery on my knee tomorrow."

"Surgery?"

"It's been bothering me the last six weeks or so," he said quietly.

"It didn't seem to bother you during the playoffs, Bobby."

"Aw, not much," he shrugged. "It's nothing serious. Anyway, I'll see you in June, eh?"

"June?"

"In Victoria," he said.

"What's happening in Victoria?"

"We're going fishing, aren't we?"

"It's news to me, Bobby," I said.

"Hell, you phoned me about a month ago about a fishing show on television," he said. "Victoria. June. I said okay."

"Bobby, that's another Red Fisher," I explained. "He's been doing that outdoors show for a lot of years. He invites celebrities all the time. I'll never understand why he didn't invite me, though. Sounds neat, don't you think? Red Fisher a guest on the Red Fisher Show."

"You didn't call me?" Orr asked.

"Nope."

"Geez, that's the only reason I agreed to go. I was sure it was you," he said.

"Have fun, Bobby," I laughed.

"Geez," he laughed.

I'm not sure if Bobby kept his television date with the other Red Fisher. He probably did. One date he couldn't keep, though, was with Team NHL in its eight-game classic with the Soviets that fall. His knee surgery stopped him from playing, and although a place on the team was kept open for him through a month-long training camp, his knee was one opponent he couldn't beat.

His pain threshold was remarkably high, but there's a limit. Time can diminish the talent of the greatest stars, but injuries have been their most formidable opponents as long as games have been played. No exceptions. Not Orr. Not anybody. Not even Douglas Norman Harvey, who was the second-best defenceman I've ever seen.

The year was 1958 and Doug Harvey was muttering darkly as the Montreal Canadiens' bus pulled away from their Detroit hotel. Whose idea was this, anyway?

The night before, a Sunday, the Canadiens had been involved in yet another vicious, hard-hitting game with the Red Wings – the rule, rather than the exception, in those years when the NHL was a six-team league and teams would meet fourteen times during the regular season. The Canadiens' schedule called for them to leave for Toronto that night, at midnight. With no ice available at the Detroit Olympia, Toe Blake had this bright idea: a mid-morning tour of the Ford plant.

"A tour of a plant, for Chrissakes," sniffed Harvey at the back of the bus. "We really need that, don't we?"

Blake thought it was a good idea. A lot better, at least, than allowing the players to visit Detroit bars on an off day. With an organized tour, he'd know where everyone was.

Fifteen minutes later, the bus stopped in front of the Olympia.

"Why are we stopping here?" Harvey asked. "Hey, Toe, why are we stopping?"

"The Red Wings are coming with us," muttered Blake.

"You're kidding, Toe, right? Tell me you're kidding," said Harvey, his voice rising.

No answer. Harvey leaped out of his seat and reached for his overcoat. "Not with me, they aren't," he snapped. "They tried to knock off my head all last night. Now you want me to go on a tour with them? Forget it. I'm gone. See ya later."

Harvey strode quickly down the aisle and marched out of the bus without a backward glance. Blake continued to sit in his front seat, not saying a word but with the colour rising in his cheeks. This, after all, was a coach who always wanted to be right, but he knew when he was wrong. He also knew Harvey, who was the best defenceman of his time until Bobby Orr came along. Once Harvey made up his mind, nobody could change it for him. Nobody. Not his family. Not his friends. Not the people who employed him. Nobody.

Harvey played the same way: his way. He wasn't merely the game's best defenceman for a long time: he controlled the game. If speed was needed, Harvey had it. If slowing down a game was a better idea, Harvey could do that, too. He loved a challenge – on and off the ice. It didn't matter where it came from: the opposition or constituted authority. All that mattered was that it was a challenge, something which had to be addressed and overcome. Telling a highly respected coach like Blake to take his tour and stuff it was a challenge.

The Canadiens and Red Wings spent a good part of the afternoon touring the giant Ford plant – without Harvey, of course. Then, the teams went their separate ways, the Canadiens back to their hotel, the Red Wings to their homes. Harvey was nowhere to be seen at the hotel, but several hours remained before the Canadiens were to leave for Toronto, where they would play the Leafs two nights later. When the team bus came to take the team to the train station, Harvey still wasn't around.

One minute before the train's departure, the errant Harvey appeared on the station platform. He was running . . . running . . . stumbling, dragging his large bag behind him, a broad grin lighting up his face. Staggering now and then . . . the grin becoming wider as several of his colleagues cheered him on from the rear platform of the train.

"C'mon, Doug . . . faster! This thing's gonna leave you behind . . ."

Now he was puffing heavily, a grin lighting up the wetness on his forehead.

"Faster . . . faster, Doug! We're takin' off . . ."

He made it . . . barely.

That was Doug Harvey, always living on the edge, whether it was waiting until the last possible split-second to make a winning pass, or holding out on signing a contract until the last day of training camp. He was stubborn, aggravating, unselfish, hard-drinking, fun-loving – and the best defenceman, by far, in Canadiens history.

Hockey was his game, but Harvey also excelled in baseball and football. What he was best at was winning – no matter what it took to do it. Pain? He didn't merely tolerate it: he played through it and, on many nights, inflicted it. I remember one game in which the Canadiens had only three defencemen on hand. Harvey was one of them – and he played fifty-one minutes of the game with a cracked ankle. On the ice, he was in control. Off it, life controlled him. He was the best of everything – and, at times, the worst. He enjoyed the good times, never complained about the bad. He was a good person, too.

One morning, he telephoned me at my home and asked if I was doing anything. When I said I wasn't, he invited me to join him and some friends in painting the cabins at a camp for children.

We spent most of the day at the camp, about twenty miles outside the city. Harvey and the rest of us left with a lot of the paint on us, but nobody enjoyed the day as much as hockey's greatest defenceman. There was so much of the kid in him!

I knew Harvey as well as anyone and better than most people. Winning was everything – on and off the ice. Win or lose, he refused to shake hands with opponents. He didn't socialize with them during the off-season. At the same time, he cared about other players. Indeed, nobody was surprised in the 1957-58 season when Harvey's name was among the half-dozen players mentioned in news stories as a key figure in the formation of the National Hockey League Players' Association. Detroit left-winger Ted Lindsay was its president. Harvey was the group's first vice-president; Boston's Fern Flaman was its second vice-president, and Chicago's Gus Mortson, third vice-president. Toronto's Jim Thomson was the association secretary and Bill Gadsby, of the Rangers, treasurer.

"Actually, we don't have many grievances," explained Lindsay, "but we felt we should have an organization of this kind. The idea was brought up at last year's All-Star Game in Montreal. We talked the whole thing over and felt this was the way to do it." The association, Lindsay said, needed a better pension plan. The league, he said, could afford it. A law firm, experts in the pension field, had been hired to represent it.

The pension plan in force at the time called for a player with two years' service to receive a pension of about fifteen dollars a month, starting at age forty-five. Increased payments would be made on a graduating scale based on experience. Only one player had refused to join the association.

"We haven't talked to the owners yet," said Lindsay. "In fact, I don't believe they know it was in the works."

Lindsay had that right. The NHL's owners didn't even suspect that their players were organizing. They wanted no part of it. Instead, the suggestion was made that the players could accomplish as much through direct, informal representations as they could through a union or association.

NHL president Clarence Campbell, for example, leaped on president Lindsay's statement which said that the players didn't have many grievances. "The statement by Ted Lindsay represents about the finest public relations tribute which the NHL could hope to have from its players," Campbell said. "It is evident that the officers of the new association have no fault to find with the treatment of the players either individually or collectively. In light of Mr. Lindsay's statement, it would be interesting to know what rights, interests, or privileges require the protection of a formal association."

Asked if he knew the association had been in the works, Frank Selke, the Canadiens' general manager, said he didn't. "I knew there was a meeting of some kind taking place in New York because Harvey asked permission to remain there after our game in Madison Square Garden, but that's all I know about it. Nothing more."

"Well, then, are you angry, sad?" Selke was asked.

"I have no comment," he insisted.

Of course, the truth is that Selke and others at the executive level were stunned by the report. Hockey players didn't do things on their own in the late 1950s. They didn't do anything without the owners' full agreement. What they did was do as they were told. What they surely didn't do was form a union.

Selke was the most powerful general manager of his time, a man with short-cropped hair who carried a big stick. He and other general managers and owners made the rules, players followed them. Selke didn't even like small surprises, and this was a huge one.

He had had a lot of good and useful things to say to a young reporter in the few years leading up to this moment. His office door was always open, and once or twice a week I would visit with him for an hour or so. He always had time. There was always something to learn. I admired him a lot. I didn't have a problem with his refusal to comment on the union. Harvey, on the other hand, couldn't stop talking about it. Much of what he said was written under my name the next day.

A few days later, I telephoned Selke on another matter.

"Why don't you run down the street and ask your friend Harvey about it?" he suggested.

"Excuse me?"

"That was a pack of lies you had in your column," he said. "Harvey told you a bunch of lies."

"Maybe so, Mr. Selke, but if they're lies, they're Harvey's, not mine. You may remember that I called you first and asked if you had any comment. You said no. That's when I called Harvey. He had lots to say."

"Lies," said Selke.

"Harvey doesn't think so," I said.

"My office door always has been open to you. I want people in my office I can trust," he stormed, and the line went dead.

The names and faces change, but the constant among high-profile hockey people is that they have long memories. Cross 'em and, sooner or later, they get you. It was sooner for some of the players who turned up on the association executive, even though the group expired in a matter of days when the Detroit Red Wings walked out. Selke waited several years before deciding to trade Harvey, although in fairness to the general manager, it could also be that the time had arrived for a change. Cracks were starting to show in the dynasty.

On the other hand, did it make sense from a talent standpoint to send Harvey, fresh from a sixth Norris Trophy as the league's top defenceman, to the New York Rangers for Lou Fontinato, whose strongest suit was toughness? After all, as a playing coach, Harvey responded to the stunning trade by winning another Norris and leading the Rangers into the playoffs for the first time in four years, only to have his team fall to the Maple Leafs in six games. Several nights after the Rangers were eliminated, my doorbell rang at the ungodly hour of 1:00 a.m. Doug Harvey stood on the door step. He told me he was planning to quit as coach of the Rangers.

"Whoa!" I exclaimed. "Am I hearing right? Your team made the playoffs for the first time in four years. They've got banners hanging from the roof in Madison Square Garden saying: 'Doug, We Love You' and you want to quit? Are you nuts?"

"I'd rather be with the boys," he said.

"Listen," I said, "in three years you could be general manager of that team. If you quit now, you're dead."

"Aw, Muzz [general manager Muzz Patrick] needs the job. He's got that big house in Connecticut . . ."

"If you don't get the job, somebody else will," Harvey was told.

"Aw, I don't think so."

We argued for the next couple of hours and looking back on it, even now, my biggest mistake was trying to convince Harvey he was making a major mistake. With Harvey, if you said black, he said white. If you said white, Harvey held out for black.

Two days later, the Rangers announced that Harvey had quit as coach. He would stay with the team as a player. Halfway through the following season, he was in the minors. Three seasons later, Emile Francis replaced Muzz Patrick as Rangers general manager. For most of the next two decades, Doug Harvey's life was a blur of booze, bad jobs, and bizarre public behaviour. In 1989 he was dead.

IO

Big Jean

Hockey has been blessed with the very best down the middle during the past four decades.

I have watched Wayne Gretzky from the first moment he and the Edmonton Oilers joined the NHL. Who has done as much for the game since he burst upon it with numbers which may never be matched? Has anyone in any sport been a better ambassador – or as good?

What's there to be said about Mario Lemieux, who overcame terrible adversity to become what he now means to hockey?

Henri Richard, who was on a record eleven Stanley Cup teams with the Canadiens, brought flaming intensity and speed to the position. Phil Esposito was a giant talent whose numbers have been eclipsed by Gretzky, but who will live forever in our minds as the player who made it happen in the 1972 series against Team Soviet. Bobby Clarke was the leader in Philadelphia when that expansion team won two consecutive Stanley Cups.

I have watched all of them and rejoiced in what they brought to hockey, but the centreman I have seen and admired the most is Jean Béliveau.

Béliveau: ten Stanley Cups in eighteen seasons, one scoring championship, two Hart trophies, one Conn Smythe Trophy.

Béliveau: 507 goals and 712 assists in 1,125 regular-season games, 79 goals and 97 assists in 162 playoff games. Béliveau: retired on his sixty-second birthday after four decades on the ice and in the Canadiens' front-office. Béliveau: grace, class, dignity. A decent human being.

Has any game ever produced a better role model? A better leader – or as good? Has hockey ever had a player who made skating more of an art? I have known him as an athlete and a friend for forty years and I don't think so.

Shortly after the Canadiens' Stanley Cup victory in 1971, the great Frank Mahovlich spoke of Jean's genius. "When I was a kid, Jean, I guess, was about five years before my time, so I never played against him when I was a junior. But when I was a kid, we kept hearing about this guy in Quebec City who was getting fifteen suits and a car as a junior. Well, fifteen suits . . .

"Then one night in Toronto, I finally get to see this Béliveau. Bert Olmstead gives him the puck and Jean, he's about ten feet inside the blueline when he lets it go. The net balloons. Nobody shoots better than that.

"If you're on his team or you're playing against him, what do you say about Béliveau? Look at him as a player. What's his strongest point? If he's better in one particular area, I'd have to say it's his skating. For a big man, he's a remarkable skater. Great balance. Strong. Always moving. Some people, some of them say Frank Mahovlich can skate, but I say he can't skate like Béliveau. I go in spurts. He's moving all the time. And strong? I've tried to knock him down, but he's got that great balance even after he lets the shot go. That's what the big superstars are all about. Most of the hockey players, they shoot, and they're off balance after they let the puck go. Not Gordie Howe. Not Bobby Hull. Not Béliveau.

"Everybody knows about his class, his talent. The remarkable thing about him, though, is that he has been able to lead this team for so long. Some guys can be a leader. Can Frank Mahovlich be a leader? Was I a leader with the Maple Leafs? Off and on. No more. Not consistently. In my case, I think it's because I didn't really get along with the coach. To be a leader, you've got to get along with management as well as with the players. It's a two-way street. From what I can tell, Jean always has managed to get along exceptionally well with management.

"He's alert to what's going on. He's aware, and he knows what to do about it. It's why he's such a great captain. It's not easy . . . you take Army [George Armstrong] in Toronto or Alex [Alex Delvecchio] in Detroit. They're captains. Good ones, too. But they're not like Béliveau. Once in a while, Alex would take a day off from practice. But Jean, I don't think he'd do it unless he was injured or unless management ordered him to take it.

"You can talk to him. I've talked to him. A guy has a problem, maybe he's in a slump, things aren't going right, maybe. He talks to you and pretty soon your problem isn't as big as you thought it was. How do you describe it? Class? I suppose so. Leadership? I guess so, too. He makes you feel comfortable. That's also part of it. Like I said, he's alert to everything. Even when it comes to his own game, he's alert. If he has a weakness, he's aware of it. He works at it and takes care of it."

Mahovlich was saying these things for everyone who ever played against Béliveau – or alongside him. There was an aura about him, a kind of majesty. No player had it before him, and none since – perhaps because everything that was Béliveau came from within. He cared about people – and they for him. Other players sensed his care for the game he played so brilliantly for so long. They played hard against him, but they cared for him.

Gretzky, great as he is, has his critics. So does Lemieux. So did Henri Richard, Esposito, and Clarke. But I don't recall any player lashing out at Béliveau. I don't remember a time when Béliveau has criticized other players. He was almost too good to be true, and still is. Too many among the old-time players I know recoil at the money hockey players earn today, but Béliveau goes the other way. He's glad for them. He'd like to see some of the hooking and slashing and holding taken out of the game, because he's truly concerned about these things, but that's where it ends. Lemieux is earning more than $6 million a year? Good for him, says Béliveau. Gretzky? No amount is too much, says Béliveau. He is gracious about today's stars, as he was for those who played in his time. Gordie Howe, in particular, held a special place in his heart.

I remember asking Jean about Howe when hockey's greatest right-winger was retiring – for the first time – after twenty-five years with the Red Wings. Would there ever be another one like him, I wondered.

"If there is," said Béliveau, "I'll be very surprised. For another Gordie Howe, it will take a long time." Béliveau was awed by Howe's strength, as well as his natural ability. "Physical strength is a very important part of the game. It always has been," Béliveau told me, "and I would have to say that there are probably a lot of hockey players who are very strong physically, but they don't have the ability to go with it. They don't have the polish. Howe always had everything. He could do everything right, and so beautifully. Some of the people, they say that Howe did not skate too fast. He knew what he was doing all the time, so he did not have to skate too fast, they said.

"All I can say is that up until near the end of his NHL career, the players who had to cover him should be asked how fast Howe could skate. And if you caught him, that great strength of his was too much. There are people like Howe in every business. There are some who will do their job and do it well. That's all. It was not enough for Howe.

"Twenty-five years . . . I do not know how anybody could play that long. With Howe, his stamina always amazed me. Lots of players can go for forty minutes, but for the last ten minutes, they're hanging on to somebody trying to catch their breath. Not Howe. Go, go, go, all the time. But that's what made him special, I think. With him, it was always that little extra that really counted. Will there be another Howe? If there is, he'll have a lot to do."

Béliveau could do a lot himself, as he proved one night at the

Boston Garden. The Canadiens were playing the Bruins, but Béliveau was not among them on the ice. He had been injured a couple of nights earlier and was now sitting in the press box.

Things didn't go well for the Canadiens. The Bruins scored early. Several calls went against the Canadiens. Coach Toe Blake fumed. Eventually, he lashed out at the referee. Worse, he left his position behind the bench to assail the official.

"If you don't get back behind your bench, and stay there, you're out of the game," said the referee. "I'm not gonna warn you again."

A few minutes later, Blake again left his bench. He was out of the game. There were no assistant coaches in those days, of course, which left Blake with at least a small dilemma. He could have turned the helm over to one of the players, but Boston–Montreal games were too important, too intense – as they are now. Blake turned to the press box and motioned to Béliveau.

"Oh, oh," said Béliveau. "I think he wants me to go behind the bench."

"Have fun," I said.

The Canadiens, as it developed, closed ranks for Béliveau. He brought out the best in them and they won the game. Blake was all smiles in the dressing room. "That's the last time I put Béliveau behind the bench," he told me. Then he turned to Béliveau: "I'm gonna lose my job if you win a couple more games, Jean."

Béliveau assured Blake it would be his first and last game behind the bench. The Canadiens piled onto the bus which was to take them to the airport for the Air Canada charter home. The airline's representative approached Béliveau. "Are we ready to leave for the airport now, coach?" he asked.

"See what I mean?" said Blake.

It may seem hard to believe, but there was at least one man who didn't recognize Béliveau's talents. Of course, he wasn't a hockey man.

Gene Mauch arrived in Montreal in 1969 to serve as the first-ever manager of the Montreal Expos. Mauch had been around. Once, his

Philadelphia Phillies had come as close as any team can to winning the National League East pennant. Then, almost remarkably, the Phillies allowed the wheels to fall off in the final week of the season, but that wasn't Gene's fault, right? He knew the game inside out, right? Unfortunately, the only thing Gene Mauch didn't know was how to win. He was, in short, made to order for the Expos who, having been awarded a franchise for $10 million, wouldn't be expected to win for a long, long time.

One day, the Expos held a meet-the-manager conference for the Montreal media. To say Mauch had a high opinion of himself would be an understatement. Moments after a few polite introductions, Mauch had a message to deliver to me. "I've got to tell you something," he said. "If I don't know more about baseball than you do, I've got to be pretty stupid, okay?"

"Whoa," I said, "did anybody say you didn't know more about baseball than I do? Did you hear me say I knew anything about baseball?"

"I've been doing this all my life," Mauch went on, "so don't even think of trying to tell me how to run a baseball club."

"Hey, we just met," I said. "So far, all I've said is hello."

"I know that," said Mauch. "I just wanted to let you know where we stand just in case you start getting ideas."

I liked him from the start. How could anybody dislike a guy like that? I still do, wherever Gene Mauch is, now that he's gone through a lifetime of managing without winning a damned thing. I mean, there he was with his year-round tan telling people at the Expos' press conference that he knew everything there was to know about baseball. If that's the case, though, why is it he never won anything? Some guys have all the bad luck, I guess.

"Okay, chum," I said, "but while we're on the subject, I've got to tell you that baseball or any other sport isn't quite as complicated as you're trying to make it out to be. We've had some baseball in this town, and we managed to get through it without embarrassing ourselves. Jackie Robinson played here. Don Drysdale pitched here. Roy

Campanella caught here. Tommy Lasorda . . . a bunch of others. We've seen it before. We know at least a little bit about the sport."

"Yeah, but don't think you know as much as I do," he said.

"I surrender," I said. "You win."

"Okay," said Mauch. "As long as we understand each other, we're gonna get along fine."

"No problem, Gene," I said. "Pleased to meet you. Welcome to Montreal."

"Glad to be here," he said. "Now, can you do me a favour?"

Mauch told me he wanted to attend a practice session of the Canadiens. Could I arrange it? I told him it was no problem and we agreed to meet at the Forum the next day at 10:00 a.m.

Mauch watched the Stanley Cup-champion Canadiens the next day from a seat high in the Forum. He didn't say a word for close to thirty minutes. He just watched everything intently. Finally, he pointed a finger at the players on the ice. "That guy couldn't play on my team," he said.

"What guy?"

"That one," he said. "The big guy's been loafing. Number 4."

"You sure number 4 is the one you don't like?"

"Yeah, that's the one," said Mauch.

"I've got news for you," I said.

"What?"

"Do you know who he is?"

"No," said Mauch.

"His name is Jean Béliveau."

Mauch stared straight ahead.

"He's one of the greatest players in the National Hockey League."

"I know," he said. "I've heard."

"Let's make a deal," I said. "You may know all there is to know about baseball, but don't even begin to tell me anything about hockey."

"I promise," said Mauch.

11

The How[e]itzer, the Rocket, and the Flower

There was nothing mysterious or complicated about Gordie Howe's game. The native of Floral, Saskatchewan, simply went out and did his job better than anyone else, with more control and greater consistency. Was he better than Maurice "Rocket" Richard? Many of the numbers say so. After all, Howe held NHL records for most goals (801), most assists (1,049), and most points (1,850) in twenty-six regular seasons of play, while the Rocket had 544 goals and 421 assists for 965 points in eighteen NHL seasons. Then again, Howe's 1,767 games produced .45 goals per game whereas Richard produced at the rate of .56 goals per game in the 978 contests in which he played. Where Richard reached new levels, however, was in the playoffs. His 82 goals in 133 games withstood the challenge of time until Wayne Gretzky redefined everyone's notion of what goal-scoring could be.

Howe was Mr. Hockey, and still is. He had everything as a player except, perhaps, the charisma needed to sell tickets. At the same time, none of the players I've known over the four decades are more warm and decent. None fills a room as much as he does when he walks into it. None commanded as much attention when he played. Few do even now.

Richard, of course, remains a legend because of the gut-churning intensity he brought to the game. He reached into souls and, during his greatest years, brought out the best in both players and fans. He was also capable of bringing out the worst.

There was a hint of snow in the air on that St. Patrick's Day morning in 1955. The sky was grey, but nobody was thinking about the weather. The Detroit Red Wings were in town for the penultimate game in the 1954-55 season and trouble was on the way.

"Go down to the Forum," I was told by my sports editor. "Just hang around. See what's happening. See if Richard's there. The Red Wings probably will be practising. Talk to Howe. Ask him about the Rocket. See what he thinks about this business."

The black night of what was to become known as the Richard Riot was rooted in a wild stick-swinging affair involving Richard and Boston defenceman Hal Laycoe that had occurred several days earlier in Boston. Laycoe had struck Richard on the side of the head with his stick. Richard responded by high-sticking Laycoe on the shoulder and face. Then, when Richard's stick was taken from him, he grabbed another and struck Laycoe twice on the back. Linesman Cliff Thompson, who was trying to restrain Richard, was struck in the face by the Canadiens' right-winger.

Richard had been involved in a similar incident three months earlier, which is why, three days after the ugly incident in Boston and the day before this Red Wings–Canadiens game, NHL president Clarence Campbell had brought down a decision which shook the hockey establishment in general, and Canadiens fans in particular. Even Richard was prepared for a suspension, but nothing approaching the Campbell ruling. The Rocket, Campbell said, would be suspended for the remaining games of the regular season and for the entire playoffs. It was an edict heard around the world, or at least the hockey world.

What my newspaper wanted from me that March 17 was atmosphere and colour. How did the people feel? Were they angry? Sad?

It's why I had been supplied with a seat in the stands, rather than in the press box. I didn't become a regular on the Canadiens' beat until the start of the 1955-56 season, but this was an interesting way to get my feet wet, so to speak. At the time, of course, I didn't realize how wet they'd become. Nobody did.

"Forget about the game," I was told. "This is Richard's night, and he's not playing. Write about the people. Talk to some of them."

No more than ten seconds into the game, I was struck by an egg thrown by a fan. Two minutes into it, Canadiens defenceman Tom Johnson was penalized. Then Dickie Moore went off for charging. Red Kelly scored the game's first goal five minutes into the game. Six minutes later, Howe sent Earl Reibel into the clear for a second goal. Then it was Kelly again. Calum MacKay scored for the Canadiens, but Reibel followed with his second goal before the period ended.

President Campbell, who had been advised not to attend the game by Montreal mayor Jean Drapeau, had arrived at his seat several rows above ice-level halfway through the period. Campbell's appearance was ill-timed, because by that time the Red Wings led, 2–0. The fans were unhappy and started turning ugly when Campbell was spotted. They brayed at the president. Eggs and tomatoes were thrown. At the end of the first period, with the Wings leading, 4–1, a fan walked up several steps toward Campbell, offering to shake hands with the president. When Campbell reached for his hand, he was struck in the face. Jimmy Orlando, a Montrealer who once played for the Red Wings, had followed the fan toward Campbell. He was too late to deflect the slap, but he was there in time to render the fan senseless in a one-punch fight.

Seconds later, a tear-gas bomb exploded. The thick, yellow fog sent fans screaming toward the main lobby. People were choking, coughing, retching, their eyes streaming tears. Many yelled "Fire!" Miraculously, no one was seriously hurt or died in the crush of hundreds of fans trying to get out of the Forum.

Within minutes, most of the smoke had cleared away or, at least, had diffused throughout the building, but hundreds were still trying to make their way out with handkerchiefs clasped over the mouths and noses. Others were milling around inside the arena. Eventually, the fans were ordered to clear the building and the game was forfeited to the Red Wings.

Inside the building, things were returning as close to normal as possible. Outside, however, thousands were milling about. Someone smashed a window. A gun went off. Small groups began to overturn cars.

Within minutes, I was on the telephone to the night city editor, John Maffre. "There are thousands of people rioting outside the Forum," I told Maffre. "Somebody put a bullet through one of the windows. They're starting fires, and pretty soon they'll be marching downtown. It's ugly now, and it's going to get worse pretty damned soon."

"Here's what you do," Maffre suggested. "Go out there and mingle. Circulate in the crowd."

"Why don't you come up here and circulate in the crowd?" I asked. "I'm heading back into the Forum and see what the Red Wings players have to say about what's happening."

Not surprisingly, it was left to Detroit general manager Jack Adams, a Canadiens hater from far back, to do all of the talking. "I'm sick, deathly sick and ashamed," he raged. "I've spent all my life helping to build this game of ours, and then this happens. Let me tell you who I blame for all this. I blame you fellows, the newspapermen who have built Richard into a hero, an idol, a man whose suspension can transform these great hockey fans into a shrieking band of idiots.

"Now hear this," he continued. "Richard is no hero. He let his team down. He let his public down. He let the league down. And he let hockey down. When you start to think about this in the summer months, you'll recognize how right I am. I tell you this: this man is no hero. He makes me ashamed, at this moment, to be connected with the game."

Jimmy Skinner was ending his first season as the Red Wings'

coach. "I still don't believe it," he muttered, "and it seems that there's nothing else to say at this moment. Jack seems to have said it all."

Almost, but not quite. "This could never have happened in any other sport," Adams chimed in. "It never would have been permitted to happen. If Babe Ruth had pulled some of the stuff in which the Rocket has been involved during the past few years, he would have been banned for life. No single figure, no matter how great he is, is big enough to dwarf the game!"

The Detroit Red Wings have been in the NHL since the 1932-33 season but they've won the Stanley Cup only seven times, with four of those wins occurring during the Howe years. Three (1952, 1954, 1955) were in Stanley Cup final series against the Canadiens. Not surprisingly, there was nothing complicated about the Canadiens' game plan whenever the Red Wings were the opposition: Stop Gordie Howe. Forget about everything else, winger Claude Provost would be told: he's your man. Later, Gilles Tremblay, a superb two-way player, inherited the job when Provost started getting long in the tooth.

Howe's strength, stamina, and his nose for the net ensured that his shadow or shadows would have to pay a price. Some nights, it would be goals. On those rare nights when he was shut down, the price was pain. Go into a corner chasing a loose puck with Gordie Howe and, more often than not, blood would be spilled. It rarely belonged to Howe.

The opposition tried to check Howe, but only the foolhardy challenged him. A better idea was to stay out of his way as much as possible. Lou Fontinato, the designated tough guy with the New York Rangers in the 1950s, had other ideas – for a little while, at least. He and Howe had clashed briefly in one game. Nothing serious, really, but Fontinato chose to regard it that way. Howe, he warned, had better keep his head up the next time the teams met in Madison Square Garden. Louie had plans for him.

For days leading up to the game, Fontinato was the media's "pinup boy," explaining in some detail what he planned to do the next time he and Howe were on the ice.

As it developed, something got lost in the translation. Fontinato, as promised, did go after Howe and the fight was bloody, ugly, and quick. But all of the blood was from Fontinato's nose, which was left mashed, smashed, and listing at a forty-five-degree angle.

Howe was forty-five when he came out of retirement to play with the Houston Aeros in the World Hockey Association with his sons, Marty and Mark. The following season, he was named to the WHA all-star team assembled to face the Soviets in an eight-game series. One of the training-camp games was against a junior team in Saskatoon.

Early in the game, a young, well-built defenceman with a growing reputation for toughness ran at Howe, elbows high. Howe stared at him . . . and skated away. Twice more in the first period, same thing. Howe merely shrugged and skated away.

Early in the second period, the boy took another run at Howe. This time, Howe's elbow came up sharply, and *thwack!* the young defenceman found himself sitting on the ice, his nose reddening almost immediately. Then he looked up quickly and blurted: "Good God, Mr. Howe!"

Howe turned and skated away, laughing. He wasn't bothered again.

The next day Howe and I went for a walk in the crisp Saskatoon air. That morning, there had been a practice in the old, cold civic arena where many of the NHL's biggest names, including Howe, had watched and learned about the game that would be their lives.

"Lots of memories in this town," he was saying, as we walked along Saskatoon's main street toward our hotel, two miles away. "I love it here."

A young boy, ten, maybe eleven years old, walked toward us, a hockey stick, blade up, gripped firmly in his small fist. He looked neither to the right or left, but several steps past Howe he stopped suddenly, threw a quick glance over his shoulder, and ran back. He stopped in front of Howe, breathed deeply, thrust his stick toward Howe and said: "Sign this."

"Whoa," said Howe, "what's the magic word?"

The boy bit his lower lip, stared at Howe, breathed deeply again and said: "Uh . . . please."

"That's right," said Howe. "Now, put it all together."

The boy stood on one leg, then the other. He fidgeted nervously. His eyes narrowed. He breathed deeply again, thrust his jaw and stick at Howe again and said: "Would you please sign my goddamn stick!"

Everything about this giant talent of a right-winger was right: the way he played the game on the ice, the way he represented hockey off it. He played with the best and excelled against the best. The Rocket, for example. On the other hand, he didn't see nearly enough of another right-winger, who was the best of his time: Guy Lafleur.

Now, among right-wingers, Howe is generally perceived to be the best. I don't dispute that, particularly since I covered the Rocket only during his last five seasons as a player. I saw flashes of his greatness, but time had eroded the genuine article. On the other hand, has there been a more exciting right-winger than Guy Lafleur? Sure, Howe was stronger, scored more goals, and lasted much longer, but was there anyone more exciting than a Lafleur, golden mane flying, skipping and dancing beyond one man and then another and then, in one motion, releasing that wonderfully accurate shot of his?

At his best – in 961 regular-season and 124 playoff games with the Canadiens – Lafleur was not merely hockey's finest and most exciting player. He was its artist, its sculptor. With his speed and hissing shot which produced 518 Canadiens regular-season goals, he could turn games into things of beauty.

You want numbers? Lafleur had them. He was the National Hockey League's scoring champion (Art Ross Trophy) three times. He was named the league's most valuable player (Hart Trophy) twice.

He won the Conn Smythe Trophy once, which goes to the outstanding player in the playoffs. He was on the NHL's First All-Star Team six times. He scored fifty goals or more in six consecutive seasons, and led the Montreal Canadiens to five Stanley Cups.

He was, simply, the very best of his time, and was treated that way on and off the ice. Big money. Fast cars. Glitzy restaurants. Fan worship. And that was the way it was until November 24, 1984. The season was nineteen games old at that point and Lafleur had scored only two goals. He had played against the Detroit Red Wings that night, but after the game didn't accompany the Canadiens to Boston.

"Did you hear about the Flower?" Chris Nilan said quietly after the Detroit game.

"What about the Flower?"

"He's not making the trip to Boston."

"Why not?"

"Groin injury. I'm driving him home before going to the airport."

"Groin injury? He was on the ice about two minutes before the end of the game. He was skating faster coming off the ice after a long shift than most of the guys starting a shift. That doesn't sound like a groin injury to me."

Nilan shrugged.

Jacques Lemaire was coaching the Canadiens at the time, having taken over from Bob Berry midway through the preceding season. He had been a long-time linemate of Lafleur's during the team's four consecutive Stanley Cup triumphs in the second half of the '70s. Playing alongside a Lafleur at his best was a pleasurable adventure. Coaching him, Lemaire learned, wasn't quite as much fun. The two often disagreed on how much ice-time Lafleur should get.

Unlike most coaches, Lemaire didn't sleep much on the afternoon of a game. Often, he could be found killing time in the hotel lobby. He was there the afternoon of the Boston game. I asked him if Lafleur was hurt.

"Check it out," said Lemaire. "You could have a hell of a story."

Nobody answered the Lafleur telephone because, as I learned later, the night before he had said to his wife, Lise: "I am empty. I have no more energy left for hockey. Even if I had a big offer, I can't do it any more."

So on Sunday morning, long before Lemaire was telling a guy to "check it out," the Lafleurs left for his home town of Thurso, on the Ottawa River. There he discussed his future with his parents. He returned home about 10:00 p.m., his mind made up.

Canadiens general manager Serge Savard wasn't home, either, so there was no real way to confirm Lemaire's hint. Still, as one looked back, there were signs that Lafleur had had enough. He had been struggling on the ice from the start of the season. Anyone who knew him could tell he was, somehow, breaking up inside because he, better than anyone else, knew the Lafleur of old was now merely an old Lafleur.

Groin injury? A groin injury wouldn't stop a Lafleur from travelling with the team to Boston, even if he knew he couldn't play. He liked being with the team. He liked Boston.

"Check it out," his coach had suggested. "You could have a hell of a story."

A hell of a story is a Guy Lafleur playing his last game only nineteen games into a season. A hell of a story is the end of an era, the end of a career which had been stunning in its beauty.

There I was, three hours before game time, sitting in front of my computer and wondering where – and if – to start. The nearest thing to a confirmation was Lemaire's strong intimation that Lafleur had played his last game. Normally, that's not enough, but Lafleur was special. Go for it, I thought.

Monday morning, Lafleur told Serge Savard and team president Ronald Corey that he was through. At noon, Canadiens management announced an important news conference would be held at the Forum at 4:00 p.m.

At 4:05 p.m. on November 24, 1984, a white-faced, drained Lafleur entered the crowded room with Savard and Corey. At

4:06, Savard said: "This is a sad day for all of us, because I must announce . . ."

He stopped. His lips trembled. He swallowed hard. Finally: ". . . the retirement of Guy Lafleur."

Savard swallowed hard again, and went on: "His contribution to the Canadiens was unbelievable."

In fact, Lafleur was unbelievable. He was one of those rare talents who was a man even while he was a boy. He was an amalgam of everything that was good and great about the game – all the more so because his speed, his quickness, his thunderclap of a shot, and his matinée-idol good looks had a deep-rooted French flavour to them.

Night after night, game after game, he would electrify all of us who watched him. There was menace implicit in every stride he skated, every shot he lashed at a goaltender. Some people called it a magic quality, but there was much more to it than that. He was hockey's royalty, its sweet prince. He was a national figure before his teens, as the star of the Quebec peewee tournament. At fourteen, he was a full-blown celebrity with the junior Quebec Remparts. He was a player teams schemed for, as the Canadiens did when they traded Ernie Hicke and their first round-choice for François Lacombe, cash, and the California Seals' first-round pick in the 1971 draft.

In Canadiens management's view, he was born to wear the CH. Nothing else made sense. It was destiny. What could be better? A poor boy from a pulp-and-paper town continuing the line of pre-eminent French-Canadian superstars starting with the Rocket, and onward to Jean Béliveau. Now Lafleur, bringing as much glory to the sweater as any of the great players before him who had lifted the torch skyward.

There was, in short, a rightness to Lafleur. He and the times and the Canadiens were right because Lafleur seemed to symbolize a new and different Quebec. He was a boy during the Quiet Revolution of the early 1960s, and a man when Quebecers began to express their sense of identity and collective power in more direct ways. That made him a big part of everything that was happening in areas and professions other than his own. Like the Rocket and Béliveau before him, when the Canadiens and Lafleur won, Quebec won. When Lafleur scored goals in the way only he could, Quebec scored. When Lafleur and the Canadiens brought home Stanley Cups five times on sun-washed spring days, all of Quebec hitched a ride on their float as it inched along St. Catherine Street.

Lafleur was blessed with the best skills of hockey's best players. When he gathered his legs beneath him deep in his zone for the start of one of his rink-length rushes, he conjured up visions of the first, most exciting players in National Hockey League history. When his eye-blinking puck-handling swept him beyond one man and then another, he was Béliveau. When he danced with a spray of ice into the opposition's zone and released his marvellously accurate shot, he was a composite of all of the great shooters who had ever worn the Canadiens sweater. He was all of them, but most of all, he was uniquely Lafleur.

Even the name always has had a special flavour and ring to it. Lafleur. The Flower. Delicate, yet indestructible.

I have seen them all since the mid-1950s – Rocket Richard, Béliveau, Harvey, and Henri Richard. I have watched Moore, Geoffrion, and Plante, Dryden, Cournoyer, and the matchless Big Three of Robinson, Savard, and Lapointe. Each brought something special to the arena.

Lafleur, though, pulled people out of their seats more often than anyone.

Lafleur was speed. He was unflinching dedication to winning. He was the game-maker and -breaker. Hockey was his life – and a life without hockey was unacceptable. It's why he came back to the game with the Rangers in 1988 after an unsettling, unhappy retirement of almost four full seasons. It's why he went on from there to the Quebec Nordiques.

Lafleur was fire and flame on the ice, and sometimes he was the same way off it. On the ice, his decisions were things of beauty. Off it, now and then, he had a talent for being involved in controversy –

much of it self-inflicted. He was easily influenced by the events of the day – or night. Like most individuals bathed in the glare of attention hour after hour, day after day, he often spoke when he should have been listening. Evasiveness, on and off the ice, was not his strong suit. He liked to tell it the way he saw it – which can be a dangerous game for someone whose game is his life.

Lafleur was also a pussycat of a man, kind and generous almost to a fault. I remember him walking over to me at that retirement press conference in the Forum and warmly shaking my hand. "My wife cried when she read your column this morning," he said quietly. "I think I cried a little, too."

Another time, a few days before Christmas, Lafleur walked into the Canadiens' dressing room wearing a full-length black mink coat. Greeting him was Gaétan Lefebvre, now the team's sports therapist, then its assistant trainer.

"Nice coat," Lefebvre said to Lafleur. "I hope you're not going to jam a beautiful coat like that into the small cupboard space we've got."

"You don't have a fur coat?" asked Lafleur.

"Are you kidding?" replied Lefebvre.

Lafleur shrugged out of his coat and tossed it at Lefebvre. "Try it on. See if it fits."

"It fits," said Lefebvre.

"Merry Christmas," said Lafleur.

There is no question that his first retirement was a mistake, a terrible example of over-reaction on both sides. In the final analysis, though, he has only himself to blame. It was Lafleur, nobody else, who allowed himself to be stampeded into retirement. Others may have thought so but, in 1984, Lafleur wasn't ready to go.

His retirement dominated the sports news for several days, of course. Even today, people wonder aloud whether or not he should have left the game – for the first time – when he did. For its part, Canadiens management wasn't particularly pleased over the need to play catch-up with the report which had appeared in the *Gazette* with my byline.

Serge Savard suspected that someone within the organization had spilled the beans. He thought that a team trainer or a player had said something he shouldn't have.

A few days later, coach Jacques Lemaire had a question for me. "Serge wants to know where you got the Lafleur story," he said.

"Really? Don't you know?" I asked.

"No," said Lemaire.

"Check it out," I replied. "You could have a hell of a story."

12

The Old Redhead

Referees and linesmen are among my favourite people. They can use a friendly hand now and then, because, face it, they're the enemy everywhere they work. Hockey players, coaches, general managers, and owners don't make mistakes; referees and linesmen do. I have known most of them on a first-name basis until recent years – that is, when expansion brought more and more officials into the league.

They're a decent, hard-working group with no family life to speak of except during the off-season when they're not travelling. They're also, with few exceptions, terribly insecure because they have always been without direction, forever at the mercy of NHL management.

Roy Alvin "Red" Storey was everybody's favourite referee in the 1950s. He was an all-round athlete who excelled in football. In fact, he was Canada's best football player one afternoon in 1938 when he scored three touchdowns for the Toronto Argonauts in the Grey Cup game. He almost made it to baseball's major leagues, and was among the best of Canada's lacrosse stars. As a referee, Storey was one of those officials who allowed the players to play. In other words, he was dedicated to the principle that a referee was merely an extension of the game. It wasn't his responsibility to determine the outcome. He called 'em as he saw 'em, with no regard for the score or the period of the game.

This is what I saw him doing on April 4, 1959, in Chicago where the Blackhawks and the Canadiens were playing game six of their Stanley Cup semi-final series. These days, the regular season doesn't end until mid-April. That night, the teams already had played five games of their best-of-seven series, and the Canadiens were leading three games to two.

Years later, Red told me the story of that night this way:

"Can you imagine what it feels like to stand at centre-ice in a hockey arena with twenty thousand people screaming and spitting and throwing things at you? I do. I know how it feels to have people coming at me, hating my guts, screaming for my blood and ready to tear me apart.

"I'll never forget what happened that night. A lot of things have changed between then and now, but one thing hasn't: it doesn't matter what game you have – whether it's the first game of a season or the last, the tension is there. But when it's a playoff game, the pressure is ten times greater. There seemed to be more tension than ever going into that game, and to understand it you've got to know a little bit more about the Chicago team.

"First of all, there were only six teams in the league in those days. There were more stars in Chicago than on most of today's top teams, but even with their stars, Chicago had been finishing at the bottom of the league year after year. I can remember going into Chicago when there'd be only 3,500, 4,500 fans in the stands. Things got so bad, they'd take games to Indianapolis, they'd take games to Omaha, they'd take 'em to Minneapolis. They took them all over to get crowds and to liven things up a little.

"If it hadn't been for the Norris family, I think the city would have gone out of hockey. What had happened over a period of a couple of years, though, was that Frank Selke – who was running the Forum in Montreal – and Conn Smythe, who was running the Gardens in

Toronto, decided to help Chicago. I guess a few other people got into the act, too, because Glenn Hall and Ted Lindsay wound up there, Glen Skov wound up there, Jimmy Thomson, Danny Lewicki, Eddie Litzenberger. They wound up with some pretty fair talent being donated, practically, by Montreal, Toronto, and Detroit.

"A lot of people didn't like [Blackhawks owner Jim] Norris. I did. The people who didn't like him didn't know him. They didn't like him because he was in boxing. They didn't like him because he was richer than perhaps anybody had a right to be. But you couldn't find a better, more generous guy anywhere. You'd have to go pretty far to find somebody who did more for hockey than Jim Norris.

"Norris never could resist a touch, and one of his best clients was a character named Jockey Fleming. Every time Norris came to Montreal, Jockey was there with his hand outstretched. One day, he's in Jim's hotel room, and now Jim has to get ready to go to dinner. He has to shave and shower. So he says:

"'Jock, I'm going in there. I'm gonna have a shave and a shower and I'm leaving my money on the mantelpiece. I want you to start clapping your hands and don't you stop clapping until I come out of that bathroom, because I want to know where your hands are every minute of the time.'

"So the Blackhawks are in the playoffs, and I think it got through to every fan in the building: 'Hey, we've got the Canadiens and if we beat them tonight we're going to seven games and they're the greatest team in the world. Hey, maybe . . . I think we can win the Stanley Cup!' I actually think that's what the team and the fans thought at the time. That's the way they were thinking when the game started.

"The tension in the building was something like the night of the Richard Riot at the Forum four years earlier. I was in that one, too. I didn't let that interfere with the way I handled a game, though. A referee only feels good if he's doing a job that's fair to both teams. I don't say good or bad, but fair. My style of refereeing was to let more go. I let the players play. Hell, that's what they were there for. I felt that when there's body contact in a game, you can give a penalty any time two

146

players come together, but I didn't think hockey should be refereed that way. I still don't.

"I let them play hockey that night and, as the game went along, I think more and more fans were building up to the Stanley Cup. It had been a terrific game and, if I say so myself, that was one game I refereed well. Litzenberger is coming out of his own end, and the crowd is really enjoying it because Eddie had scored a couple of goals for the Blackhawks up to then. He was the club's top scorer. Anyway, it's 3–3 and there's about seven minutes to go in the third period. Marcel Bonin goes in to check Eddie and he went in facing him. Bonin's stick is flat on the ice. I'm pretty damn close to the play and I'm sure Bonin's stick isn't off the ice. Eddie doesn't hit the stick. He steps on the stick and falls on his ass and now everybody on the Chicago team is looking at me for the penalty. I'm not calling a penalty, see, but they're waiting for me to blow the whistle, and while they're waiting, Dickie Moore picks up the puck and scores. Sure he does! What else is the guy supposed to do?

"Well, things weren't too healthy. The fans are a little peeved. As a matter of fact, you might say they're a little hot. It's now 4–3 and the fans can now see that maybe we're not gonna win the Stanley Cup and maybe this is the last game of the season. Somebody is gonna catch hell, and it might as well be that son of a bitch out on the ice, which was me!

"Anyway, we get the game started again and Lindsay scores for the Hawks. Everybody is happy again. Terrific. But now – I think there was about a minute and a half to go – Bobby Hull is coming down the wing and when he gets to the blueline he cuts right across it. Junior Langlois hits him with a hip and Bobby might have been the first guy in outer space. Well, once again everybody is looking around at me for the penalty. There's no penalty. Langlois hit him with a hell of a hip, so what am I supposed to do? One thing you've got to realize: the easiest thing for me to do that night would be to give the Canadiens two penalties. Hell, I was in Chicago. The crowd would have loved me.

"They're waiting around for the penalty, and while they're waiting, Claude Provost goes down and scores. This ball game is over! The season is over! There's still a minute and a half left, but it's over, and the people don't like it. I've never worried about people. I mean, people screaming at me don't scare me. When you've got twenty thousand people on their feet screaming at you, anybody with a brain in his head has to be scared. I wasn't scared, so I guess the answer is I didn't have a brain in my head. Let 'em yell.

"Now, though, they're throwing all this garbage, and I figure: 'Well, damn it, if they're gonna start throwing, I'm gonna get to centre-ice. Any son of a bitch who's gonna hit me is gonna need a good arm. So I'm at centre-ice and all of a sudden somebody yells at me to look out. I turn around and this guy had come off the Chicago bench, a fan. He threw one of those plastic cups of beer right in my puss. I grabbed him. I was so teed off, I was really gonna clean his clock.

"I'll never forget Doug Harvey as long as I live for what happened next. I've got hold of the fan on one side and Doug's got hold of him on the other side. Doug says: 'Red! Red! You can't hit a fan. Don't hit a fan!'

"I let go and Doug piles him one right in the kisser. I'm still mad, though, and Doug can see I'm still mad as hell. He says again: 'Red! Red! Don't hit a fan. You can't hit a fan!' Then Doug hauls off and hits him another one before he lets him go. The fan staggers off.

"By this time, you wouldn't believe the noise in the place. Rudy Pilous, the Chicago coach, is giving me the choke sign from behind the bench. Doug is facing me, about three feet away.

"'Look out!' he yells at me again.

"I turn, and there's another guy coming at me. Here's this guy in mid-air about to jump on my back, so the ol' redhead dipped a little. The guy is off his feet, Doug stabs him with his stick and cuts him. Oh, he cuts him bad. It's an eighteen-stitch job. He goes off the ice and he's bleeding like a war hero. That puts an end to any more of the fans coming on the ice, but by now the players are so scared for their own safety, they're sitting on the ice next to the boards so that the stuff coming over the screens – there was no glass in Chicago back then – won't hit them. I'm out in the middle of the ice. Harvey is there, and so is Tom Johnson.

"By now, we've gone thirty, thirty-five minutes. Stuff is coming down from upstairs all over the place and players are hiding underneath the screens. I'm saying to myself: 'What the hell am I gonna do? Should I call off this game?' I'm saying it, but I knew I wouldn't. I don't think any professional game should not be allowed to finish.

"Never mind what the players think, what the fans think, a game has to finish. The Richard Riot thing was different. It couldn't finish because of the tear gas. Somebody tosses the tear gas at the end of the first period, and we were told to get out of the Forum. I decided, though, that maybe I shouldn't have to make that decision. I could see Mr. Campbell [league president Clarence Campbell] sitting behind Norris. I requested that Mr. Campbell come to the penalty bench. He never came.

"Now we're getting ready to finish this game. Tod Sloan is facing off for Chicago. Before I drop the puck, he looks up at me, and believe me, the tension can be cut with a razor. He looks up and says: 'Red, tell me something: if you had known that first guy was gonna throw a beer in your face, would you have opened your mouth?'

"I started to laugh and he started to laugh.

"We finished the game, and Danny Lewicki skates over to me. He gives me his stick and says: 'Red, you're gonna need this more than I do now.'

"When the referees go out in Chicago, they go down the stairs at one end of the rink. The crowd was waiting at the top of the stairs. They didn't look happy, and I must say I opened up a few heads before I got down the stairs. They were spitting and throwing things and trying to get at me and I guess I combed about six of them. If I hadn't, I wouldn't have been able to get out of there.

"Now, I get down to the bottom of the steps, and who's standing there but Ted Lindsay. He's really teed off. Of course, in his playing days and my refereeing days, Ted and I weren't exactly bosom buddies. As a matter of fact, I don't think Ted ever wound up a bosom buddy of anybody he ever had contact with. He had his stick in his hands.

"'I'm going to cut your goddamn head off,' he said.

"'You make your first shot the best shot you ever had,' I said, 'because this is the first time we've both had a stick, and I'm gonna cut you in two.'

"Norris came along and saw what was going on. He grabbed Lindsay with two hands and threw him into the dressing room. 'Get in there, you little bastard,' he said, 'and leave Red alone.' Then he turned to me: 'Red, you don't have to take that in my building or anybody's building. You go to your room and have a shower. Forget about this.'

"Roger Strong and George Hayes were the linesmen in the game. They couldn't do much while all this was going on, except make sure they didn't get hurt. They couldn't protect me. I didn't need any protection. I figured that, one on one, I could take anybody in the building. I always felt that way.

"We're in the officials' room and I'm having a few beers. When a game is over, that's it. That was the end of that nonsense. Now where do we go tomorrow? I knew I'd had a tough game, but mentally it didn't bother me. Mr. Campbell came into the room and I might say he was very pale. He didn't say anything. He seemed to be in a state of shock.

"'Why didn't you come to the bench when I called for you?' I asked.

"'I feared for my safety,' he said.

"Fair enough. Good answer. Twenty thousand people against one. He'd seen what had happened at the Richard Riot. He gave me an honest answer, and I can't ask for more than that. Putting up with some of the things with management over the years, I knew he didn't lack for guts.

"'Do you want a ride downtown with us?' I asked.

"'No,' he said.

"Now we're ready to leave – but there's a crowd waiting for us upstairs. 'We can't let you out that way,' a guy says. 'There's five thousand people up there waiting for you.'

"'What do we do? Where do we go?'

"'There's a car downstairs.'

"'Downstairs? Hell, we're already downstairs.'

"'No, go down another floor.'

"So we go down another floor and there's a big station wagon waiting for us. George and Roger and I get in. The driver yells to somebody upstairs: 'All clear?'

"'All clear,' a guy yells back.

"We go up this winding thing. The tires are burning and we go out through the parking lot. The crowd smells this, and they're going for their cars and now the chase is on. We're going down one street screaming and sliding, down another screaming and sliding, just like one of those cops-and-robbers movies. All of a sudden, we round the corner and the guy stops the car.

"'Get in that car beside the road,' he yells at us.

"Geez, we jump out with our bags, jump into this car, and slam the door. He takes off and five thousand people are chasing him downtown and we're sitting at the side of the road watching them go by. We go down to the hotel and hang up our stuff. I went out and had a few beers, and stayed over in Chicago the next day. On Monday, we're off for Boston – ready and rarin' to go. There's another playoff game to referee the next night, right?

"The Chicago game was on a Saturday night. Monday was our travelling day. Tuesday was the next game. I got into Boston, and it's maybe 5 o'clock. There was a message to call my wife, and that bothered me. Helen and I had an arrangement that we wouldn't call unless it was serious. Phone calls upset me. They upset her, too, so unless it was something important, we never called each other. To me, this was urgent. I called.

"'Have you seen Mr. Campbell?' she asked.

"'No, why?'

"'He phoned here and said there's going to be some things coming out in the paper. He said not to pay any attention to them. What did he mean?'

"'I don't know what he meant,' I said. 'I haven't read any papers.'

"Now I get a call from Carl Voss. Carl is the referee-in-chief and, well, he's my boss.

"'Come up to Mr. Campbell's room,' he said.

"I went up to the room.

"'Have you read anything in the papers?' Campbell asked.

"'No, I haven't.'

"'Well, there were some things said, and they weren't meant the way they came out.'

"'Mr. Campbell,' I said, 'there's been an awful lot of things written about me in my lifetime. I've been called lots of names, I'm sure you couldn't say anything that would hurt me.'

"'Fine, fine,' he said. 'I just wanted you to know before you read about it.'

"I went downstairs and got George and Bill Morrison, who were my linesmen for the game the next night. I got Eddie Powers, who was the stand-by referee. We went over to Jack Sharkey's bar for a few beers. It's Monday. We're entitled to have a few beers like everybody else, right?

"We're sitting there and the kid comes running through with the papers.

"'Hey, come over here,' I said. 'Leave one of everything.'

"He leaves his papers. Christ! Headlines! STOREY CHOKES. The next one: STOREY CHICKEN! I read the papers and the statements were not about my refereeing but about my character. I was a chicken, I was a choke artist. I was gutless. Hell, if they had said I was a bad official, I would have said, yeah, at times I've stunk out the joint. But don't call me gutless and don't say I'm chicken. Don't say I choked. Don't say things that aren't true. If you're going to run me down, say things that may be right. I read the papers and going through my mind is a picture of my kids going down the street and other kids telling them their old man is gutless.

"Now, I'm boiling. 'Don't drink too much tonight,' I said to Eddie. 'You're the stand-by official for tomorrow night. You're refereeing. I've refereed my last game. I won't be there.'

"'Come on,' said Eddie, 'don't talk stupid.'

"'Eddie,' I said, 'I was never more serious in my life.'

"'Sleep on it,' Powers said. 'Think it over.'

"I've got all these newspapers in my mitts where the stories are quoting the league president saying I'm gutless and I choked, and this guy wants me to sleep on it! 'Like I said, Eddie, get a good night's sleep. You're refereeing.'

"We called it a night because I wanted to make sure these guys got to bed early. But there was no way I could sleep. There was no way I wanted to sleep. I walked the streets, instead. I walked Boston. I saw every corner you could think of. At about 8 o'clock in the morning, I knew I had to talk to somebody. I put in a call to a couple of newspapermen in Boston.

"'I'd like to see you in my room,' I told them. 'It's getting on to 9 o'clock. I'd like to see you at once. I don't know whether it's important to you guys, but I've got something to say.'

"I asked Powers and Hayes and Morrison to come to my room, too, and that's when I told them I was finished. That's when I told them I couldn't work any more.

"Then I went to Voss's room. I told him I was through just like that! . . . He didn't give me any encouragement. He didn't tell me to think it over or to do anything.

"'Are you going to tell Mr. Campbell?' he finally asked.

"'No,' I said, and I didn't see or speak to Mr. Campbell for another five years.

"I remember checking out of the hotel a little while later. By that time, everybody knew I had quit. The first guy I saw was Kenny Reardon, a pretty outspoken ex-player who was there to scout the game for the Canadiens. He looked me up and down and finally said: 'Red, you're making a big mistake.'

"I looked at Kenny and just kept on walking out of there. I didn't say a word. But I remember thinking to myself: How's that guy supposed to know how I feel? How's he supposed to know if I was making a mistake? Was he out at centre-ice in Chicago? Was he the one who was being hammered in the press by the president of the league? In my mind I know I didn't make a mistake even though at the time I was in my forties. I had no job. I still had a family to raise. I suppose that ninety-nine people out of a hundred would have taken that crap, but I couldn't.

"I was angry. I was sore. I was humiliated. I could have stayed, I suppose, but if I had I don't think I could have lived with myself. Even today, I look back on it and I know I couldn't have lived with myself.

"I've always felt the most depressed people in the world are those in professional sport. The money was lousy in my time, but even today I run into more depressed people in professional sport than anywhere else. It's because of the nature of the whole thing. You don't last long. There are injuries. You're afraid all the time. You're afraid of getting hurt. You're afraid of coaches. You're afraid of kids coming after your job. It's unreal. I think you have to live with it to understand it and I've lived on both sides of it – as an athlete as well as a referee.

"I've had a lot of sad and fearful days because I've had a lot of injuries, but that day had to be the lowest. I can't remember a sadder time in my life."

The biggest loser in the wake of Red Storey's resignation was the game itself. It should never have happened and I'm certain president Campbell for a long time regretted that it happened. The source of Storey's rage was an interview Campbell had given Ottawa sports editor Bill Westwick after the NHL president had arrived at his hotel in Chicago. Campbell was still shaken by what had happened at the arena. Things were said that should not have been said. To add insult to injury, Campbell the next day declared that he had no idea he would be quoted on the matter. Why would he expect otherwise?

Storey's abrupt departure was an embarrassment to the game, but it didn't hurt his popularity with many of the players and some of the owners. In 1967, he became the sixth referee admitted to the Hockey Hall of Fame as a builder. He's also been one of Canada's most sought-after speakers.

I believe Storey when he says he has never regretted doing what he did. Now and then, not often, he laughs about it – perhaps because he's too old to cry. On the other hand, Storey has gone through life with a laugh not far away. It's why he's always been special to a lot of people. It's why one of my favourite newspaper stories involves Storey.

"I've sent down a new story for the second edition," I said one day to a colleague at the *Montreal Star*. "Throw out the story that's in the paper now. Put the new one in."

Minutes later, the composing-room man was told: "Red's story is dead. There'll be a new story in the next edition."

A few metres away, another composing-room man dropped what he was doing, and telephoned his wife.

"Did you hear about Red Storey? He's dead. We've got a story going in the next edition."

"Oh my, that's terrible," she said. "The poor man."

Minutes later, she was on the telephone to a Montreal radio station. "My husband works at the *Star*," she said. "He just telephoned to tell me that Red Storey is dead."

Pat Curran, my assistant, almost ran me over getting off the elevator. "Boy, I'm glad I bumped into you," he said. "Did you hear about Red Storey?"

"What about him?"

"He's dead. I heard it on my car radio on the way to work."

"I spoke to Red on the telephone yesterday," I told Curran. "He was fine."

"I heard it on the car radio," he insisted.

Minutes later, I was on the telephone to Storey's wife, Helen. "How are things?" I asked. "Everything okay?"

"Everything's fine," she said. "How are you?"

"Your husband there?"

"Here he is," she said.

Storey came on the line.

"Red," I said, "have I got a story for you!"

13

The President

Few men in professional hockey have commanded more respect than Clarence Campbell, who was the NHL's president from 1946 to 1977, when he was succeeded by John Ziegler. Campbell, a Saskatchewan native, was a Rhodes scholar in 1925-26 and a lawyer who was a prosecutor at the Nuremberg War Trials.

Hockey was Campbell's life. Having married relatively late in his years, Campbell had succeeded in making the league his baby, his hobby, his vocation, his *raison d'être*.

What made Campbell special was that, unlike Ziegler, his office was your office, his free time yours. Everything he did was dedicated to making the game greater and healthier. He would defend it against any danger, real or imagined. Nothing else mattered but the game. And like most people who put the game above everything else, including family, he was unforgiving with those who, in his perception, had harmed it.

Campbell enjoyed everything about hockey: the owners, the players, even most of the media. A good day for him was a day in which he would be surrounded by hockey people. Such a day occurred in June 1970, when he met with the NHL's Board of Governors and read them his confidential financial report. The news he brought them was what they wanted to hear. He was especially proud and delighted with one section of the report, which he highlighted with a yellow tracer pencil. One sentence read: "Even though our return to the players last season was at an all-time low, our profits were at an all-time high."

Smiles greeted this news. Clearly, business was better than ever. Profits were soaring and overhead was at rock bottom, thanks to the fact that the minimum NHL salary was less than $10,000 and three-year $25-million deals simply a pipe dream.

Each of the twelve owners received a copy of Campbell's report, of course. Good news always was good reading.

A few days after Campbell had delivered the good news, Alan Eagleson, executive director of the NHL Players' Association, was on the telephone to me.

"I've got something here that might interest you," he said.

"What?"

It was Campbell's heretofore secret report to the NHL board.

"There's some pretty strong stuff in there," said Eagleson. "Interested?"

What reporter wouldn't be? Eagleson suggested I fly to his office in Toronto where he'd show me the report and we could talk. I agreed. And, yes, the Campbell report was everything Eagleson had said it was. Everything in it was dedicated to making owners smile.

"Do you think, maybe, this paragraph about record profits and a record-low return to the players would help the association the next time we sit down with the owners?" he asked with a chuckle.

I told Eagleson I'd like to borrow the purloined report. He had no objections. Back in Montreal, I informed the *Star*'s editor-in-chief, Frank Walker, that I'd like to do a five-part series on the report.

"Sounds good," said Walker. "Make sure we promote it in the paper a couple of days before we start carrying it."

The report, of course, was filled with startling numbers, promises, and conclusions. It dealt with salaries, benefits, and other material

Campbell, in particular, and the NHL's owners, in general, ordinarily would be loath to make public. Given the wealth of data, several days were needed to write the series. The day before the first of the five parts was to run, a promo ran on the first page of the *Montreal Star*. It read: "Tomorrow, the first of five parts dealing with National Hockey League salaries and benefits . . ."

Seemingly moments after the newspaper appeared on the streets, the telephone rang on my desk. Clarence Campbell was on the other end. "This series you're starting tomorrow . . . I don't recall talking to you at any time about players' salaries and benefits."

"You haven't, Mr. Campbell."

"In that case, how can you be quoting me on those subjects?"

"Because all of the quotes are contained in a copy of your confidential report to the Board of Governors," I replied.

Silence.

"Mr. Campbell . . ."

"If I'm misquoted, you'll hear from our lawyers," he snapped.

"I assure you, there's no chance that you'll be misquoted. I have a copy of your report."

End of conversation.

The series, needless to say, created a small sensation. It was not difficult to imagine the Players' Association's officers walking into their next bargaining meeting with the NHL owners and pointing out: "Uh, you people are always complaining there's no money to increase benefits to the players. It says here in Mr. Campbell's report to the governors that profits were at an all-time high last year, but that the percentage of return to the players was at an all-time low. Presumably, gentlemen, that's an accurate statement."

In fact, the players did walk away from their negotiations with increases in many areas. In the meantime, Clarence Campbell smouldered. He had to explain to the owners how the copy of his report had fallen into the wrong hands. As far as the leak was concerned, Campbell, in fact, was completely blameless. One of the owners had been clumsy with his handling of the report, and had left it behind in the meeting room. Eventually, somehow, it fell into Alan Eagleson's hands. For his part, Campbell strongly suspected that the owner of the St. Louis Blues, Sid Salomon, Jr., and his son, Sid III, had passed the report to me. He knew the Salomons and I were friendly.

Well, the five-part series went on to give me my first National Newspaper Award for sportswriting. (Much later, when he was told about the award, Campbell harrumphed: "That's the first time anyone has won an award for thievery.") Campbell had been embarrassed. Players' salaries would rise to an average of $85,000 per year in 1975. Somebody would have to pay. And pay I did, in the summer of 1970.

For years, I had been a fairly regular member of the *Hockey Night in Canada* gang. "The Fisher Report," which was the brainchild of HNIC executive producer Ralph Mellanby, had become a useful feature. It also helped pay the rent, because linked with it was a radio analyst's job for all of the Canadiens' games.

Each year, before the start of the season, Mellanby would telephone to renew my participation. It was always an oral agreement. Written contracts were for the big hitters. An oral agreement with Mellanby, who's now responsible for the television feed at the 1996 Olympic Games in Atlanta, didn't present a problem. He was fair. He was a man of his word.

A couple of weeks after the series on Campbell's report appeared, Mellanby was on the telephone to me. "We're changing our intermission format," he said. "I'm sorry, but we can't use you."

"Seems to me we made a deal a few weeks ago, Ralph," I replied. "This new format must have come up in a hell of a hurry."

"Sorry," said Mellanby.

"Don't lie to me, Ralph," I said. "I know why you can't use me any more. David [Canadiens president David Molson and his two brothers owned the team] told you to get me off the air."

After several moments' pause, Mellanby stammered: "Uh . . . I'll deny it if you write, but it's true."

"Tell me something, Ralph, do you really think I'd write about this? Do you really think the people who read my newspaper care one way or another whether or not I'm on *Hockey Night in Canada?*"

"Uh . . ."

"Radio, too, Ralph?"

"Yes," said Mellanby.

"See you around, Ralph," I said.

David Molson, of course, had every right to stop anyone from appearing on a television or radio broadcast of his team's games. Owners have that right to this day. It's in their contracts with the television and radio people. Should Molson have argued the point with Campbell? It would have been nice because David and I had a completely cordial relationship. On the other hand, word had apparently come down from the president's office. It had to be done. Somebody had to pay.

I didn't write anything about the episode, but others in Canada and the United States did. It wasn't that big a deal as far as I was concerned, but others leaped happily on the scenario of an individual blackballed on television and radio for something which had appeared in a newspaper. They saw red. So did my bosses at the *Montreal Star.*

A couple of weeks later, publisher Derek Price stopped by my desk. "Frank [Walker] tells me you've been kicked off *Hockey Night in Canada,*" he said. "True?"

"That's right."

When he asked why and I told him, he was not amused.

"You can't be serious."

"That's what the television people have confirmed to me," I said. "Anyway, it's no big deal. NHL teams have the final word on who appears on their television and radio broadcasts. I don't have a problem with that."

"How much is that going to cost you?" he asked.

"Not much," he was told. "Oh, a fair amount, I guess, but I've always regarded that kind of work as temporary, at best. If you're asking if I depend on that money, the answer is no."

He rubbed his hand across his chin. "Don't you have a son who's starting at M.I.T. ?"

"Ian started classes about a month ago."

"Didn't he finish number two in the province when he matriculated from high school last June?"

"Right."

"How come he wasn't awarded a scholarship by the McConnell Foundation?" asked Price. "We like to do something for our employees' kids who do that well."

"I don't know. It never really crossed my mind," he was told.

"Obviously, it was an oversight," said the publisher. "Let's see what we can do about it."

For the next four years, the McConnell Foundation contributed $5,000 each year toward my son's tuition at the world-renowned Boston school. Nice.

In the meantime, Clarence Campbell continued to hold firmly to his belief that the Salomons had been the cause of his embarrassment.

Late in the 1970-71 season, the Canadiens were in St. Louis. Only minutes after our group arrived at our hotel, the telephone rang in my room.

"It's Sid," said Sid Salomon III.

The owner's son reported that he had "just got off the phone with Clarence Campbell and he's accused me, again, of giving you that report."

"So?"

"Here's what I want you to do," said Sid III. "Hop into a cab and come down to my office. I've got [St. Louis Blues' lawyer] Jim Cullen in the office with me."

"So?"

"When you get here, I want you to sign an affidavit to the effect that I didn't give you the report."

"Sid," I said, "you know I can't do that."

"Why not?" he asked.

"Because you know you gave it to me."

Click!

14

Jumpin' Jacques and the Jet

Jacques Plante peered into the mirror in the Canadiens' dressing room and ran his fingers lightly alongside the fresh stitches. Seven had been needed to close a savage cut that ran from the corner of his mouth, along his cheek, and through his nostril.

"Looks pretty ugly," I told the Canadiens netminder.

"Not bad. I've seen worse. This was gonna happen sooner or later," he shrugged.

The day was November 1, the year, 1959. A little more than three minutes into the first period of this Canadiens–Rangers game in New York, Andy Bathgate had moved in on Plante and backhanded a puck which struck the goalie in the face. The Canadiens star promptly sprawled on his stomach, his head cushioned in an ugly pool of blood. Bathgate raced to the fallen goalie and lifted his head. Blood poured from the wound onto the New York player's fingers. Bathgate shook his head and skated away.

A moment later, Plante struggled to his feet. A towel was placed over his face, but still the blood dribbled down his sweater and fell in droplets on the ice. Plante swallowed some blood as helping hands guided him to the medical room, but once inside the area, he shook off the supporting arms.

"Lie down on the table," he was told.

Plante shook his head. Instead he moved in front of the mirror.

"Before you do anything," he told the doctor, "I want to see what it looks like."

The doctor scraped away bits of loose flesh from the wound before inserting the stitches. Plante lay there, soundless, his fingers locked, as the needle knifed through the raw flesh.

Twenty minutes later, Plante left the room and skated back onto the ice to the sound of thunderous cheers and a lively rendition of "For He's a Jolly Good Fellow" from the Garden organist. He went directly to the Canadiens' room, where coach Toe Blake was waiting.

"How bad is it?" Blake asked.

"It's sore," Plante replied.

"Why don't you wear your mask for the rest of the game?" suggested Blake.

For some weeks, Plante had been making small noises about doing precisely that. Why not, he argued. Was it really necessary for goaltenders to stand there while pucks came at them through thickets of players? Players were shooting harder. Curves were starting to appear on the blades of sticks. Deflections were becoming more and more dangerous. Who needs it?

He had spent a lot of time with equipment manufacturers, throwing ideas at them. Why not a face-fitting mask? Yes, maybe it would be difficult to see a puck lying at his feet, but why not? Wasn't that better than no mask at all?

"I don't think I can go back in without it," Plante told Blake. So wear the mask he did. Prior to his injury, Plante had stopped three shots. After donning the mask, he was beaten only once on twenty-five shots. Now, at game's end, he sat in the dressing room, fresh blood dribbling from under the patch that covered his wound. Another patch, caked with dried blood, covered a five-stitch cut on his chin, a souvenir of a Canadiens game against Chicago a week earlier.

"After the puck hit me," he told the throng of reporters, "I didn't think any bones were broken. But what bothered me most of all was that I swallowed some blood. I didn't feel too good and my teeth felt numb."

What about the mask? Could he see properly with it? Did he feel more confident with it?

"I wouldn't have played without it," said Plante. Then he added: "Well . . . maybe I would have."

Toe Blake wasn't an instant convert to the cause. He knew Plante had been experimenting with masks. "He can practise with one, if he wants," he had snapped earlier, "but no goaltender of mine is gonna wear one in a game. We're here to win."

Plante didn't wear the mask in the Canadiens' next game. But he wore it in the game after that, and, once he did, goaltending and the game were changed forever.

Jacques Plante was different. He wasn't intimidated easily. He had firm ideas about what was good for his game and for him. The puck stopped with him, and nobody else. He would do what he felt was right for him – on and off the ice. What was good for him, he insisted, was right for the Canadiens. If Canadiens management didn't think so, well, there were other teams.

On their seven regular-season visits to Toronto in the six-team era, the Canadiens always stayed at the Royal York Hotel. Nice place. Bright, clean rooms. A superb location in downtown Toronto, just a brief subway ride to Maple Leaf Gardens and only a short walk from favourite bars and restaurants.

Plante, however, was not an enthusiast.

"I can't stay in this hotel any more," he told Blake one day.

"Why not?"

"My asthma. I get an attack every time I come to this place. I'm sure it's the bedsheets. I'll stay at the Westbury. It's right next door to the Gardens."

Blake reluctantly agreed.

Later that season, Blake and the Canadiens were in Toronto for another game. That morning, Blake invited me to go with him by subway to the Leafs' practice in the Gardens.

The ride is only six or seven minutes. There's a short walk along the platform, up a short flight of steps to Carlton Street, and a two-minute walk east to the Gardens.

Blake and I started up the steps, turned a corner – and there was Plante walking towards us, a lady friend on each arm. We passed on the steps.

"Well, good morning, Mr. Plante," boomed Blake. "Nice day, isn't it?"

"Ah, good morning," muttered Plante, who continued to walk down the steps toward the subway platform. He turned the corner, and disappeared from view.

Blake started to laugh. "How d'you like that?" he grunted. "Asthma. Bedsheets. I should never have let him change hotels in the first place, but he's gonna make one more move the next time we're in town."

That night, after the game, Plante visited Blake on the train.

"Uh, Toe, about this morning. They're my cousins, you know."

"Sure they were," said Blake.

"I have cousins in every city," argued Plante.

"Sure you do."

"My asthma . . ."

Blake broke in, "The next time we're in Toronto, you're gonna have to get used to the bedsheets at the Royal York."

Case closed.

Blake loved Plante, the goaltender, but didn't like him as a person. The Canadiens coach didn't like surprises, and Plante was full of them. On some nights, Blake would arrive at the arena to find Plante waiting for him. "I don't think I can play tonight," Blake would be told.

"What's the problem?"

"Asthma."

Later, Blake would fume. "That son of a bitch is driving me nuts. I never can be sure when he's playing, but he always ends up playing. I don't know how much more of this I can take."

At the same time, Blake always insisted Plante was the best goaltender he'd ever seen. "Especially those five years we won the Cup, eh? I played with [Bill] Durnan, and he was best I'd seen up to that time. Plante was better during those five years."

Blake knew it. So did Plante. So did his teammates, even though he stretched their patience from time to time. It's true he played behind many of hockey's best players, starting with Doug Harvey on defence. There were nights when the Canadiens were so dominant, his workload was minimal. But he always made the big stops when the Canadiens needed them. No goaltender I have known had as much confidence in his own ability.

Take the 1961-62 season. Harvey had won his sixth Norris Trophy as the NHL's top defenceman in 1961. Plante, however, had missed the Vezina (fewest goals against during the regular season) for the first time in six seasons. Yet despite his dominance at his position, Harvey, the NHL's best defenceman, was traded to the New York Rangers for Lou Fontinato. It was a trade which didn't make any sense at all. Was it because the Canadiens had failed to win the Stanley Cup for the first time in six seasons? That's unlikely. Was it, as I've suggested elsewhere, Canadiens management's way of finally getting back at Harvey for the role he had played in the formation of the short-lived Players' Association in 1958? Probably. Was it the first shot in the breakup of the dynasty? Definitely.

"How much is this team going to miss Doug?" I asked Plante on the first day of training camp.

"I figured that would be the first question I'd be asked in training camp," he said with a grin. "Listen to this: Doug Harvey is the greatest defenceman in the National Hockey League. All of us, and especially me, owe him a lot. He helped me win five Vezinas in a row. But now I'm going to show you how good Jacques Plante is. I'm going to win the Vezina without him."

"Do you really think you can?"

"Watch me."

Despite the absence of Harvey, the Canadiens allowed only 166 pucks to pass the goal line that season, twenty-two fewer than the previous year. They finished in first place with 98 points, six more than the previous year and thirteen ahead of the second-place Toronto Maple Leafs. Plante played seventy games, enjoyed a modest goals-against average of 2.37 – and won his sixth Vezina. He also won the Hart Trophy, which goes to the NHL's most valuable player.

Two years later, though, Blake had had enough of his star goaltender and Plante was traded to the Rangers. Blake stayed with the Canadiens where he won three more Stanley Cups in the next five years – but only after going four seasons without one. That empty streak had started with a semi-final loss to the Chicago Blackhawks, where the best left-winger in NHL history was making good things happen.

Yeah, Bobby Hull, like Plante, another guy with firm ideas about what was good for him and good for hockey.

The Golden Jet was on the telephone. He had a problem.

"My folks are in town for tonight's game at the Forum," Hull told me. "I didn't expect them. Can't find a ticket anywhere."

"What about the tickets set aside for the visiting teams?" he was asked.

"Gone. Can't find a spare one. I need two."

"Sounds like you have a problem, Bobby, but I guess we can't have your folks sitting in the hotel without tickets."

"That's why I'm calling," he said. "Do you know where I can buy a couple?"

"I can do better than that," I said. "You can have mine."

It's no longer the case, but for a long time, one of the perks linked with covering the Canadiens' beat was a pair of season tickets. There was nothing sinister about it. The tickets were for family and friends, and Hull was a friend going back to the time he and Stan Mikita came to Chicago out of junior hockey within a year of each other in the late '50s. Until they arrived, the Blackhawks had made a career out of missing the playoffs. They missed the playoffs in Hull's first year, the eleventh time in twelve seasons. Three seasons later, Chicago had won its first Stanley Cup since 1937-38.

Robert Marvin Hull jump-started the organization in a lot of ways. His shot terrorized the opposition to the point where it wasn't unusual for a visiting goaltender to develop a groin injury during the pre-game warmup. The sound of Hull's hundred-miles-per-hour-plus shot hitting the boards was ample reason for a visit to the clinic. Then, there was his skating and his strength. Add his uncommon good looks, and he was everybody's pinup boy, blessed with an upper body which, somehow, appeared to grow larger the more items of clothing he removed. He took the game by storm everywhere he played and he had time for everybody. He was also Chicago's – and hockey's – hope for the future.

"You're sure I'm not taking away the tickets from somebody else?" asked Hull that March day in 1963.

"Of course you are, but you need a pair for your parents, right? You've got 'em. One small problem, though. Your folks will be sitting in the same section as the players' wives."

"That's no problem," said Hull before he rang off.

That night, Mr. and Mrs. Robert Hull's boy was on top of his game. He scored twice and Chicago won, 3–2. The Hulls had a lot to cheer about.

The same couldn't be said, however, for the Canadiens' wives and fans sitting in their section of the Forum.

"You shouldn't be cheering for the Blackhawks," Bobby's mother was told at one point. "Those are Red Fisher's seats."

"I'll cheer as much as I want to," snapped Mrs. Hull.

More words were exchanged as the game wore on. Also more cheering, for good reason, from Bobby's mother.

The next day the Canadiens' trainer told me that the wives of the Canadiens planned to complain to Frank Selke, the team's managing director, about what had happened. I said I was sorry but there wasn't too much I could do about it. The incident, to my mind, was a tempest in a teapot and, in fact, it seemed to be forgotten quite quickly.

Until, that is, a few weeks before the start of the next season. One morning, as I had done for years, I asked one of the *Star's* office boys to go to the Forum to pick up my season tickets.

He returned empty-handed one hour later. "The box-office man said he doesn't have the tickets. Mr. Selke has them."

"Anything else?"

"All he said was Mr. Selke wanted to talk to you about the tickets."

Several weeks later the telephone rang in my office. Frank J. Selke was on the line. "You haven't picked up your tickets," he said.

"As a matter of fact, I sent an office boy for them a few weeks ago, like I always do," I said. "He was told I had to talk to you first."

"You know, you had a couple of hustlers sitting in your seats late last season. They got into a shouting match with Mrs. Blake and some of the wives."

"I heard a little bit about that the next day," I said, "but what I'd like you to know is that the hustlers, as you describe them, are named Mr. and Mrs. Robert Hull. They have a son, Bobby, who plays for the Chicago Blackhawks."

The line fell silent.

"I heard there was a little shouting when Mrs. Hull cheered for Chicago," I continued, "but it didn't sound too serious to me."

"Well," Selke replied, "a lot of the people sitting there were upset. I got a lot of complaints." he said.

"Sorry about that," I said. "His parents needed tickets. Bobby called. I gave them the tickets."

"How would it be if I moved your tickets to the other side of the building?" Mr. Selke asked.

"I've got a better idea," I said. "My wife uses the seats now and then, but I don't. I've never sat in those seats. I don't need them. Why don't we just forget about them?"

"No, no," he said, "that's not what I have in mind at all. Why don't you come down and check out the new seats. If you don't like them, you can have your old seats back."

"I really don't need them," I said. "I really don't want them."

"Why don't you talk it over with your wife?" he asked.

The seat locations were changed. Several months later I got the chance to tell Hull the story. "I'm not surprised," he grinned. "My mother's as quiet as a mouse at home, but every time she watches me play, she gets pretty excited. I'll make sure to get my own tickets the next time we're in town."

"Please do," I said.

Hull's parents, of course, weren't the only ones to be excited by Bobby. When he arrived in Chicago, the Blackhawks hadn't made the playoffs since the 1952-53 season. The team in 1957 was playing to crowds of 4,500. Some games were shifted to other cities. The noise heard in Chicago Stadium was the franchise's death-rattle. Hull changed that, particularly when Stan Mikita's arrival for the 1958-59 season lifted the Hawks into the playoffs and started to put more fans in the seats.

Hull was as big in Chicago, bigger in some respects, than any of the great stars in Montreal. He sold tickets in every city in the league. There was a magical quality about him which set him apart, on a higher level, from all of the NHL's other left-wingers. Moreover, he went out of his way to sell the game. It didn't matter how long he kept a team bus waiting, if there was one more autograph to sign, he found time for it.

How much did Hull mean to hockey? Let me count the ways. The NHL expanded to twelve teams from six in 1967-68. Two more teams were added in 1970 and another two in 1972. This growth was prompted, in part, by the realization that if the NHL didn't expand, other cities in Canada and the United States would form a league of their own. At the same time, a lot of NHL owners were dismissive when the World Hockey Association was incorporated in 1971. Where would the players for the WHA come from, they asked. All of the game's great stars were locked into the National Hockey League. Sure, there would be some defections, but how could a new league even think of challenging the old boys' network of the NHL?

Hull was the answer when Winnipeg entrepreneur Ben Hatskin made him an offer he couldn't refuse. He became hockey's first million-dollar player, and the WHA, against all odds and much to the dismay of NHL owners in general, and Chicago's Bill Wirtz in particular, went into business. Hull carried the new league into 1972 on his shoulders. Without him, there would not have been a WHA. Without him, the glow was lost from the Chicago franchise.

When Hull hung up his skates in 1980, he had scored 610 goals and 560 assists in 1,063 games, most of them played with Chicago. His sixteen NHL seasons also included some time with Winnipeg and Hartford after those cities merged with the NHL in 1979. But how many would he have scored had he remained in the NHL for all twenty-two of his seasons as a professional? How many more Stanley Cups would the Blackhawks have won besides that one in 1960-61?

Hull's defection shook up the hockey establishment. In truth, they never forgave him for it. He went to the WHA the same year hockey's best professionals faced the Soviets in their classic eight-game series, but Hull wasn't among them. Only NHL players were to be invited, the league explained, which represented to many a classic case of changing the rules halfway through the game. Hockey fans across Canada were furious. Politicians raged. Even the Soviets objected to the idea of playing the series without a Bobby Hull on the team – to no avail. He was in Moscow two years later, however, wearing a WHA sweater, still selling the game. Everywhere he went, kids followed him. He signed autographs. The team bus waited for him.

Players always have known where they stand with Hull. So have owners, general managers, and coaches. He held nothing back, still doesn't.

Rick Ley, who's now with the Vancouver Canucks as an assistant coach, was a defenceman on the 1974 WHA team that went to the Soviet Union. The team played well in Canada, but the Soviets' superior skills took over in Moscow. The WHA players became more frustrated day by day, from game to game. The Soviets were too strong on the ice. Off it, Soviet officials went out of their way to make things difficult for their visitors. Promises were made, then broken. Accommodations were poor. Players' wives complained. Just after the sixth game, which Team Canada lost, 5–2, Soviet superstar Valery Kharlamov made a derisive gesture at Ley. The defenceman exploded. He grabbed Kharlamov, beat him like a drum, and received a game misconduct.

Later, in the WHA dressing room in Moscow, Hull shrugged out of his equipment. Ley undressed a few yards away. Neither exchanged a word.

Hull nodded in Ley's direction. Then, quietly, he said to me: "We don't need animals like that on this team."

"What's that?" I asked.

Hull shrugged his shoulders and didn't say a word.

"Tell you what," I said. "There's nobody else around, so I'll forget what you said if you forget it."

"All right," he sighed.

A couple of minutes later, Hull was surrounded by a group of North American reporters. "We don't need animals like that on this team," he said, nodding in Ley's direction.

Hull didn't pick his spots on the ice. Off it, like Lafleur, he would often speak when he should have been listening. This hasn't diminished his stature as a superb player, but he has paid a price for being a rebel with a cause. Hull was as big as any of the game's greatest stars before and after his time. I'm certain there would have been a job for him in the Chicago organization if he had broken the ice with Blackhawks owner Bill Wirtz. Instead, Hull waited for Wirtz to come to him. It didn't happen.

Nobody's perfect.

15

Cream of the Crop

Having been a sports reporter for more than forty years, I've seen a lot of hockey games. When I say a lot I mean more than four thousand regular-season and playoff games, plus exhibition jousts, Canada Cup games, and World Championships. I've seen games in Stockholm and Saskatoon, Prague and Helsinki, Vienna and Leningrad, Charlottetown and Victoria, London and Moscow. I've seen games in every NHL town, from Montreal to San Jose, Tampa Bay to Vancouver.

Not surprisingly, people occasionally ask me to name my favourite game or games. Of course, there have been good games and bad ones, great and only acceptable ones. Then there are those which have stirred the soul and remain locked in my mind forever.

Game eight, of course, in the 1972 Team Canada–Soviet Union series, was one of those. I know I'm not alone in that. Millions of Canadians have memories of Paul Henderson's historic goal which provided Team Canada with a 6–5 victory after they had entered the third period trailing, 5–3. The Goal also provided Team Canada with a 4–3–1 series victory, sending most of Canada on an emotional roller-coaster the likes of which has not been seen before or since.

As good and as emotional as that game was, it's not the best I've ever seen. That accolade goes to game three of the 1961 Stanley Cup semi-final between the Chicago Blackhawks and the Montreal Canadiens. It started at 8:00 p.m. on Sunday, March 26, and ended almost six shirt-twisting hours later on Monday, March 27.

There is no hockey crowd anywhere quite like the one in Chicago Stadium. There are no individual sounds in the arena. Instead, there is a sort of white noise, a steady kind of roaring hum which engulfs them, and on this night there was a good reason for it. This, after all, was the Canadiens team which had won a record five consecutive Stanley Cups, and there was no real reason to believe that the torch would finally be passed. The Canadiens had finished the regular season in first place with 92 points, Chicago in third, with 75. The Canadiens had scored 254 goals, the Blackhawks, 198. The Canadiens had allowed 188, the Blackhawks, 180.

Here they were, after splitting the first two games of their best-of-seven series in Montreal, where visiting teams almost never win in the playoffs. Jacques Plante versus Glenn Hall, Jean Béliveau versus Stan Mikita, Bobby Hull and Dickie Moore. The Rocket had retired during training camp, but his brother Henri was there.

What occurred that night in Chicago was, arguably, the greatest performances by two goaltenders in NHL history. From the start, the game belonged to Plante and Hall. Breakaways, long shots, slapshots, close-in shots – they saw them all and stopped them all for the entire first period and most of the second. Then, with less than two minutes remaining in that period, a gritty, hard-nosed left-winger named Murray Balfour, who had been "sold" to the Blackhawks by the Canadiens in June of 1959, scored the game's first goal. The crowd erupted.

Could Hall do it? Could he hold on? Could the Blackhawks do it? Hell, could the Canadiens do it?

The third period was a clone of the first two. Scoring chances on both sides. First Plante. Then, Plante again. Hall. Hall again. As the teams approached the final minute of regulation time, Balfour's goal continued to stand straight and tall, like a sentinel. Would it be enough? After all, these were the Canadiens. There was Béliveau. There was Richard. Yes, Bernard Geoffrion had been injured and was out of the game, but there were Moore and Doug Harvey.

There were only forty seconds left in regulation time when Toe Blake motioned to Plante to head for the bench. The Canadiens' net stood empty as the teams awaited a faceoff in the circle to Hall's right. Richard was there, lightly scuffing the blades of his skates on the ice, waiting for the puck to drop. If Henri lost the faceoff, the game would be over. If he won, there was still a chance.

The puck dropped, Henri got control of it, and, in one motion, lashed a short shot past a stunned Hall. The crowd, which had been on its feet for longer than a minute, was stilled. How could this have happened? How could the Blackhawks hold off the Canadiens for more than fifty-nine minutes, yet now, with only thirty-six seconds left, overtime was looming. How? Why?

Early in the first overtime, Béliveau went in alone on Hall, and shot wide. Ralph Backstrom swept in and lost the puck at the last moment. Bill Hay, who's now the president of the Calgary Flames, shook himself loose and skated in alone on Plante. The puck hurtled toward an open, upper corner, but Plante lunged desperately and deflected the puck with the shaft of his stick. Hall stopped Moore. Minutes later, the puck is twisting and turning in the Canadiens' crease, but referee Dalton McArthur whistles the play to a halt when several Canadiens fall on it. At the end of the first overtime, Plante had made eight stops and so had Hall.

There were more scoring opportunities by both teams in the second overtime. Once, Donnie Marshall slapped a puck out of the air and watched it drop behind Hall, but referee McArthur promptly ruled that Marshall's stick was above his shoulder when he made contact with the puck. No goal. In fact, no goal was scored in the second overtime period.

Early in the third overtime, Chicago's Ron Murphy was penalized. Seconds later, Béliveau swept in on Hall, but the Blackhawks' goaltender made yet another one of what would be fifty-three stops.

Seconds later, Chicago's Tod Sloan had an open net – and missed. Then, Hall stopped Marcel Bonin and Junior Langlois. Richard, the hero of regulation time, broke in alone, but a split-second lunge by Hall at the last possible moment stopped him. Claude Provost had an open net, but shot wide.

As the clock neared the twelve-minute mark of the third over-time, referee McArthur whistled down the Canadiens' Moore with a minor penalty. Borderline stuff, particularly considering the time, the game's tempo, and the game's importance. Put it this way: there had been occasions earlier in the game when far more obvious penalties could have been called – against either team. Twenty-eight seconds later, at 12:12, Murray Balfour put the puck behind Jacques Plante from a scramble in front of the net. It was all over – except for the bedlam which followed.

The instant Balfour scored, twenty thousand fans leaped to their feet, their wild cries sweeping the arena. Strangers hugged and kissed. The ice was littered with debris. The Canadiens, who had reached a special high when Richard scored the tying goal with only thirty-six seconds remaining in regulation time, and a low when Marshall's apparent winning goal was disallowed in the second overtime, stormed after referee McArthur. Why the penalty? How could he call a penalty at that stage of the game?

Behind the Canadiens' bench, Toe Blake had another protest in mind, something a little stronger than words. He reached for the gate leading onto the ice, shrugged off the restraining hands of sev-eral players and took off in a slow, uneven trot toward McArthur, who was leaning over the official scorer's bench on the opposite side of the rink.

McArthur still had his back to Blake when the Canadiens coach flung a punch which struck the referee on the shoulder and deflected onto his jaw. It was only then that McArthur turned, his eyes widen-ing in surprise at the sight of Blake. That was also the moment when several Canadiens players wrapped their arms around their coach and led him from the ice.

It was a wild finish to one of hockey's greatest games, and certainly my greatest. It was also, as it developed, the start of the end of the Canadiens' dynasty. Sure, they won the next game in Chicago, but then Hall shut out the Canadiens in game five in Montreal, and held them scoreless again in game six at Chicago. The Blackhawks went on from there to meet the Detroit Red Wings and won their first – and as it turned out, only – Stanley Cup since 1938. The Canadiens, meanwhile, didn't see another Stanley Cup until May 1, 1965, when they beat, yes, the Blackhawks in seven.

After the game, I approached NHL president Clarence Campbell in the referee's room. "What happens now?" I asked.

"I don't know," said Campbell. "I really don't know. I'll have to go by the book. Rule 67B says that if a coach or manager holds or strikes an official, that coach or manager will be immediately suspended for the balance of the game and fined substantially. He will also be ordered to the room. It happened at the end of the game . . ."

"Does that mean Blake won't be suspended from the next game?"

"The rule applies only to this game," said Campbell. "The incident has nothing to do with other games, but frankly, I don't know . . ."

The next afternoon Blake was still fuming over the incident. He was also worried – or at least he should have been. It's one thing to protest a controversial loss, and he had a good case for one, but coaches don't go around punching officials, or they shouldn't. In short, there was some explaining he had to do. For that matter, Blake didn't have far to go: Campbell's room was just down the hall from Blake's.

"How could you do something like that?" Betty Blake asked her husband. "That was stupid."

"Yeah, pretty damned stupid," I seconded.

"He doesn't allow a goal in the second overtime, and Moore's in the penalty box for what – hooking – when they get their goal," Blake snapped back. "That's what's stupid."

Blake wondered what would happen to him. I said a suspension was unlikely, but a fine was a definite possibility. "Just pay the money, whatever it is," I told him.

"Yeah? How much?"

"Two thousand." (Blake's annual salary at this time was $18,000.)

"Well, it better not be more than five hundred dollars," snorted Blake.

"Pay," he was told.

Moments later, there was a knock on the door. "Mr. Campbell wants to see you," Blake was told.

"I'll be there soon," said Blake.

"He wants to see you right away."

Blake left for Campbell's room, but was back in a matter of minutes. A flush suffused his cheeks.

"Suspended?"

"No."

"Fined?"

"Yeah."

"How much?"

"Two thousand."

Blake, of course, went on to coach for another seven seasons and three more Stanley Cups. Dalton McArthur wasn't that lucky. He was fired before the start of the 1961-62 season.

16

The Wrestling Rabbi

Hockey has been the focus of my career as a reporter. But, of course, I've covered other sports, other athletes, other celebrities.

Wrestling and boxing promoter Eddie Quinn was unlike anyone I have ever met in sports. He was, in every way, an unforgettable character. He met people from every walk of life – athletes, milkmen, youngsters, accountants, office help, show people, strangers looking for handouts – and talked to each and every one in the same way. He made no distinctions. Period.

He arrived in Montreal in 1939 at the invitation of Canadiens' general manager Tommy Gorman. Before that, he had promoted wrestling in his home town of Waltham, Massachusetts, where he once scuffled for a living as a carpenter and a cabbie. In Montreal, prior to Quinn's arrival, the only sound heard at most wrestling cards was the sound of silence. Attendance at the Forum measured in the hundreds. Wrestling needed a quick fix and, in Gorman's view, Quinn was the doctor who could do it.

Quinn was different. His face resembled the map of Ireland, but he was a handsome man, with eyes which always seemed to be laughing above a year-round tan. A spit-and-polish guy. He was a fashion plate, with made-to-order silk suits and shirts, and never a hair out of place. Then, there was his voice: as loud and as harsh as an old file on wood. It announced his presence long before an audience could see him.

Wednesday night was traditionally wrestling night at the Forum. But few honoured that tradition. Quinn needed an attraction, a reason to make people come, and, in Montreal, Quinn knew that his man had to be a French-Canadian. Someone with colour and style. He had to be a husky, good-looking performer who would appeal to the ladies.

Yvon Robert was the answer. He was a big, athletic guy blessed with matinée-idol good looks. Quinn had first met him on the circuit in Waltham and, sure enough, he brought back the people. In his time, he was as big in Montreal as Rocket Richard. On some nights, bigger.

Quinn wasn't merely wrestling's promoter: he was its royalty. His arms reached out to most of the major cities in Canada and the United States. Lou Thesz, Nature Boy Rogers, Argentina Rocca, The Angel, the Dusek brothers, Killer Kowalski, Gorgeous George, Don Leo Jonathan, Yukon Eric, and others turned up in St. Louis, Toronto, and other major cities – all of them an extension of Quinn's promotional genius. In Montreal, Robert was king, but there were others in his court: Larry Moquin and Johnny Rougeau, for example, and later, Edouard Carpentier.

Television was an important piece of the puzzle and, in time, Quinn arranged for that as well. The marriage of Robert, who quickly became the Montreal version of the heavyweight champion of the world, and Michel Normandin's play-by-play was made in heaven. By the mid-1950s, crowds of fourteen thousand were filling the Forum each week while silk suits filled the closets of Quinn's fashionable Town of Mount Royal home. Several streets away, Robert frolicked in his pool. Life was grand. Quinn was pocketing $350,000 a year. Trouble is, he was spending $360,000. Eventually, it would become more trouble to Quinn than even he could handle.

Eddie didn't merely enjoy life: he rejoiced in it. He made it sing, and he wrote the songs and the lyrics. The city's sleekest convertibles were his toys. Show-business people were his passion. He knew and was friendly with people in high and low places. Many, like Jackie Gleason, Dean Martin and Jerry Lewis, Billy Daniels and Eartha Kitt, worked for him at the El Morocco, the glitzy nightclub he owned in downtown Montreal. He loved show people because in so many ways, Quinn was show biz too.

He loved to tell stories.

"I'm sittin' in my office at the Forum one day, and it's hot outside. I've got my shirt open. I'm not wearin' a tie. I'm just sittin' back and thinkin' about the fight we had comin' into the building. It was [Dave] Castilloux and [Johnny] Greco, and it's gonna be a big one.

"There's a knock on the door and I yell: 'Are you gonna stand there all day, or are you comin' in?'

"This little guy walks into the office, and his hands are together and he says to me: 'I'm Frank Selke. I'm the manager of this building now.'

"'Holy cow,' I says to myself, 'what do I do now?' I mean, here's the new boss of the building and he sees me in this condition: no tie, shirt open. I looked like a bum.

"'Mr. Selke,' I said, 'you have my deepest sympathies.' Then we both laughed.

"'I've got this fight comin' into the building,' I told him. 'It's a big one. It'll outdraw anythin' we've had in the place. Do you want to help me with it?'"

"He helped me," Quinn said. "He helped me for years. I loved that little guy."

Selke, who went on to create the Canadiens' dynasty which won five consecutive Stanley Cups, loved Eddie Quinn. It was easy to love Quinn.

"You've gotta do me a favour," Eddie said to me on the telephone one morning in the late 1950s.

"Name it."

"The guy wants to quit. He's got one fight under his belt, he still hasn't been hit by the other guy, and he wants to quit. Can you believe it?"

"You mean. . .?"

"Yeah, Buchanan," said Quinn. "You've gotta talk to him. You've gotta tell him what he's throwin' away."

Bucky Buchanan was a blond, blue-eyed heavyweight boxer who had attracted a huge following as an amateur. He could hit. He was Irish. He was blessed with baby-faced good looks. He was money in the bank.

Quinn had been talking to this heavyweight from Rosemount, Quebec, for some time. It took a while to convince him to turn professional, but the night he did, ten thousand fans nearly filled the Forum to watch him against a made-to-measure opponent, the first of many Quinn had in mind.

A minute or so into the fight, Buchanan threw a long, overhand right which, to ringside spectators, missed by roughly a foot. No problem. Buchanan's opponent crashed to the canvas and thrashed around like the proverbial beached whale. Ten thousand fans celebrated. A white hope was born.

"Sounds like you have a problem," Quinn was told.

"A problem? You kiddin', or what? The Irishman tol' me this mornin' that's it for him," said Quinn.

"Why?"

"He says he doesn't want to get his pretty face cut up. I tol' him he'd be pullin' in a hunnert grand per fight in less than a year, but he won't listen. Talk to him. He's at the joint across the street."

"I'll be there in thirty minutes," I said.

Buchanan was sitting alone in the empty El Morocco.

"It's not what I want," he said. "I don't need this. I don't want this."

"You're throwing away lots of money," I said. "It's not as if you got hurt last night."

"I know . . . I know, but it's not what I want."

"He doesn't want it, Eddie," I told Quinn later. "He's not kidding."

"I'm gonna send him to New York to see Jack. Maybe Dempsey can change his mind."

Buchanan went to the former champ's restaurant in New York. Dempsey even sparred lightly with him, all the while trying to convince Buchanan to stay, to give it a try. "The money's there, kid," Dempsey said. "You're good. You can do it."

Buchanan didn't waver. He retired after one professional fight. His record may even be listed somewhere.

It fell to Johnny Greco, born in the Notre Dame de Grace area of Montreal, to become the Northern Dancer in Quinn's stable of boxers. He was a knockout puncher.

One day the telephone rang in Quinn's office. "This is Senator Murphy," said the voice at the other end of the long-distance line. "Senator Murphy" was Frankie Carbo, a not-so-silent partner in the International Boxing Club which promoted fights in Madison Square Garden. Jim Norris, who was a powerful figure in hockey largely because his father, James, Sr., owned the Detroit Red Wings and pieces of the Chicago Blackhawks and the New York Rangers, was IBC's owner of record. Besides his IBC affiliation, Carbo was a practising lieutenant in the notorious Brooklyn-based gang of assassins known as Murder, Inc.

"You've got a fighter up there named Greco, right?" said Carbo.

"Yeah, Johnny Greco," said Quinn.

"I think we can do something with him in New York," Carbo told Quinn. "I want you to send him down here."

"When?"

"Next week," said Carbo. "He'll do good here."

"He's on his way," said Quinn.

"One thing more," said Carbo, "I'm your partner from now on."

"Sounds good to me," said Quinn. "I'll have my guy draw up the papers."

"No papers," said Carbo.

"No papers," said Quinn.

Quinn could be loud, profane, harsh, and unforgiving – but he was the city's softest touch during his twenty-five years in Montreal.

Once, he was in Boston to pick up his share of the receipts for a wrestling show at the Garden. His representative brought the money to Quinn's suite, where I happened to be visiting. Eddie dropped the packet of money into the inside pocket of his jacket.

"Aren't you going to count it?" I asked.

"Naw. My guys don't make mistakes."

"How much have you got there?"

"Five t'ousand."

"Let me count it."

There was $4,950 in the packet. Another count verified it. "You're short fifty dollars," I said.

"Impossible," said Quinn's Boston man. "You made a mistake."

"I'll count it again," I said. And again Quinn was short.

Quinn fixed his eyes on the man. "If you needed fifty bucks that badly," Quinn said quietly, "why didn't you just ask me for it?"

"I swear I counted out five thousand at the office," the man stammered. "Somebody must have lifted a fifty."

"Out," said Quinn. "If you're not out of here in ten seconds and out of my sight forever . . ."

The man ran from the room and out of Quinn's life.

A lot of people ran out on Eddie with a lot of his money over the years. By the late 1950s, business fell off. Many of his big wrestling names, including Robert, lost their appeal. The crowds of fourteen thousand dwindled to three thousand.

One fall day, Eddie was on the telephone. "I've got a new guy coming in next week," he said. "The Wrestling Rabbi."

"Say that again."

"The Wrestling Rabbi."

"Eddie," I said, "I love you like a brother. I'll do anything for you, but don't get me involved in that stuff."

"I'm tellin' you, he's a rabbi."

"I don't believe you," I said, and hung up.

Several minutes later, my phone rang again.

"Eddie Quinn asked me to call you," said the caller, who identified himself as a rabbi from a Montreal synagogue. "The wrestler he was talking about to you a few minutes ago is a rabbi."

"Rabbi, I don't believe you're a rabbi. Give me your number and I'll call you back."

Several minutes later: "That you, rabbi?"

"It is."

"Okay. I checked out the number. So tell me about the Wrestling Rabbi."

"I don't know much about him, but I can tell you he's a rabbi. He's been working at Madison Square Garden in New York."

That day, a short story detailing the impending arrival of the Wrestling Rabbi appeared in the *Montreal Star*.

Several days later, 7,500 fans – an increase of 4,500 from the previous week – pushed their way into the Montreal Forum. Many were from an orthodox Jewish group. Black hats. Large black coats. Beards.

"Good crowd tonight," Quinn said in the moments before the main bout. "It's about time. Hope we have a good show. I can use that guy."

Benny the Barber, a Quinn employee, walked into the office. "We've got a problem, Eddie," he said. "The Wrestling Rabbi doesn't want to go in the ring."

"What's his problem?"

"Says he has a cold."

"Send the son of a bitch in here," snapped Quinn.

Moments later, the Wrestling Rabbi was telling Quinn about his cold. He was clean-shaven, fairly tall and muscular. He looked like an

187

athlete. Quinn wasn't convinced by his new headliner's explanation.

"Listen, pal, I've got 7,500 people out there. If you bail out, most of them will start throwing rocks at my office windows. I can't afford that," said Quinn. "I'm sorry you've got a cold, but if I were you, I'd get my ass into that ring right now, because having a cold is a lot better than two broken legs, if you know what I mean."

The rabbi quickly saw the wisdom in what Quinn was saying. "I know, I know," he said. "I'm going, I'm going."

"Now, get the other guy in here," Quinn snapped at Benny the Barber.

The Wrestling Rabbi's opponent was ushered into the office.

"Where do you go from here?" he was asked.

"St. Louis."

"Okay, you've got a ten-second stop here, if you know what I mean," said Quinn.

Then he crooked at finger at me: "Let's go out there and see what happens."

The Wrestling Rabbi was in his corner. His opponent was on the apron outside the ring. The bell rang, and the Rabbi raced across the ring toward his opponent. A flying head-scissors whipped his opponent onto the mat and one! two! three! It's over!

The mere appearance of the Wrestling Rabbi had started a murmur among the crowd. Now, though, pandemonium! Hats flew in every direction. People stood on chairs, cheering . . . saluting their new hero, who almost had to fight his way through his new fans en route to his dressing room.

Quinn stood there, taking it all in. For the first time in a long time, he was smiling broadly. "What a match, eh?"

The Wrestling Rabbi promptly left on a road trip and never returned to the Forum again.

Quinn seemed to enjoy life more than any other sports character I ever knew. Maybe, in fact, he enjoyed life a little too much. A warm-weather Sunday rarely passed without his home in Town of Mount Royal being filled with wrestlers and other friends. If he wasn't at his

Forum office, he'd be across the street at the El Morocco with his show-business friends. Everywhere, there were stories to tell. The money rolled in and rolled out. Easy come, easy go. Then, in 1959, he suffered a mild stroke – and the vultures started to circle.

One day, in the spring of 1964, Eddie phoned me from, of all places, North Hampton, New Hampshire.

"What are you doing there?" I asked.

"We've got a place here now," he said. "I had to get out of the country." Eddie had been living too high for too long. Money had dried up. Taxes hadn't been paid. Now, with the Canadian government moving in, Eddie moved out to bucolic New Hampshire where his son-in-law, an American, had bought a nursing home for Eddie and his wife, Gert, to run. He was calling from his small house, which was part of the nursing-home purchase package. No more bright lights. No more fun.

"Geez, Eddie, couldn't you have called before you left?"

"No time," he said quietly. "There wasn't any time to say goodbye. The house is sold. Everything's gone."

"When do I see you?" I asked.

"Soon," he said. "Soon, I hope. But you'll have to come here. I can't go back there."

Six months later, the Canadiens were in Boston for a game and so was I. Tom Johnson, who knew and loved Quinn during his fifteen years as a defenceman with the Canadiens, now was with the Bruins. A broken leg had left him with a toe-to-thigh cast and out of the Bruins' line-up. Before the game, Johnson suggested I stay over an extra day and the two of us and his wife would drive to Eddie Quinn's home in New Hampshire.

The next day, we found Eddie's place and settled in for a good gab. Eddie sat in an easy chair. I was a few feet away from him at one end of a sofa, Doris Johnson sat at the other end. Tom lounged against the wall near the door leading out of the cottage.

A green panel truck moved slowly along the driveway to the front door. Quinn rubbed his hands together. "Boy, this has to be a red-letter day," he said. "We've been workin' to get the place into shape, but do you think a guy can get a refrigerator delivered? Two months we've been waitin' for that refrigerator, and I guess you guys must have brought us luck. That must be the refrigerator comin' now."

We talked for a long while in the living room of that small cottage, a place too far removed from the big city streets and brassy noises Eddie Quinn loved. We talked for more than four hours and memories marched like soldiers on parade. Then Eddie fell back and his lips moved soundlessly.

At the other end of the sofa, Mrs. Johnson paled and she half-rose to her feet.

"Give him a few seconds," I said quietly. "He hasn't been feeling well."

Seconds passed without any sign of improvement. It was then that I leaped to my feet and tore his shirt open at the collar.

Gert Quinn looked in from the kitchen. Her hand flew to her mouth, muffling a scream. Her eyes opened wide. "Eddie! Eddie!"

"Call the fire department," I yelled.

No more than two minutes later, several firemen rushed in with their life-saving equipment. They worked feverishly on Eddie for the next five minutes. He was dead.

Later, in the gathering dusk, a few old friends came to the Quinn cottage. Jack Sharkey, the former heavyweight boxing champion of the world, lived just down the road. He talked for a long time about the man he called his dearest and closest friend. The telephone rang constantly. A neighbour's son, no more than fourteen years old, walked quietly into the cottage, sat numbly for a few minutes. Just before he left he said, "Eddie Quinn was a nice man."

Yes, he was, and he was dead at fifty-eight.

ve: Riding the Moscow subway during the famous 1972 Summit Series. *Below:* Hanging out
Bobby Hull in Moscow's Red Square during the Soviet-WHA series of 1974.

Above: Making a point with (from left) Hall of Famers Tom Johnson and Bernie "Boom-Boom" Geoffrion. *(Peter Brosseau) Below:* Here I am talking with Serge Savard the day the Canadien defensive star announced his retirement. After a stint in Winnipeg, Savard rejoined the Canad in 1983 as general manager. *(Michael Dugas)*

re: With the great Stan Mikita of the Chicago Blackhawks. *Below:* With Bobby Clarke, the
of the great Philadelphia Flyers teams of the 1970s.

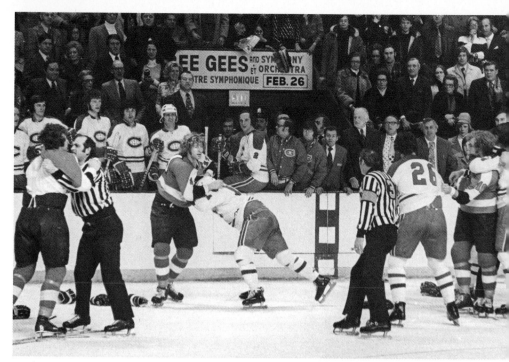

Above: The Canadiens and the Flyers rough it up at the Forum in the early 1970s. I'm with Jo MacDonald at the far left end of the Canadiens bench. Among the celebrities in the crowd are and Mrs. Robert Stanfield, Brian and Mila Mulroney, and cP president Ian Sinclair.
Below: Having a drink flanked by Hall of Famers Frank Mahovlich (left) and Gordie Howe.
(Doug Ball/Canapress)

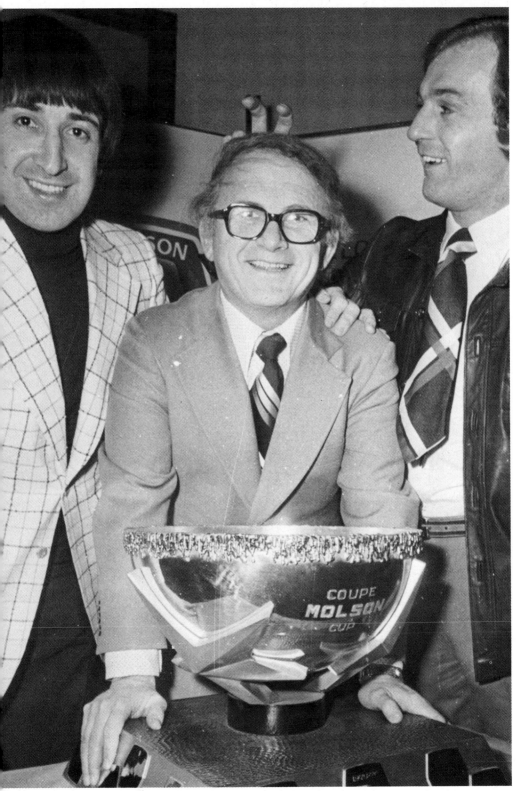

wning around with the Canadiens' Guy Lapointe (left) and Guy Lafleur.

Phil Esposito in 1971 with the second of the five Art Ross Trophies he won during his stellar tenure with the Boston Bruins.

ove: Yes, that's me with Edmonton Oilers coach and general manager Glen Sather (left) and
nd Johnny Golka (centre). *Below:* The infamous "Indian painting" episode comes to a laugh-
d conclusion. Glen Sather (left), former NHLer Jim Neilson (centre), and me.

With my wife, Tillie, the night in 1985 when I was inducted into the media section (Elmer Ferguson Memorial Award) of the Hockey Hall of Fame.

17

The Gladiators

Hockey has always been my passion, but boxers are my favourite people.

They're different. The ones I've known are as gentle and friendly outside the ring as they are dedicated to violence inside it. I've never met a world-class fighter I didn't like. They keep alive an ideal of manly courage whose greatest value lies in its preservation of the notion that rational man can survive any ordeal, once he braces himself for it.

Forty years ago, world-title fights in New York or anywhere else were almost always an adventure, if only because all of the stars came out to shine. There, sitting at ringside, would be Frank Sinatra. There was Humphrey Bogart, or Hugh Hefner and his barbie doll. Elizabeth Taylor would be there.

The New York writers shone as brightly as any of the stars at a time when readers in that city had their pick of as many as ten newspapers. Jimmy Breslin and Red Smith were with the *Herald-Tribune*, (Smith later joined the venerable *Times*, in 1972), Frank Graham and Jimmy Cannon with the *Journal-American*. The *New York Mirror*'s Dan Parker had to be read because of his hatred for International Boxing Club owner Jim Norris. Milt Gross was with the *New York Post*.

Why this fascination with people in a so-called blood sport? One reason was my close friendship with Montreal boxing promoter Eddie Quinn, whom you've met earlier. He knew everybody. Former world heavyweight champion Jack Sharkey was a close friend, only a telephone call away for refereeing assignments. So were Jack Dempsey and Rocky Marciano.

Sugar Ray Robinson was the best fighter I ever saw, Rocky Marciano the nicest, and Muhammad Ali the best heavyweight. I was in Madison Square Garden on March 8, 1971, for Ali's first fight with Joe Frazier, and Ali was this good: Frazier won a fifteen-round decision against a memory who had been away from the ring for more than three years. Boxing people still look back on it as one of the great fights of all time. I remember it as the most exciting event I covered in a year that also included the Canadiens, led by a rookie named Ken Dryden, winning the Stanley Cup.

That night in Manhattan, Frazier had faced a clowning, talking, slowed-down ghost from the past, and left the twenty-nine-year-old Ali with a balloon-sized cheek and a broken jaw from the left hook that had produced the only knockdown of the fight. From the beginning of the bout, it was clear that this was not the Ali who had dominated his profession until 1967 when his right to fight was taken away after he suggested he "had no quarrel against them Viet Cong." The showmanship was still there. The dancing around the ring was there. The furious footwork before the opening bell got the reaction he wanted from the crowd. But Ali wasn't moving the way Ali once did. He didn't control his man from the start, as he always had.

There were, of course, flashes of his former brilliance. I remember him poking fun at Frazier in the early rounds, and shaking his head when Frazier landed what appeared to be solid left hands. Is that all there is, Joe? he seemed to be asking. He knew better. Once in a while, he would challenge Frazier to throw at him, then he would pull his head back an inch or two, as he used to do. Some of Frazier's blows landed, though. They crashed into his jaw, slapped at his ears, and slipped off his shoulders. And when they did, he looked sad, as if he suddenly realized that things that shouldn't be happening were happening. A man who had always been in control, no longer had all of it.

Several years earlier, when he was known as Cassius Clay, Muhammad had toyed with his opponents – among them Canada's George Chuvalo. His fifteen-rounder against the Canadian champion in Toronto on March 29, 1966, was no more than seconds old when he raised his arms and said to Chuvalo: "Here, hit me. Hit me!"

Chuvalo blinked in surprise, put his head down and pounded his gloves into the champ's unprotected side.

My ringside neighbour was the brother of Angelo Dundee, who trained Clay. "What's he doing?" asked Dundee.

Clay grinned at Chuvalo: "Harder," he urged. "Harder!"

Chuvalo hit Clay again.

"Dammit, will you cut that out," Dundee screamed at Clay. Then he turned to me and said: "He's liable to bust a rib that way, the idiot."

For almost the entire round, Clay taunted Chuvalo, inviting him to take a free shot. A few landed, many didn't. At the end of the round, Clay was grinning broadly. The only man who suffered truly from the Chuvalo punches was Dundee. "That man," he said, "is gonna kill me some day. I tell you, when he fools around like that, I'm gonna die."

For the next fourteen rounds, Clay stopped the clowning. He hit Chuvalo with everything. His hands were left bruised and swollen after hitting Chuvalo's head hundreds of times. Chuvalo's eyes were blackened and there were ugly red marks on his chest and arms after the fight, but he walked from the ring secure in the knowledge that the heavyweight champion had failed to knock him down or even stagger him.

Another memorable fight occurred in 1958 when light-heavyweight champion Archie Moore brought all of New York's writing stars to Montreal for the champ's first fight with New Brunswick's

Yvon Durelle. They were there to watch Moore, nobody else. Durelle, "the fighting fisherman from Baie Ste. Anne," wasn't given a chance, but he would have won Moore's title if the referee, former heavyweight champion Sharkey, hadn't messed up. It also would have helped if Durelle had been a better fighter. Admittedly, he could hit and he hurt Moore that December night in the Forum.

The initial damage was done only one minute into the fight, when Durelle came out of a crouch with a left hook to Moore's heart, then followed with a right to the chin. Moore, who had held the light-heavyweight title for six years, froze, then fell heavily to the canvas. He struggled to his feet at the count of nine. Seconds later, Durelle half-hit, half-pushed Moore to the floor. Moore staggered to his feet almost immediately. Moore moved away from Durelle, who by now was swinging rights and lefts at the stunned champion. Moore sighed and slipped to the canvas again. He got to his feet at the count of seven. The bell saved him.

Moore survived three knockdowns in that first round, but he should have been out of the match after that first, numbing punch by Durelle. It's true Moore rose to his feet at the count of nine. What's also true is that the referee didn't start his count until four or five seconds had elapsed. The champ got the long-count – and got away with it.

Moore recovered sufficiently from his three knockdowns in the first round to punish Durelle with his jab in the second, third, and fourth rounds. In the fifth, however, Durelle worked Moore along the ropes, feinted with a left, then, with the hardest punch of the night, threw a right hand which sent Moore sinking to the canvas for the fourth time. He took a six-count, held off Durelle with his jab for the next round, and then, finally, went to work on the fisherman from New Brunswick. He floored Durelle in the seventh and tenth rounds.

Moore was late leaving his corner for the eleventh round, but by that time, everyone could tell Durelle was on the way to becoming Moore's 127th knockout. Moore almost ran across the ring, throwing punches. Durelle fell to the floor for a nine-count. Moore leaped in again with rights and lefts which sent Durelle to the floor. Blood dribbled from his nose, mouth, and a small cut alongside his eye. His legs twitched as he tried to get to his feet. By the time he did, the count had reached ten. This time, referee Sharkey had started the count on time.

Moore made Durelle his knockout number 129 the following August – in three. A little more than two years later, he added my pal, promoter Quinn, to the list.

The first fight with Durelle had attracted a record $90,000 gate at the Forum, along with $100,000 for television rights. Moore's share was $75,000. His second fight attracted a $140,000 gate, plus hundreds of thousands of dollars in television revenue. Moore's share was $250,000.

Clearly, Montreal boxing fans had taken to Moore. They wanted to see more of him and, no doubt, he of them. In 1961, Robert Cleroux was given the nod as Moore's next victim. Cleroux was a Montreal heavyweight with marginal talent who had been brought along carefully. In other words, he had been fed the right diet of fighters. He was money in the bank. He couldn't afford to lose. His fight with Moore, though, was deadly serious. December 5 would be Cleroux's biggest payday, by far.

Moore and Cleroux were to meet at the Forum in early December. The night before, I was in Toronto to cover a Floyd Patterson–Tom McNeeley world heavyweight championship fight. I flew into Montreal the next morning, and there at the airport were Moore, his wife, his manager Jack Kearns, and two handlers.

"What are you doing here, Archie?" I asked. "Don't you have a fight tonight?"

"I'm goin' home," he said.

"What do you mean you're going home?"

"The fight's off," he said.

Two days earlier Quinn had met with Kearns and Moore. The promoter explained that the advance sale was small, and since Moore was the drawing card, Quinn felt he should take a licking along with everybody else, including Quinn. Eddie asked Moore to fight for a percentage rather than the $50,000 guarantee he'd been promised.

Archie walked. So there he was at the airport talking about how shocked he was that the bout had been called off – a lot more shocked, let's say, than he left others when he had twice postponed his second fight with Durelle. Moore pointed out that he had trained for two months in San Diego and had come to Montreal two weeks before the fight to fulfil his contract. He couldn't believe it when his manager told him the fight had been put on hold.

"You'll kill Eddie with this," I told Moore. "He's been pretty good to you the last couple of years."

"I signed a contract," he shrugged. "Now he's trying to change it. I'm walkin'."

"You had a contract for your second fight with Durelle," I said. "You postponed it twice."

"I'm walkin'," he said.

The telephone was ringing when I arrived home. Sports columnist Elmer Ferguson from the *Star* was on the line. "This is a terrible thing Archie Moore is doing to our friend Eddie," he said. "You should take a run at him in your column tomorrow."

"Elmer, seems to me you've got a column tomorrow, too. Why don't you take a run at Archie?" I asked.

"Everybody knows I'm Eddie's friend," said Elmer. "It wouldn't look good."

"I see," I said.

I don't think I ever completely forgave Elmer for turning his back on Eddie when he needed him most.

The promotion had two strikes against it from the start. The big guarantee to Moore was a mistake, particularly since the television networks hadn't shown any interest in the fight. Another mistake was the high ticket prices. As a result, Moore–Cleroux never took place, and the Montreal Athletic Commission's response to Moore's walkout was almost predictable: an indefinite suspension of Quinn's licence to promote.

Five years earlier, I had been in Chicago to see Moore lose, by a fifth-round knockout, to up-and-comer Floyd Patterson. Patterson was little more than a light-heavyweight when he won the heavyweight championship in 1956, but I regarded him as a lightweight from the moment I "went down swinging" against one of the curves he learned to throw early in his reign.

A Brooklyn boy who had learned his craft in a correctional institution in upstate New York, Patterson, like Mike Tyson, had problems handling the attention which came with the heavyweight championship. There was no position like it anywhere else in sport. While there could be championship teams, there was, after all, only one heavyweight champion of the world. Everybody, including the New York media, wanted a piece of him, but Patterson wanted no part of it. He preferred to let his manager, Cus D'Amato, do most of the talking for him. Now and then, the champ would simply disappear. All that did was put the New York hounds on his trail.

One morning, in 1961, I got a telephone call from a friend.

"Do you know that Floyd Patterson is in town?" he asked.

"You're kidding," I said. "Only the other day I was reading he'd dropped out of sight. Nobody in New York knows where he is."

"I saw him last night. He's staying at the Windsor Hotel," I was told. The Windsor was a swank hostelry on Peel Street in downtown Montreal.

"Nobody by that name is registered at the hotel," the operator insisted.

"He's not here," said the hotel manager. "I wish he was."

I called my friend back to tell him I was firing blanks. He insisted Patterson was at the Windsor. "I shook his hand."

I hustled myself down to the Windsor where the doorman was certain of only one thing: Patterson wasn't registered at the hotel.

"Is it possible he's here and you wouldn't know about it?"

"It's impossible," he said.

"Okay, thank for your trouble," I said, then I slipped him two one-dollar bills. It wasn't a bad tip in those days.

"Patterson," said the doorman, "is in rooms 130 and 132."

A DO NOT DISTURB sign hung on the doorknob of room 132. I knocked.

Cus D'Amato opened the door.

"I'm told that Patterson is registered in this room. Is he here?" I asked.

"No, he isn't," he said. "You know, I don't know how you found out he's here, but you're absolutely right. Trouble is, you're out of luck. The champ left about an hour ago. We checked in last night, sorta passing through, you know, but now he's gone."

"Since I'm here, do you mind if I ask you a few questions?"

"Go ahead," he said. "Anything you want to know."

"Is he going to England? I read somewhere he's going to England."

"Probably not," said D'Amato. "You see . . ."

At that moment, the connecting door between the rooms opened and there stood Floyd Patterson, a towel slung over his shoulder, an embarrassed smile on his kisser. D'Amato coughed quietly.

"What brings you to Montreal?" I asked Patterson.

"Well, uh, it's got something to do with my manager's troubles with the International Boxing Club," he said. "Say, you're not from United Press, are you? You see, I'd hate for it to get back to New York that I was in Montreal. No, sir, I surely don't want it to get back there."

Patterson didn't say why he didn't want anyone in New York, including perhaps a Mrs. Patterson, to know he was in Montreal – and I didn't ask.

"Maybe you can do me a favour," he continued. "Don't tell anybody I'm in Montreal. I'd sure appreciate it. I expect to be back in maybe ten days, two weeks at the outside, and if you see your way clear to keep quiet about this visit, I promise I'll call you from New York the day before I leave. Then you can come up and talk and ask questions and take pictures. Anything you want," he said.

"But why are you in Montreal today?" I asked.

"I can't tell you any more about it," said Patterson. "Not right now, I can't. It's just that my manager wants me to get out of the United States from time to time. I used to go to Hamilton, but somebody down there on the desk was telling reporters, and every time I visited the place the reporters wouldn't give me a minute's rest. I'd sure appreciate it if you didn't mention I was here."

"Yeah, the champ would sure appreciate it," said D'Amato. "I promise I'll have him call you as soon as he's ready to come back here. Maybe I'll call you myself to make sure. Just don't mention he was here."

"I'll be back in two weeks," repeated Patterson. "I'll call you. You can count on it."

A ten-day wait, two weeks at the outside, wasn't really a long time – particularly when the heavyweight champion of the world was asking it as a favour. What's more, he was a nice guy, wasn't he? He spoke softly and earnestly. He was persuasive.

The ten days, two weeks at the outside, stretched into two months, without a call from Patterson. That's when I finally wrote a column about it. A few days later, Dan Parker of the *New York Mirror* devoted his entire column to what he described as the "big Montreal mystery." He gave me full credit for tracking down Patterson. I've kept a copy of that column all these years.

A couple of months later, Parker wrote another in which he was kind enough to mention me prominently again. It was in reply to a column I wrote about Truman Gibson, who was an aide to the owner of the International Boxing Club, Jim Norris. Parker had always hated anyone connected with the IBC. I liked Norris. I also liked Gibson which, I assume, is why Parker referred to me in his column as the "the open-handed youth from Montreal." I didn't keep a copy of that column.

On the other hand, a few paragraphs dealing with Pulitzer Prize winners are framed and hang in a place of honour at my home. The National Newspaper Award is the most prestigious prize a journalist can win in Canada. The Pulitzer goes to Americans who have distinguished themselves in journalism, fiction, non-fiction, poetry, drama, and music.

One day in 1976, my wife, Tillie, looked up from her newspaper. "Did you win an award recently?" she asked.

"Not to my knowledge," I said. "Why do you ask?"

"It says here you won an award," she said.

"Let me see that," I said.

The *Montreal Star* carried a "Week in Review" column each Saturday. This one led off with the year's Pulitzer winners. It started:

"Saul Bellow won the premier Pulitzer Prize for his latest novel *Humboldt's Gift*. In 1960, a jury's recommendation that he receive the award for his novel *Henderson the Rain King* was over-ruled by the advisory board. Ironically, Bellow allows Humboldt, the prize-winning book's chief character and a poet, to observe: 'The Pulitzer is for the birds – for the pullets. It's just a dummy newspaper publicity award given by crooks and illiterates.'"

The item continued:

"Prizes for journalism were won by two staff members of the *New York Times*: Sydney Schanberg for his coverage of the Communist takeover of Cambodia; and Walter Wellesley (Red Fisher) for his sports column."

I'm still waiting for that Pulitzer. I guess it got lost in the mail.

18

The Fighters

Alfred's on Sutter Street in San Francisco was a favourite media watering-hole and restaurant in the 1960s and 1970s, and on this Tuesday night in November 1970 there were at least a dozen people sitting around the table. I was among them, having been in the city by the bay for the last two days to cover a Canadiens–Oakland game.

The food was good, the drinks plentiful – which was good, since I was the guest of honour of the media gang. When the party really started to warm up at 8:30 or so, 11:30 Eastern Standard Time, I knew I had to go. Earlier that day, just before the party started, I'd received the news from a colleague at the *Star* in Montreal: John Ferguson, probably the roughest, toughest player ever to don a Canadiens sweater, was planning to return to the team.

Fergie joined the Canadiens in the 1963-64 season, after the team had failed to capture a Stanley Cup for a third consecutive year. He had decided to pack his skates before the start of the 1970-71 season and devote his time to his knitwear business and a column on horse handicapping for the rival Montreal newspaper, the *Gazette*.

As far as I knew, the Fergie story was known only to me. There was a chance he might have passed the information to his newspaper, but I didn't think he had.

However, how could I leave my own party on such short notice? What possible reason could I give? Finally, I hit on a standard: "I think I've had a little too much to drink. Gotta go, guys. Thanks for everything."

"Naw, you can't leave now," moaned Gilles Terroux, who was there for the French-language newspaper *La Presse*.

"Sorry," I shrugged, "I've got this splitting headache. You guys stay. I'll grab a cab back to the hotel. I've really appreciated this."

If Fergie was indeed returning to the Canadiens, it was big news. The team had not been doing that well since Ferguson had told general manager Sam Pollock he wouldn't be playing the 1970-71 season. "My mind isn't one hundred per cent on hockey," Ferguson had told Pollock just before the Canadiens' season opener against the Philadelphia Flyers. Later he told me: "If I can't give a hundred per cent, I'd rather not play at all. I know I can't give a hundred per cent." The Canadiens, he said, had been "wonderful . . . and that's why I feel I shouldn't play. My business is taking more and more of my time and leaving me with less and less for the game."

Ferguson's decision prompted expressions of dismay, surprise, and disbelief from his teammates. After all, it was Ferguson's muscle and leadership that had brought the Canadiens four Stanley Cups in five seasons, three with Toe Blake and one with Blake's successor, Claude Ruel.

Centreman Ralph Backstrom was his closest friend with the Canadiens. "I don't know what to think," Backstrom said. "Fergie told me he was thinking about it after he was hurt," – hand injuries and a six-game suspension had kept Ferguson out of the lineup for twenty-six games in 1969-70, a principal reason for the Canadiens' failure to make the playoffs for the first time in twenty-two years – "but I didn't give it too much thought. I felt he was just depressed. Training camp isn't the happiest time of the year for players."

"My wife woke me at 7:00 and told me about it," said Henri Richard. "It's a lousy way to wake up. I don't believe it and I think he'll be back. He's like everyone else. He'll be tempted."

"I spent last night at the track with him," said Peter Mahovlich, "and he didn't mention it."

"This is a real shock," said goaltender Rogie Vachon. "He must be tired and fed up. I hope somebody talks to him because everyone's counting on him."

"He's been one of my big leaders," said coach Ruel, "and I hope he changes his mind. He told me on the phone last night, and it's a shock, but these days everything's a shock and you have to learn to live with them. Two years ago, when he was healthy, he was the guy who came through for me in all the games."

"He's not just a policeman, he's a twenty-goal scorer," said Jean Béliveau. "Some teams have policemen who score five goals, so he's a pretty valuable guy. And I don't have to tell anybody what he means to us in the dressing room."

Defenceman Terry Harper probably had the best – and pithiest – assessment of Ferguson's retirement: "Help!"

This unhappiness with Fergie's sudden departure proved justifiable as the 1970-71 season progressed. Suddenly, teams were roughing up the Canadiens – something that hadn't happened when Ferguson was around. Prior to coming to the Canadiens in 1963 Ferguson had been an all-star left-winger with Cleveland in the American Hockey League. He was the AHL's top policeman, its best fighter, a surly, mean, and menacing competitor.

Back then, the Canadiens' general manager Frank Selke had dispatched his scout, Floyd Curry, to Cleveland to see what he could find. What Curry saw was John Bowie Ferguson firing a puck at teammate Terry Gray when he caught him talking to a player from the opposing team during the pre-game skate. That was enough for Curry – and for Selke. It was Selke's view that one of the main reasons the Canadiens had fallen into a three-year drought after winning five consecutive Stanley Cups was the team's lack of muscle against squads like the Boston Bruins. Ferguson, Selke felt, would take care of that and, indeed, he did: ten seconds into his first game he became involved in a free-swinging scrap with another tough guy, Boston's

Ted Green. He also scored two goals, pacing the Canadiens to a 3–2 victory.

Of course, rumours of Ferguson's return to the fold were many once the season got under way. Fergie's partners in his knitwear business were starting to realize that Ferguson, the player, meant more to the buying public than Ferguson, the ex-player. Pollock had met with Ferguson several weeks earlier. Everybody knew about it. But comeback? Don't be silly, said Pollock. "We're old friends," he explained, "and Fergie wants to play for the Oldtimers. He could use his skates."

Earlier that day in San Francisco I had reached Ferguson in Washington, D.C., where he was attending the Laurel International. "I really don't know how I'd feel about coming back," he told me. "I'm a Canadien, and have always been a Canadien. There are a lot of things involved. I have my partners and my company to think of. It would involve a lot of people talking to a lot of people before I could play. Right now, there is no meeting scheduled."

No meeting scheduled, the man said. However, my man in Montreal had told me that a meeting was, in fact, set for Thursday, that Fergie would sign the next day and that Fergie's agent, Gerry Patterson, had confirmed the whole thing.

As midnight neared in San Francisco, I was putting the finishing touches to my Ferguson story. Just then, Gilles Terroux walked into my room, unannounced. He looked over my shoulder at the sheet of paper in the typewriter. The lead paragraph read: "Canadiens management will meet with John Ferguson tomorrow to hasten what will be an early return to professional hockey by the sweater manufacturer and part-time handicapper . . ."

"Is that why you left early?" he asked.

"Uh . . . I guess."

"What about me?" he asked. "What about my paper?"

"What about your paper?"

"You're gonna make me look bad if I don't have something about it."

"Tell you what," I said. "This goes in my paper first so, obviously, you can't use it for your first edition. Take whatever you want from the story, but you've got to promise it won't appear in your paper until the second edition."

"I promise," said Terroux.

My colleagues spent a good part of the next day trying to play catch-up on the story. Claude Ruel and Jean Béliveau didn't say much. In Montreal, the *Gazette* tried to shrug off the story as fiction. Ferguson, for his part, continued to deny he was returning right up to 2:00 p.m. on Friday, November 13 – which was the moment he signed with the Canadiens.

Later, at the press conference: "You must have some pretty good contacts," he said to me out of the side of his mouth.

"Not bad," I said.

John Ferguson wasn't the best fighter I've seen in the NHL, but he surely was among the best. Nobody was meaner. He fought to hurt. No exceptions. He fought almost everybody there was to fight, and a few he should have avoided. Bobby Hull, for example.

Then, as now, there are certain players who get a pass when it comes to fighting. Does it make sense for anyone to beat up on Wayne Gretzky? Mario Lemieux? You don't mess with the best players, particularly those who don't look for trouble. Chicago superstar Hull qualified in every way. He could take care of himself, but nobody challenged him. There was no need to challenge Hull.

On the other hand, Fergie didn't need a reason to fight, or not to fight. Often, he would hit people simply because they were there. Hull was there one night in Chicago. It was a good fight, too, but unfortunately Hull came out of it with a slight crack in his jaw. It wasn't serious enough to force the Golden Jet out of the lineup for long, but he was forced to wear a bulky protective device for several weeks.

Hull was still wearing it when Chicago visited the Forum a little more than a week later. Early in the game, Ferguson and Hull collided. Hull fell heavily to the ice – and lost his protective mask in the process. Even now, Ferguson remembers the incident.

"He had his jaw wired, of course, and now the lights are reflecting off the wires. I'm lookin' down at him wondering what to do, and the first thing that crosses my mind when I see the light reflecting off the wires is: 'Fergie, if you hit this guy, you're gonna be the biggest rat in Canada.'

"The crowd booed me that night," Ferguson recalls, "but I didn't hit him. I swear."

Eric Nesterenko, another Blackhawk, was a Ferguson victim at the Forum on another night. Nesterenko had size, but he wasn't much of a fighter. Ferguson's first punch sent Nesterenko staggering, unconscious, to the ice. Minutes later, Nesterenko was peering into the clinic mirror, running a finger along an ugly gash over his left eye. "Who hit me with his stick?" he asked.

"That wasn't a stick," Nesterenko was told. "That was Ferguson's right hand."

"No way," mumbled Nesterenko. "It was a stick."

In another game, Ferguson and Red Wings defenceman Gary Bergman became involved in a verbal sparring match. Things started to heat up when Bergman tried to toss a punch at Ferguson over the heads of several players. Detroit defenceman Bryan Watson, Ferguson's closest pal off-ice, put out the fire by jumping on Ferguson's back.

Watson still was grinning over the incident in the Detroit dressing room after the game. As I was heading out to an after-game watering-hole frequented by the Canadiens, Watson asked me to do him a favour.

"If you see Fergie over there, tell him I said I saved his ass by jumping on his back. Bergman was ready to clean his clock if I hadn't jumped in."

"You serious?"

"Tell him that for me," laughed Watson.

Later, Ferguson left a group of players and walked over to a table I shared with another Montreal hockey writer. "What was that stuff with Bergman?" I asked.

"Aw, nothing much," said Ferguson.

"Watson says he saved your ass by jumping on your back," I said.

Ferguson paled. Then he reached for a chair and smashed it against a wall. "That yellow son of a bitch wouldn't have even thought of throwing a punch if there weren't a bunch of guys between us," he thundered. "I can take three of him any day in the week." Then he smashed another chair against the wall before leaving the saloon.

A white-faced Claude Larose and several other players came running. "What did you guys say him?" asked Larose.

"Nothing much," Larose was told.

"What made him yell like that?" Larose asked.

"Can't take a joke, I guess," I said.

Like it or not, fighting has been a part of hockey as long as the game has been played. Players fought before the formation of the National Hockey League in 1917, and they've fought since. In recent seasons, rules have been introduced to turn off that part of the game in the hope that in time, the fighter will become as rare as the *grus Americana*. It is a noble undertaking, but fighters simply won't go away in a sport in which machismo reigns. Fighting isn't as important as it was, say, in the six-team era when the sheer frequency of match-ups ensured enduring feuds, but the fraternity remains alive and well.

Who was the best? Ferguson, as I've said, ranks close to the top, but the best fighter on skates I ever saw was Orland Kurtenbach, who played for thirteen seasons (639 games) in New York, Boston, Toronto, and Vancouver. He earned 628 penalty minutes, roughly one half of Ferguson's total even though Fergie played in 139 fewer games.

What that means is that while Ferguson went looking for trouble, Kurtenbach could take it or leave it. If a challenge arose, he was there. He knew he was very good, and since he didn't go looking for problems, opposing players gave him plenty of room.

On the other hand, hardly a game passed without Ferguson

having his hands full, mostly with other players' faces. There was nothing complicated about his game plan: hit first, ask questions later. His attitude was that if somebody was in his way, he had to be taken out. If he happened to be a goaltender, no problem. *Bam!*

In his time, Fergie led the league in bodychecking goaltenders to the ice. Remarkably, he got away with it most of the time, because there weren't many players interested in challenging him.

Kurtenbach, unlike Ferguson, was a stand-up fighter. Jab. Hook. Uppercut. He knew precisely what he was doing and what he wanted to do. He didn't waste time wrestling with his opponents. He was too strong to be pushed around. He had size: six-foot-three. He was over two hundred pounds. Any bout was usually over quickly, with no clamour for return matches. One dance with Kurt was normally about as much as anyone wanted.

Kurt was also fearless. It's not surprising, then, that the best fight I ever saw on ice was his match-up with Ted Harris, the second-best on-ice fighter I've seen. Harris, who played twelve seasons between 1963-64 and 1974-75 (788 games) with the Canadiens, Minnesota, Detroit, St. Louis, and Philadelphia, finished his career with exactly one thousand penalty minutes. He matched Kurtenbach in height, gave away a few pounds, but came close to Kurtenbach's quality as a fighter.

They met one night when the Canadiens visited Toronto. It doesn't really matter what led up to the fight. What followed, however, was a classic confrontation between two gladiators. They adopted the position as old as Spartacus and went at each other for what seemed like a full five minutes, but probably was only three. No wrestling. No tugging. No talking. One would be knocked down, then the other. Nobody interfered. Nobody piled on. Everyone stood back to watch a punishing fight between the two best fighters of their time.

Neither gave an inch during the joust, but eventually, both capitulated to weariness. The fight had been going on for so long, with neither gaining the upper hand, that it seemed a good idea for both to drop their hands at the same time. They simply looked at each other, nodded their heads in what appeared to be a declaration of peace by common consent, then skated off side by side to the penalty box. Neither one exchanged a word.

Terry Harper was a tall, gangly defenceman who played most of a nineteen-season career with the Canadiens before landing in places such as Los Angeles, Detroit, St. Louis, and Colorado. His strong suit was his heart. He was a clutch-and-grab defenceman who led the league in starting fights and finishing only a few. He didn't win many, but who's counting?

One night, at Maple Leaf Gardens, Harper challenged Kurtenbach. Big mistake. By the time Kurtenbach had finished with Harper, the Canadiens defenceman was left with severe cuts over his eyes. The fight took place midway through the game. Harper needed seven stitches over each eye. His night's work was over.

Two nights later, the Leafs and Canadiens met at the Forum. Harper and Kurtenbach were in the starting lineups. From the face-off, the puck landed in the Canadiens' corner of the rink. Kurtenbach was there first, with Harper only a step behind and *thwack!* the Canadiens defenceman thudded heavily into the Toronto forward from behind, which is not a good idea at any time. Kurtenbach turned his head quickly to see who had delivered the cheap shot, and looked into the fresh stitches above Harper's eyes. The Canadiens defenceman grinned back at him and delivered an extra shove just to let him know he was there. Kurtenbach stared at Harper for several seconds, shook himself free, and skated away . . . shaking his head.

Ferguson and Kurtenbach never crossed paths. Ferguson and Harris never fought, either, although Fergie took on all comers. His dance card was always full.

Howie Young was a wild and free spirit with the Detroit Red Wings in the early part of his eight-season NHL career. He was also careless with his stick. Early in a game at Detroit, his stick came up on Ferguson, cutting the Canadien badly. Strange things happened to Fergie when he saw red, particularly when the red was his own precious bodily fluid.

With blood streaming from his face, Ferguson promptly went after Young. Happily for the Detroit defenceman, his opponent was held off by half a dozen arms, and was convinced to go to the clinic for repairs. Ferguson returned minutes later, and spent the rest of the night chasing Young or any other Detroit player who happened to be in the area. The Olympia had seldom seen a wilder night. Poor Paul Henderson was pounded. Gordie Howe was run into the boards. Any Detroit player, large and small, was a target, but it was Young whom Ferguson really wanted – and never quite caught up with that night.

Fergie's role with the Canadiens wasn't necessarily to win the best fights. He won the important ones. Take 1968, when the Boston Bruins were preparing for a playoff series with the Canadiens. All of the Bruins were aware of Ferguson's reputation, of course. To win, they knew they had to go through Ferguson.

"We've got somebody who'll take care of him," said Boston goaltender Gerry Cheevers several days before the start of the series. Cheevers didn't name names, but everyone, starting with Fergie, knew he was talking about Ted Green.

Green was as tough and as hard-nosed as they come, and still is. He could fight. He could use his stick, if that's what was needed. Ferguson had Green on his mind going into that first playoff game at the Forum.

It happened quickly, and was over almost as fast. The two were a few steps inside the blueline on the Boston side of the ice when they collided. In seconds, Green's sweater was pulled over his head, a disadvantage even the best fighters can't handle. Ferguson struck the helpless Green unmercifully, to the delight of the Forum crowd. On the Boston bench, heads sagged, and the Canadiens went on to win the series in four straight games.

In his own mind, Ferguson has never lost a fight, but once in a long, long while, some of Ferguson's own blood would hit the ice.

Take the time Philadelphia was in Montreal for a regular-season game. Things were going well for the home folks. The Canadiens were leading the game and the Flyers didn't appear to be interested in changing things. Ferguson ran into Simon Nolet in front of the Philadelphia bench and, even though Nolet went a long time between fights, Fergie didn't really need a reason to flail away at a Flyers sweater. Years later, when people would mention his fight with Ferguson, Nolet would explain the only reason he fought was that there was no place to run. "I fought out of fear," he said.

What made this fight different was that even though Nolet absorbed a flurry of punches from Ferguson, he also landed a few, spilling a great deal of Fergie's blood. Ferguson was forced to leave for repairs, which is as good as a win for anybody messing with Ferguson.

Or, as Philadelphia goaltender Doug Favell was to mention later: "The important thing is not whether you win or lose. It's whether you stand up and fight."

At the time, Dick Irvin and I worked on the radio broadcast of Canadiens games. The sight of Fergie's blood on the ice in a fight with Nolet was, at the very least, a surprise to both of us.

"I know the Canadiens are leading, but this game isn't over," I told the radio audience, intimating that Nolet's heroics just might be a tonic for the troops. And so it came to pass, with Philadelphia winning, 3–2.

If Simon Nolet was a reluctant pugilist, his colleague Dave Schultz was an exceptional fighter, a willing bully-boy. In his nine seasons in the NHL, most of which were spent with the Flyers, he amassed a remarkable total of 2,294 penalty minutes in only 535 games. How important was Schultz to the Flyers? Sure, Bernie Parent, Bobby Clarke, Reggie Leach, and Bill Barber were the biggest reasons the Flyers won back-to-back Stanley Cups in 1974 and 1975, but Schultz was at least a contributor.

Intimidation played a big role in Philadelphia's success in the mid-1970s. They made bullying fashionable. After they won their first Stanley Cup, goon was in, finesse was out. Not surprisingly, a lot of players hated the idea of going into Philadelphia for a game.

In 1973, the Flyers won the first game of a playoff series in Montreal. The Canadiens rallied late in the second game and won in overtime. Nobody had to spell it out for the Canadiens. They knew they were fortunate to arrive in Philadelphia with the series tied. They also knew that things weren't going to get easier with the next two games in the Spectrum. They had a lot to think about, and that's precisely what about a dozen of them were doing the morning of game three. As they sat together on their hotel patio, no words were spoken. Then defenceman Guy Lapointe joined them.

Lapointe quietly studied the tight, pinched, pale faces and let the silence hold for another fifteen or twenty seconds. Then, he lifted his arms skyward, and boomed: "Let us pray!"

Lapointe, who was his own greatest fan, led the laughter which followed. Soon, some players had tears streaming down their cheeks. Others held their sides from laughing so hard. Eventually, those three words and the laughter that followed proved to be precisely what the Canadiens needed. They were better than any motivational speeches they were to hear later in the day. They wiped out the tension most of the players had been feeling. The Canadiens went on to win their two games in Philadelphia, and the series finale in Montreal.

While Schultz was the best of the Philadelphia fighters, he wasn't a stick man, as some of his colleagues were. On those rare occasions when he couldn't get the job done with his fists, he took his lumps and lived to fight another day. Montreal people still mention the time a Canadiens defenceman named John Van Boxmeer challenged Schultz at the Forum. One punch later, Van Boxmeer was down – and out! They also mention the night Larry Robinson did a man-sized job on Schultz. But the fact is, Schultz was among the best – and the fairest.

Mario Tremblay was a feisty forward with the Canadiens whose enthusiasm frequently led to fights. Tremblay could throw 'em, ready to take on all comers. One night, he challenged Schultz, who was at this point with the Los Angeles Kings.

Several punches later, Tremblay was flat on his back, with Schultz sitting on his chest. The former Flyer drew back his right hand for one more shot at Tremblay, glanced down at the stunned Canadiens forward – and stopped in mid-punch. Then he got to his feet and skated away. Teammates helped Tremblay to the Canadiens bench.

Later, Tremblay and I walked along a hallway leading to the team bus. "Were you trying to get yourself killed?" I asked.

"I guess I didn't win that one," he shrugged.

"Schultz showed a lot of class," I said.

"He could have hurt me pretty bad if he had thrown that last one," Tremblay agreed.

At that moment, Schultz, head down, was spotted walking toward us.

"Look who's coming, Mario," I said. "Here's your chance to get even."

Tremblay looked up and broke into a broad grin. "Hi, Dave," he said with a wave of his hand.

Schultz nodded curtly and walked by.

"Nice guy," said Tremblay.

There was fighting in hockey long before I started covering the game. It was there in abundance then. It's here now.

Is there a place for it in hockey?

Some have campaigned earnestly against it. A few NHL owners have made attempts to legislate against it, largely because they feel squeaky-clean hockey would be easier to sell to American television networks. Money talks.

What the reformers will probably discover is that fighting is here to stay because the fans want it. Most of the players don't have a real problem with it. They're far more concerned with cowardly cross-checks from behind and careless use of the stick. Most of the players regard fighting as an occupational hazard. It only hurts for a little while, as long as it's controlled properly.

There was nothing quite as silly as the instigating rule, introduced for the 1992-93 NHL season, which calls for an extra minor penalty and a game misconduct for the player who starts a fight. Trouble is, what always happens with these new rules is that they're followed stringently during the exhibition season and early in the regular schedule. Then, after that, the whistle is thrown away, largely because the owners want it that way.

There's always an instigator in a fight. To my mind, an evenly matched fight is far less dangerous than any of the game's mean stick-work. Take away the fighting, and the stick takes over. What's more dangerous than a player cross-checking another from behind into the boards?

I have watched hundreds of hockey fights. Most of them were little more than a waste of time, but I can't recall a fight that left a player hurt badly. It may not seem that way, but players are intelligent enough to understand there's a limit. A Dave Schultz doesn't hit a Mario Tremblay when he's on his back and semi-conscious. An Orland Kurtenbach and a Ted Harris fight furiously for a while, and then skate off the ice, side by side. Ferguson fought often and well, but he didn't inflict permanent damage on anyone. Maurice Richard was a splendid fighter. He was a rare bird among players who were tested often: a knockout puncher. It's why he was challenged less and less from year to year. Maurice's brother, Henri, was fearless. He won a lot more than he lost at a time when fighting was a large part of the game.

As mentioned earlier, teams met each other fourteen times a season in the six-team league, which meant that grudges were carried from one game into another. Often, teams would play back-to-back games – a Saturday in Montreal, say, and another in the opposition's arena twenty-four hours later.

A young Vic Hadfield would catch Henri Richard's eye, and seconds later they'd be going at each other. Dickie Moore and Red Sullivan were frequent combatants. Bench clearings between the Rangers and the Canadiens were the rule rather than the exception. It was same whenever Boston and Montreal got together.

Hadfield was a principal figure on a night which called for one of the truly great fights of all time – without a punch being thrown.

Lou Fontinato had joined the Canadiens for the 1961-62 season in a trade which sent Doug Harvey to the New York Rangers as a playing coach. Fontinato was one of the NHL's most formidable fighters. Nothing fancy, but he let you know he was there. He had size. He had stamina. He had toughness. Fighting, though, wasn't on his mind early in March 1963 when he and Hadfield headed for a loose puck in the corner. Just as Fontinato and Hadfield were about to collide, the Rangers forward ducked, and sent Fontinato head-first into the boards. He lay there, without moving a muscle – and that's when the buzz of fear from the fans started. In seconds, it was almost a roar, as teammates, Forum sports therapist Bill Head, and team doctor Douglas Kinnear, who's still with the Canadiens, huddled anxiously around him.

"Don't touch me," whispered Fontinato. "I can't move."

He was placed carefully onto a stretcher. The crowd stilled as he was carried toward the exit behind the net. Then, hundreds gasped when one end of the stretcher slipped from linesman Neil Armstrong's hands and struck the ice.

The next day, doctors issued a medical bulletin: "Lou Fontinato sustained a fracture with some dislocation in the cervical spine. He has some paralysis in his arms but is showing steady improvement. He has not been operated on and is receiving conservative treatment." In other words, a broken neck.

I remember visiting Fontinato in hospital two months later. He was locked into a cast which started at the top of his head and ran the length of his body. He had lost sixty pounds, but he still wore his gap-toothed smile.

"I'm sweating a lot," he said. "I'm itching all over under this damned cast, but I'll beat it. You'll see, I'll beat it."

Fontinato never fought a better fight or one nearly as good. He never played again, of course, but he beat it, as he had promised. He won the biggest fight of his life. The best fighters always do.

19

Miltie and Phil

Once in a while – not often – a major story falls into the lap of a reporter. I say not often, because most of the time the uncovering, researching, and writing of a big story are hard work. Then, one day, the exception happens. Look what I found in 1967.

It was hot that June in Toronto, where hockey's large and small hitters had gathered at the Royal York Hotel for their annual meeting. What made this one interesting was that the league was at a crossroads in its history. The expansion virus had settled into the game: in just a few months the current six-team league would be joined by six new teams. New teams meant new faces on the ice and new faces in the front-office. It also meant that teams would be doing a lot of trading.

The spring of 1967 had seen the Boston Bruins miss the playoffs for the eighth consecutive season. The year before, Bobby Orr had joined the team out of junior hockey, but even the presence of a player who was to become the game's greatest wasn't enough. The Bruins needed more good players. People at the top thought the Bruins needed a lot more, and one way to get that done was to install a new general manager: Milt Schmidt.

Everybody, everywhere knew Milton Conrad Schmidt. As a

player, he wore a Boston sweater with distinction for sixteen seasons. Schmidt was what Boston hockey was all about: unflinching, tough, dedicated to winning. Bruins fans loved him, and still do.

The first time I saw him play was in 1955, when I was assigned to do a colour story on a Bruins–Canadiens playoff game at the Forum. At one point in the game, Schmidt and Canadiens defenceman Tom Johnson squared off in an ugly, one-sided fight, all of it on Schmidt's side. He was tossed out of the game, leaving behind a whipped and spent Johnson.

It seemed like a good idea to visit with Schmidt in the Boston dressing room. Maybe, just maybe, he'd have something to say about the fight. Or, perhaps, about being ejected from a playoff game. It seemed like a good idea . . .

Schmidt was sitting alone in the room, his right hand swollen to twice its normal size from the thrashing he had administered. His face was beet-red. He stared at the dressing-room floor, muttering angrily to himself.

"Could I talk to you for a minute. . .?" I started to say.

Schmidt's head snapped up. "Get the fuck out of here, kid," he yelled.

I left so quickly, there was no time to say goodbye.

How tough was Schmidt?

The teams met again two nights later. His right hand was still swollen, making it difficult to hold his stick. Schmidt solved the problem by having his hand taped to the stick. He played.

Milt Schmidt was also this tough: Red Storey, the referee, once asked me for my all-time All-Star Team. I told him I'd have Jacques Plante in the nets, Bobby Hull on the left side and Gordie Howe at right, with Jean Béliveau at centre (Wayne Gretzky was several years away from the NHL at the time), and Bobby Orr and Doug Harvey on defence. I asked Red for his team.

"Give me five Milt Schmidts," said Storey. "I'd put my grandmother in the nets, and my team would beat your team four out of five nights."

When he was through as a player in 1955, Schmidt was popular enough to be named Bruins coach. One Sunday in November 1962, the Bruins found themselves playing host to the Canadiens. However, Cliff Pennington, the team's leading scorer at the time, wasn't dressed for the game.

"What's going on? Why aren't you dressed?" I asked Pennington.

"There's the coach," Pennington said with a wave of his hand at Schmidt. "Ask him."

Schmidt gave me the full story. The Bruins had been in Toronto two nights earlier, the eve of the Grey Cup game, as it turned out. At 2:00 a.m., the telephone rang in Schmidt's hotel room. The caller identified himself as a member of the hotel's security staff. "Mr. Schmidt," he said, "you requested that we put your team in rooms in one corner of the hotel to ensure that they wouldn't be disturbed by the noise from all the football people. Now, all of the noise in the hotel is coming from your area."

"Give me the damned room number," said Schmidt. "I'll call up there right now."

Pennington answered the telephone.

"What the hell's going on in there?" Schmidt barked at his leading point-getter.

"Hey, coach, we're having a hell of a party here," said Pennington. "Why don't you come up?"

"Now do you understand why he's not dressed?" fumed Schmidt.

Schmidt coached for nine seasons and parts of another two. Now, as the 1967-68 season loomed, the general manager's seat awaited him. Hap Emms, who had held the post for two seasons, was out. Schmidt was in.

"Let's go for a walk," Schmidt said to me that June day.

"Why not?" I said. "Not too long, though. It's hot out there."

"It's hotter in here with all these hockey people trying to pick your pockets," grinned Schmidt. "Let's go."

Moments later, we were on the hot, humid streets of Toronto, walking east on Front Street.

"What do you know about Phil Esposito?" asked Schmidt.

"The kid in Chicago?"

"That's him."

"What I know for sure is that he scored the second-highest number of points in the second half of last season. Why do you ask?"

"I can get him," said Schmidt. "I told Emms about it and he told me not to make the deal, because Gilles Marotte is involved. Emms loves Marotte," said Schmidt. Marotte was a strong, well-built defenceman who had joined the Bruins in 1965. He was a good one, but hardly a great one.

"Who do the Hawks want for Esposito . . . Bobby Orr?"

"Get serious," said Schmidt. "I can get him."

"I don't know him that well, but if I were you, I'd grab him," I said. "It looks like he's going to be a good one. Mind you, he was on a line with Hull . . . and that doesn't hurt. Still, I'd grab him."

Tom Johnson, an old friend from his years on the Canadiens' defence, was now with the Bruins' front-office. (He would later coach the team for three seasons and serve as vice-president). He telephoned me the next day.

"Milt tells me he talked to you about Esposito yesterday in Toronto," he said. "What's your feeling about Esposito?" asked Johnson.

"I told Milt to grab him," I said. "What do the Bruins think?"

"We think the deal is so one-sided, there's got to be something wrong with Esposito."

"Like what?"

"Who knows? Maybe he's into the booze. How do I know?" asked Johnson. "All I know is that everything about the deal is too good to be true. I mean . . . we give up Marotte, Pit Martin, and Denis DeJordy, and they give us a bunch of players and Esposito. He's the key guy. If he's no good, the deal's no good."

"So what do you want from me, pal? I've already told Milt to grab the guy."

"What if there's something wrong with him?"

"That's your problem, not mine."

"You know the Chicago guys, don't you?" he asked.

"Sure, I know most of the Chicago guys. I also know a lot of guys on the rest of the teams."

"Can you call one of the Chicago guys for us?"

"Why?"

"Ask him about Esposito," Johnson said. "Ask him if there's anything wrong with Esposito."

"Why don't you call one of the Chicago guys?" I asked.

"Get serious," said Johnson. "He'll talk to you. He won't talk to me."

"If I call one of the Chicago players, everything is up front," I said. "I'll tell him why I'm calling. I'm telling him the Boston Bruins asked me to call."

"We'd rather you wouldn't do that, but okay, that's fine."

"That's really generous of you," I said.

"Call me back," he said.

"Collect," I said.

Stan Mikita, the Blackhawks' ace centre, was at home when I telephoned.

"Here's the story, Stan. The Bruins have been offered Esposito. The deal is so one-sided, they figure there's something wrong with Espo. They asked me to check him out with one of the Chicago players, which is why I called you. You can answer or you can tell me it's none of my goddamn business. No sweat."

"Give me that again," said Mikita. "The management guys here [Billy Reay and Tommy Ivan were, respectively, Chicago's coach and general manager] are ready to give up Esposito?"

"That's what I'm told," I said. "Schmidt told me about it in Toronto. Now, Tom Johnson tells me it's a done deal if the Bruins want it."

Seconds passed without a word from Mikita. Finally, he said: "Okay, here it is. Tell the Bruins this, and tell 'em exactly the way I'm tellin' it to you. Tell the sons of bitches there's nothing wrong with

Espo. Like the rest of us, he takes a beer after a game, but that's it. Got that? Tell 'em to grab him."

"Yep."

"Make sure to tell 'em exactly the way I said it," said Mikita.

"Exactly?"

"Tell the sons of bitches," snapped Mikita.

A few minutes later, I was on the line to Johnson:

"What'd he say?"

"He said: 'Tell the sons of bitches there's nothing wrong with Espo.' He said: 'Like the rest of us, he takes a beer after a game, but that's it. Got that? Tell 'em to grab him.' That's what he told me."

"Okay, I'll tell Milt. Who was the player?"

"None of your business."

"What are you gonna do with this?" he asked.

"The story will be in the paper tomorrow."

"Oh," said Johnson.

The next day, the Bruins announced that they had completed a deal which would bring Esposito, Ken Hodge, and Fred Stanfield from Chicago for Martin, Marotte, and goaltender DeJordy. The Bruins, armed with Esposito, Hodge, Stanfield, and, of course, Orr, made it to the playoffs for the first time in nine years, but lost in the first round. They made it to the second round the following year, and won the Stanley Cup in two of the next three seasons. Esposito went on to become one of hockey's most formidable and productive players with 717 goals and 873 assists in 1,282 regular-season games. He also scored 61 goals in 130 playoff games. He also may have contributed the greatest series ever played by anyone when he led Team NHL over Team Soviet in their classic confrontation in 1972.

Esposito and I have been friends for a long time, although I haven't seen or heard nearly enough from him since he steered Tampa Bay Lightning into the National Hockey League in 1992. Until now, he has no idea how and why he landed in Boston and, eventually, in the Hockey Hall of Fame. Okay, so the guy owes me one. Esposito probably figures I owe him one. Everyone, of course, owes him for his stunning leadership with Team NHL in '72. Without Espo's brilliance, there would not have been any need for The Goal, because the Soviets would have erased Team NHL long before Paul Henderson made life worth living with time running out in the eighth game of the series. Without Esposito, the series would have been an empty shell. He made it work. He lifted it, and all of us, at a time when nobody thought it could be done. Without Esposito, there would not have been anything to remember about a series none among us can forget.

Some of you may not remember, but there was a two-week hiatus in 1972 between the games of the Summit Series played in Canada and those to be played in the Soviet Union. In that interim, Team NHL stopped off in Sweden for several exhibition games. It was, largely, fun time. Or, at least it was supposed to be, a time to regroup for the second half of the series in which Team NHL trailed, 1–2–1. The media, however, which had been left stunned and disappointed after the first four games in Canada, was not in the mood for fun. They regarded the results of the first four games as a personal affront. How could this team of overpaid, arrogant, beer-guzzling hockey players do this to them? What was going wrong? How could this happen?

Reporters were everywhere in Sweden, and everything, on ice and off, was reported. No holds barred. Most of the time, the wrong spin was put on it. If a few players visited a strip joint in Stockholm, which players and even reporters have been known to do on occasion, it was reported. There wasn't much room to breathe or to relax or to have fun. Players weren't so much interviewed each day as they were grilled. Not surprisingly, they soon bristled at even the barest hint of criticism – real or imagined. Even the reporters quarrelled among themselves.

One day, an unhappy Pierre Gobeil, from Montreal's French-language newspaper *La Presse*, knocked on my hotel-room door. "You've got to talk to Claude St. Jean for me," he said.

"What for?"

"He's gonna kill me."

St. Jean, a former champion amateur wrestler, was a mountain of a man. He loved hockey players, which was why he was in Stockholm. His closest friend was Canadiens defenceman Serge Savard. Another was Jacques Beauchamp, who had asked St. Jean to telephone daily with snippets of gossip for the column he wrote for the *Montréal-Matin*, *La Presse*'s rival newspaper in Montreal. Claude's friendship with Savard opened doors for him, including the one to players' dressing room. While other reporters were kept waiting outside, Claude was welcomed into the room. The gossip flowed in Beauchamp's column.

Gobeil had a question in one of the stories he dispatched to his newspaper: why was someone who wasn't even a reporter allowed into the Team NHL room, while accredited people weren't? The next time St. Jean talked with Beauchamp on the telephone, Gobeil's complaint was relayed to him. St. Jean confronted Gobeil.

"What you're telling me is that Claude isn't very happy with you, right?"

"You've got to talk to him," said Gobeil.

I telephoned St. Jean later in the day and invited him to my room. When we met, I told him Gobeil was frightened. "He says you threatened him over some note he had in one of his stories."

"I'll crush him like a grape," said St. Jean.

"I guess you wouldn't have any trouble doing it," I said, "but look, do you really need the aggravation? Do any of us? All of us have been having enough trouble with the players. It's almost like a war out there. It's no fun for anybody. Why don't you back off?"

"Why would he write something as cheap as that?" fumed St. Jean. "I'm not here to make trouble for anybody. Our friend Beauchamp asked me to do him a favour by calling him every day, and that's what I'm doing."

"No problem," I told him. "Now do me a favour and leave Pierre alone. You don't have to do it for Gobeil. Do it for me."

"I'll do it for you," he agreed, "but if I hear he writes anything else about me, even one word . . ."

"He won't. Trust me," I said.

Team NHL lost game five of the series in Moscow, and won game six, even though Esposito spent a lot of time in the penalty box. What he also did was help kill off penalties for almost one third of the game. The headline in my newspaper, which I did not write, suggested that Team NHL had won the game despite "silly penalties," including a major penalty Esposito had drawn for high-sticking Team Soviet defenceman Alexander "Rags" Ragulin. The story I wrote quoted Team Canada assistant coach John Ferguson at length about Espo's silly penalties.

The only edition of the *Montreal Star* to land in Moscow during the series was the one carrying the story of that game. Esposito read the headline – and simmered.

Team Canada won game seven on September 26. Then, The Goal in game eight. A mob of reporters surrounded Esposito in the dressing room after the final game. Esposito caught my eye, and turned away to answer other questions.

In time, the mob dispersed. Esposito sat there, in full uniform, his chest heaving. He was drained. It was over. He looked up, then looked away. He started unlacing his skates. Not a word was spoken.

Finally, I asked, "You got a problem, Phil?"

No reply.

"What's your problem?" I asked.

"That wasn't a silly penalty," he whined.

"What are you talking about?"

"The story in your paper after game six," he said. "There isn't a referee in the NHL who would have called a major penalty for what I did."

"You high-sticked the guy. It was a good call. If you read the story, even Ferguson, your coach, described it as a silly penalty," I said. "What's more, who gives a shit about game six now? The only reason I'm here is to tell you that's the greatest series I've ever seen anyone play. The team couldn't have won without you. I wanted to tell you that."

Espo looked up, his eyes widening: "Gee, thanks, Redso," he said.

"One thing more," I said.

"What's that?"

"I agree it wasn't a silly penalty."

"That's what I've been trying to tell you," said Espo.

"It was stupid!"

20

Grapes

It was the evening of March 26, 1979, and Don Cherry, the man nearly everybody calls Grapes, was angry. "Really pissed" was the way he put it.

"How cheap can the guy get?" he asked.

The guy in question was the Boston Bruins' general manager, Harry Sinden. Moments earlier, the Canadiens had rallied for a 2–2 tie with the Bruins in Boston Garden. Nothing wrong with a point, except that Cherry, as coach, was convinced his team deserved something better. "We could have beaten your guys tonight," he muttered to me as we sat in the Bruins' dressing room, "but how are we supposed to win when the general manager makes it so tough for us?"

The day before, the Bruins had played – and lost – an evening game in Atlanta, while the Canadiens had played an afternoon game in Montreal, then flown to Boston afterward. Thus, while the Bruins fought to burn Atlanta, the Canadiens were "sittin' in Boston lickin' their chops because they know we've got to fly back the next day," said Cherry. "I asked Harry to get us a charter out of Atlanta. 'No way,' says Harry. 'It's too expensive,' he says. 'Fly commercial,' he says. Does that make any sense?

"It's tough enough playin' that bunch on even terms," Cherry fumed, "but when they're waitin' for you and we've got to play with only a few hours sleep . . . hell, right now, I'm burnin'."

Bad weather had swept in on Atlanta that morning. One flight was cancelled, another was delayed. As a consequence, the Bruins spent hours at the airport and hadn't landed in Boston until four that afternoon.

"Here we are, whipped from sittin' around that damned airport all day," Cherry continued, "and we've got to head for the rink when we land. Makes a lot of sense, doesn't it? If we charter, we beat these guys. Guaranteed we get another point out of it, but a charter was too expensive. You comin' into my office?" he asked.

Cherry was still steaming several minutes later when Harry Sinden walked in. Harry didn't seem too happy, either. He didn't like losing a point late in a game. He slipped wordlessly into a chair. Cherry stared at a spot on the wall, breathing heavily. Nobody spoke. At least for a moment.

"Harry, what's this about Cherry saying the Bruins didn't want to charter out of Atlanta last night?" I finally asked.

"What's that?"

"Cherry figures he would have beaten the Canadiens tonight if," I explained, "the team had a charter after last night's game. He says the Bruins were too cheap to order one."

Sinden jerked up his head quickly, his face turning beet-red. Cherry? Let's just say his face was turning cherry-red.

"Uh . . . oh, well. . . , see ya later, guys," I said, and quickly left.

I was only three steps down the hall, when the shouting started.

"Is that what you told him, that I was too cheap?" roared Sinden. "Is that what you said?"

"Well . . . not exactly," said Cherry, "but yeah, I guess you could say that's what I said. How would you describe it?" he yelled. "Yeah, we'd've beaten these guys if we'd been able to get a few hours' sleep."

Sinden stormed out of the office. He didn't look happy.

These days, Cherry almost always mentions this story when we meet, particularly when he has an audience. He likes audiences. "Say, did I ever tell you the story how I got fired by the Bruins?" he starts. Then he spends the next five minutes relating it. "That's the guy that got me fired," he says, pointing a finger at me. "That started it, you know. That definitely started it. He's the guy. Nobody else! Bang! Just like that! Fired! Where was I supposed to get another job? He's the guy!"

Donald S. Cherry has told the story many, many times, with varying degrees of accuracy. My reply is that, sure, I may have contributed to his firing, but the worst I could be accused of is taking a $30,000-per-year coach and making a millionaire out of him.

After being bounced by the Bruins in the 1978-79 season, Cherry went to the Colorado Rockies, where he managed to get himself fired after just one season. From there, he won the lottery: *Hockey Night in Canada*. Now, at age sixty, he is, in every way, Canadian television's most outrageous high-collared redneck, the medium's no-necked monster. He's also its best salesman. He has turned the "Coach's Corner" into a sort of cross-country meeting place. That strident voice carrying a big "shtick" has brought him television and radio commercials; a weekly television interview show which ran for years until he decided he could no longer fit it into his schedule; a five-times-weekly radio quickie heard from coast to coast; something he calls "Rock 'em, Sock 'em" videos; big fees for after-dinner speeches; and a string of restaurants carrying his name.

I like him – even though his act often skates on thin ice. What counts is that he's a favourite with the blue-collar crowd, and there are a lot more of them than the group wearing those high, white ones.

My old friend Cherry was in Ottawa for the Senators' first-ever game on October 8, 1992. Yes, once again he told the story about how and why he got fired by the Bruins, but only four or five times. After the morning practice, we headed back downtown and came upon a parade of hundreds of retired servicemen and women who had participated in a ceremony for the unveiling of a statue. Pipe band, police cars running interference . . . the works.

The marchers passed our downtown hotel, eyes glued to the backs of the marchers directly ahead of them. Shoulders back, steps firm – until one of them spotted Cherry's high collar out of the corner of his eye. Who can miss it, right? There was a whispered message out of the side of his mouth to the marcher alongside him, and in a matter of seconds, the word was spreading through the ranks. Hey, it's Cherry! It's Grapes!

Pretty soon, military discipline went thataway. One marcher . . . two . . . then, a half-dozen and more were turning their heads to the left toward a grinning, applauding, thumbs-up Cherry. The marchers smiled, laughed, and snapped comments at Cherry.

"You're the reason we're here, guys," Cherry yelled at the marchers. "Atta boy, guys, you're lookin' good!" Then, of course, thumbs up.

"Who's gonna win tonight, Grapes?" yelled a marcher.

"Who cares? You're the only guys that count, guys. Yeah. Nobody else."

"Hey, Grapes, welcome to Ottawa."

"Love it. Let's see a thumbs-up for Ottawa," Cherry said. "I've been telling the other guys you're the reason we're here. Yeah. Love ya."

"I love the old guys in the parade," Cherry said out of the side of his mouth. "Look at those guys march. I should be out there with them. Love a parade. Used to be in a marching band, you know. I was great."

"How could you tell your left foot from your right?"

"Very funny," said Cherry.

One large-sized group of marchers came to a halt across the street. When they were dismissed, a dozen or so hurried to Cherry.

"I need a new shirt with a high collar," a be-medalled senior marcher said.

"Ho, ho, yeah, very good, pal," Cherry said. "Lemme shake your hand."

Another pointed a finger at me. "Who's this, your bodyguard?" he asked Cherry.

"You mean you don't recognize him?" Cherry asked.

"Naw."

"Love ya," said Cherry.

"I want to shake your hand," another senior said to Cherry. "I want to tell my wife I shook your hand."

"Put 'er there, pal," said Cherry.

"I want to tell her I shook your hand because she hates you."

"Hey, good stuff," said Cherry. "Give her a big hello for me, pal. Give her a hug. Hates me, eh? On second thought, maybe you'd better not give her a hug," said Cherry.

Everybody laughed.

Six years earlier, on May 24, 1986, Cherry had been in Calgary for what turned out to be the decisive game of the 1986 Stanley Cup final, won by the Canadiens. Chris Nilan, who wasn't dressed for the game, was his intermission guest. "Gee, I hope [coach Jean] Perron uses Steve Rooney in the last period," Cherry remarked to Nilan on the air. "It would be a shame if the kid didn't get his name on the Stanley Cup."

Rooney hadn't played in the four previous games. The rules have changed since then, but in 1986, a player had to appear in at least one Stanley Cup final game to get his name on the trophy. Obviously, it had escaped Cherry's attention that Rooney had, in fact, been on the ice several times during the first two periods of the very game he was commenting on.

The press box at the Saddledome is located near the roof of the building. The television studio is in the basement. To get there from the press box, it's necessary to walk down a couple of flights of stairs, turn right for about sixty feet, and left for another thirty to an elevator which goes to the basement. Then, a short walk to the television studio. No big deal, but it's at least a little out of the way.

Cherry was in the studio with his executive producer. "Got a minute?" I asked Cherry from the doorway.

He joined me outside the room.

"In case you find it necessary to mention Rooney again before the end of the game, I just wanted you to know he was on the ice a few times in the first two periods," I said.

"Geez," snapped Cherry, "after all the good things I've mentioned tonight, is that all you've got to tell me?"

"Listen, Grapes," I said, "I didn't have to do this. I've just come all the way down here from the press box, which is way up there. The only reason I'm here is to stop you from embarrassing yourself in front of a national audience – and that's your reaction? Hey, screw you!" I turned, and started to walk to the elevator.

"Hey, wait a minute," sputtered Cherry, "I didn't mean . . ."

"Like I said, Cherry, screw you!"

Several days later, a letter (written in red ink) arrived at my home. It read: "Just a note to thank you for coming down from the press box to help me, not many guys would do that; only true friends.

"I am sorry I acted like a asshole.

"Love Grapes."

"Read this," I said to my wife, "and tell me what you think. Should I answer it?"

"Of course," she said. "He made a mistake. He's sorry. He took the trouble to write. Haven't you ever made a mistake? No," she quickly added, "don't answer that."

I replied to the letter. It read: "Dear Grapes: Thanks for your letter. You did, indeed, act like a asshole."

We've always remained friends.

21

French–English Thing

If there's a constant, other than winning, with the Montreal Canadiens, it's the "French–English thing." I heard about it when I first
started travelling with the team – yet saw no evidence of it. Forty
years later, I still hear about it and I still don't see it. It's one of those
things that seems to exist in the minds of people who should know
better. Reporters, for example.

What is this thing they call French–English?

Let's go back to 1976. Mario Tremblay was upset. The aggressive
sophomore right-winger hadn't played for the second consecutive
game of a lengthy road trip. Instead, he watched from the seats this
night as the Canadiens toyed with the hapless Cleveland Barons,
eventually winning by a score of 8–1.

Returning to his hotel room at 2:30 a.m., Tremblay's roommate
Peter Mahovlich found his entry barred by the chain on the door.
Tremblay was in the room with several other Canadiens and for a
long time they ignored Mahovlich's repeated requests for entry. "Go
away," he was told. "Take a walk."

Mahovlich continued to pound on the door. Eventually, it was
opened, whereupon Mahovlich became involved in a shoving match

with Tremblay. Mahovlich fell back against the corner of a table. Fifty-five stitches were needed to close the wound to Mahovlich's thigh.

Mahovlich and Tremblay had been roomies since the start of the season. Until this evening, there hadn't been even a threat of an incident. They were made for each other. Each was a fun-loving, free-spirited guy. Where they differed was that Mahovlich was a regular on a line with Guy Lafleur and Steve Shutt, while Tremblay was a relative new kid on the block, trying to get there. It's never easy for a young player to earn a regular job with the Canadiens – at least it wasn't in those days. Patience was, indeed, a virtue.

But such nostrums were of little consolation to Mario Tremblay that dark morning in Cleveland. He didn't like the idea of waiting his turn.

I can remember when he and Doug Risebrough, who is now the general manager of the Calgary Flames, arrived at the Forum in 1974, fresh out of junior hockey. They worked hard. They hustled. They scrapped. Trouble is, the numbers of players and the positions they could fill didn't add up. With Henri Richard still with the team, where was centreman Risebrough to fit? Tremblay, a right-winger, had a similar problem. There was just no room.

I mentioned this fact in one or two lines at the end of a training-camp story. The next day, as I stepped aboard the team bus, coach Scotty Bowman shouted: "Hey, Mario, Fisher says there's no room for you on this club."

Bowman was pulling Tremblay's chain, of course. Trouble is, when you're still a teenager with big ideas and bigger dreams, it's often difficult to see the humour in things.

"Yeah," snapped Tremblay, "the fucking grand-fodder."

I don't really have a problem with thin-skinned players – particularly the young ones. They're in a tough business. They desperately want to make it as soon as possible and stay in the business as long as possible. What they should understand – and don't – is that it doesn't

233

really matter what a reporter thinks about them. All that counts is whether or not management likes him. In fact, fans can do more to drive an athlete out of a city than any reporter I've known.

Tremblay, who went on to play a total of twelve productive seasons with the Canadiens, still remembers the Cleveland incident. And Risebrough continues to tell people that I was responsible for his demotion to the minors, because twenty-four hours after my lines appeared at the end of the training-camp story, both he and Tremblay were sent to the Nova Scotia Voyageurs, the Canadiens' farm team based in Halifax.

Anyway, I was proved both right and wrong about Tremblay and Risebrough. Six weeks into the season, Richard broke his ankle. The next day, both Risebrough and Tremblay were recalled for a game in Boston. They excelled. They stayed.

What really counts, though, is to stay and to play, which is why Tremblay and Mahovlich had this, uh, tiff. It was an incident that cried out for damage control. Not surprisingly, the Canadiens players quickly closed ranks, agreeing to keep the early-morning fracas within the family. The next day, however, the story was leaked to a media person. Mahovlich, among others, was livid at the stories that ensued.

"Stupid, that's what it is," he fumed. "Stupid. Tremblay and I have been roomies since the start of the season. I liked him before this thing happened, and I like him now. What I can't understand is why somebody on this team would tell a reporter about it. If all of the reporters had been there and had seen precisely what had happened, not a word of it would have appeared in the papers. They wouldn't have regarded it as important enough to write about. There wasn't a punch thrown. There was noise and some shoving, nothing more. But then one of our players tells a reporter about it, now it's a French–English thing."

Now any time I hear the term, I remember Rocket Richard's declaration about not being a politician, only a hockey player. Hockey players don't score goals in two languages. They score goals, period.

That's why the French–English thing has never become a problem. Sure, I have heard French and English players poke fun at each other about their respective mother-tongues. This hardly makes them unique. On a road trip, I frequently see a group of four French-speaking players sit at one restaurant table and another group of English-speaking players sit at another. Is that what French–English is all about? Not to my mind. It's nothing more than friends having dinner with friends.

When the Canadiens leave defenceman Sean Hill open in the Expansion Draft and protect J.J. Daigneault, is that a French–English thing? If it is, then what about protecting Paul DiPietro and leaving Jesse Bélanger open? Was something lost in the translation?

What the French–English thing is not is this: the Canadiens are faced with having to trade one of, say, two players of equal calibre. One is English-speaking, the other French-speaking. It's the English player who will go, and there's nothing more sinister to it than good business sense in a predominantly French-speaking city. Where it becomes a French–English thing in the minds of some media people is when a Mike Keane sees a lot of ice time and a French-language player doesn't. Or when a press colleague looks down on the Canadiens players on the ice and says: "Look at that: five English players on the power play!"

The guy was kidding, of course. Or was he?

When Henri Richard lashed out verbally at coach Al MacNeil during the 1971 Stanley Cup final, calling him the worst coach he'd ever played for, was that a French–English thing?

It certainly wasn't for Richard. It didn't matter who the coach happened to be behind the Canadiens' bench. When Richard exploded it was simply a prideful player venting his frustration at having to spend a lot of time on the bench. And wasn't that John Ferguson who, after leaving the bench, smashed his stick and trashed the clinic when he wasn't used as much as he thought he should be during one of the games of the 1970-71 Canadiens–Minnesota series? That's John, not Jean.

Where MacNeil was concerned, it was a matter of going with the players he felt could win for him. Nothing more.

Wasn't that Dickie Moore leading a charge from the bench after Frank Mahovlich had lashed a puck directly at Henri Richard late in the second period of a Canadiens–Toronto game in the early 1960s?

The Canadiens were in Toronto on this night, and late in the second period Richard moved in to check Mahovlich, who was leaving his zone with the puck. There was more than enough room to deal off the puck to linemates on either side of the rink, but Mahovlich had been growing increasingly frustrated in the game. Instead of passing the puck to his right or left, he let it fly directly at the on-rushing Richard. Blood poured from an ugly gash on Richard's face.

Moore leaped off the bench. In seconds, both benches had emptied. Many minutes passed before order was restored.

Canadiens general manager Frank Selke, who had once described Moore as the best junior in Canada, raced down to the team's room between periods.

"Don't put out Moore in the third period," he instructed coach Toe Blake.

"Why not?"

"I don't want any more trouble out there," said Selke. "We're in control of this game. I don't want Moore and Mahovlich getting into it."

Moore was on the ice for third-period faceoff.

To this day, Mahovlich insists he wasn't aiming the puck at Richard. "It was an act of God," he explained as recently as the 1993 All-Star Game in Montreal, where he and Richard were honorary captains of the teams. "I was trying to pass it off, but somehow, it hit Henri in the face. Why would I shoot a puck at Henri?"

"Have you told that to Henri?" Mahovlich was asked.

"Several times," he said.

"Did he believe you?"

"No," answered Mahovlich with a grin.

French–English?

Frank was to join the Canadiens during the 1970-71 season, and two years later, during a road trip, teammate Yvan Cournoyer approached him with a request.

"You've got your own room on this trip, eh, Frank?"

"Yep."

"Do you think I could use your room?"

"No sweat," said Mahovlich.

Later, Cournoyer opened the door to his lady friend. After she agreed to have a drink, Cournoyer placed a call to room service. "I need some ice and six glasses," he said.

"No problem. What's the name, please?"

"Mahovlich," said Cournoyer. "Frank Mahovlich."

"How do you spell that?"

"M-a-v . . . M-h-l-c . . . M-o-l-i . . . aw, to hell with it," said Cournoyer, slamming down the phone.

The reality is that the French—English thing has been twisted and shaped by the media, then shaped again into something grotesque by the fans. There's no question that there's a French—English thing in the Province of Quebec, and elsewhere in Canada for that matter. People have carried their adherence to their mother-tongue and culture as proudly as they would a flag or a first-born. But in trying to take the language "problem" to the ice, they're attempting to create a situation that's not there and never has been. Certainly, French-speaking Montreal in particular and Quebec in general have taken special pride in the triumphs of the Canadiens, and the achievements of such native sons as Maurice Richard, Georges Vézina, Yvan Cournoyer, Henri Richard, Jean Béliveau, Guy Lafleur, and Serge Savard. Who wouldn't get a sense of empowerment, a sense of identity, from this? But would the Canadiens rank as the most successful franchise in professional hockey if their ranks had been constantly riven by internal strife?

Others have imagined it, but I haven't seen it. In all the years I've covered this team, I have never met a player who has given me even the slightest problem in terms of language. Most of my questions have been delivered in English to Québécois Canadiens, and I can't remember one time when a reply was made in French. What I'm saying is that the French–English thing has never been an issue of any kind in terms of my job. There has never been a reason for it.

It's teamwork that's made this club great, teamwork that's won them twenty-four Stanley Cups. Canadiens coaches bark out instructions in English without complaint from the French-language players. French-speaking players snap at each other in their language and English-speaking players do the same. That's where it begins. That's where it ends.

22

Danny

There are good and bad times in this business. Rarely, however, does good news come calling late at night or early in the morning. Montreal radio-station CJAD program director Ted Blackman confirmed this truth when he telephoned my home at 8:04 a.m. one cold Friday in February of 1993.

The news was bad. Danny Gallivan, for thirty-two years "the voice of the Canadiens," was dead at seventy-five. A friend of four decades, asleep forever. A partner on so many nights in so many different cities, gone. The previous day, his son-in-law had become concerned when telephone calls to Danny's apartment on Nun's Island in downtown Montreal had elicited no response. The body was discovered on the floor of his apartment.

Danny and I had talked on the telephone four, maybe five days earlier. We talked frequently, now and then about Hockey Hall of Fame matters. He was on the Hall's original nine-man players' selection committee when it was formed in 1958, and had been its chairman for a decade.

"I've resigned, you know," he told me the last time we talked. "It'll be official at our meeting in March."

"Are you sure that's what you want?"

"Time to move on," he said. "Time for somebody else."

He mentioned Guy Lapointe who, along with Serge Savard and Larry Robinson, had comprised the Big Three on the Canadiens' defence corps of the late 1970s. No team ever had been blessed with three defencemen of that quality. It was a team that had won four consecutive Stanley Cups, and much of what made it excellent flowed from the Big Three. Savard already was in the Hall of Fame. Lapointe, with his 622 points in 884 games, had been nominated twice, but for some reason didn't get the required votes.

"He should be in the Hall," said Danny. "The deadline is March 10 but, so far, nobody has nominated him. That's not right. I'd do it, but since I won't be at the selection committee's next meeting, I don't think it's right for me to put his name forward. Would you do it?"

Done.

The telephone call from Blackman was the first of many I received that day in 1993. Television people. Radio people. Reporters. People who weren't in radio or television but whom Danny had touched in some way. How did he die? they asked. When? What made him so special? Was it the colourful language, the unique vocabulary? The enthusiasm? Was it because he cared so much about the game and most of the people in it?

Danny Gallivan was special because he delivered the genuine article. He was the voice of the Canadiens, with all the hucksterism that can imply, but he was also their severest critic when individual and team performances weren't what he felt they should be. The Canadiens teams he covered from 1952 to 1984 were among the best hockey has known, but what he saw was what his audience got. There were no "free passes" for players taking a night off.

I have known and admired most of the people who have worked behind hockey microphones during the last four decades. I did some games with Foster Hewitt. I did a few with his son, Bill. I was Dick Irvin's analyst on radio for several years. Dan Kelly was a close friend. So is Bob Cole. But Danny was the best.

He was the play-by-play man on radio for the Sunday-night broadcasts of Canadiens games carried on the coast-to-coast network of the CBC. I was a regular guest between periods and for years was responsible for selecting the three stars. Whenever Danny disagreed with any of my selections, he never failed to let me know. We'd argue about it and then we'd laugh about it – until, that is, the next time he disagreed.

I sat alongside him in a broadcast booth on some nights. He'd be there, often on his feet, clutching the microphone in his fist, his voice rising and falling with the ebb and flow of the action. He was never more comfortable than when he gripped that microphone, never more sure of himself than when he was completely immersed in the game. Somehow, he was able to shut out everything else, and that often included instructions barked into his earphones from the television truck.

I was his colour man one night for a telecast in Pittsburgh.

"We're welcoming the viewing audience from Vancouver in sixty seconds," was the message in the earphones. "Get ready, Danny . . ."

"Béliveau has the puck . . . over to Cournoyer . . ."

"Thirty seconds, Danny. Remember, Vancouver audience, Danny . . ."

"Cournoyer shoots . . ."

"Now, Danny . . . welcome the viewers, Danny. Now!"

"There's another shot . . ."

It was clear, of course, that Danny wasn't hearing a word from the truck. Seconds later, there was a break in the action. Time enough, at least, for me to say: "And now Danny, let's welcome the viewers from Vancouver . . ."

Gallivan turned, winked broadly, and, without missing a beat, said: "And the score for those viewers who've just joined us from Vancouver is . . ." Later: "You did that well," he grinned. "Yes, sir, you've got the stuff to feed the troops."

Danny joined the Canadiens two years before I joined the *Montreal Star*, and a lot of the next four decades were spent in each other's company – mostly professionally and, from time to time, socially. For years, we lived within walking distance of each other. Sometimes, there were poker games. Sometimes, there were dinners with Joe MacDonald, who was Danny's best friend – and mine.

Danny and Joe had roots in the Maritimes. It's where they grew up, where they were educated. In time, both landed in Montreal – Joe as an executive with a firm producing engineered plastics, Danny with the Canadiens as the team's broadcast play-by-play man.

"This good friend of mine, Joe MacDonald, has a son playing college hockey at Michigan," Danny mentioned one day. "I'd like you to meet Joe one of these days."

Joe was a hockey freak. His idea of paradise would have been to have his son, Barry, make it to the National Hockey League. His face lit up when I suggested that perhaps a few paragraphs could be written about Barry's progress at Michigan.

Joe MacDonald became something of a hockey celebrity himself because his seats were alongside the Canadiens' bench at the Forum. When lines were changed, the camera often caught him. When there were brawls near the Canadiens' bench, his snow-white hair always was part of the picture. "Don't let that guy push you around," he would plead with Serge Savard. "Get him, Pierre."

"Joe," I once told him, "if you're on television any more than you are now, the players are going to start complaining."

"Oh, was I really on camera?" he laughed.

Laughing came easily to Joe, as it did to his pal, Danny. Too many individuals I have known don't regard a day as being complete unless they can convince themselves, and others, that life is beating one's brains out. They don't care who knows it. If they could, they would hold press conferences to announce it. They depress me.

Not Joe. The grief was there, as it is now and then with all of us. He had his problems, as we all do, but Joe shed his tears in private.

The important thing to Joe was to reach out for the good things, whether they happened to be a seat alongside the Canadiens' bench, a good dinner with friends, a hockey fight, the warmth of a gin and tonic, or a golf game with his gang, which included Danny.

Sitting with Joe meant there were stories to be told. There were jokes, most of them old and bad, but there was lots of laughter. Long faces didn't belong at his table. He may have been breaking up inside, but he laughed.

Both Danny and Joe loved to golf. Each year Joe would organize golfing vacations for Danny and their friends. Most years, they'd travel to Florida. One year, though, the group went to southern California. The weather hadn't been that good in the winter of 1978. It rained, but what was a little rain when there was a game of golf to be played? After that, dinner. Four people in the group needed a ride to their hotel.

"I'll do it," said Joe. "No problem."

He dropped off his friends at their hotel, and headed back to the ranch where he and the rest of the group were staying. The road was slick. Joe missed a turn. The car hit a tree.

Danny was on the telephone to me the next morning. He talked about how Joe had offered to take his friends to their hotel, about how Joe, who loved to drive fast, couldn't handle the turn on the wet road. The tree.

Our friend held on to his life for a couple of days more. Then, on a Wednesday, Danny called from California to tell me Joe had died an hour earlier. The voice which thrilled so many millions on *Hockey Night in Canada*, barely made it across the long-distance telephone line. By then, his crying was over, but he had difficulty speaking. Danny didn't love many, but he loved hard.

In the course of hundreds of hockey trips together, Danny and I naturally had many good-natured arguments over the merits of teams and players – but there was none he admired more than those who had won so many Stanley Cups with the great Canadiens teams. He was the best at what he did and he loved what he did – all the more so because his colourful language was devoted almost exclusively to hockey's best team. It was Geoffrion who had "the cannonading shot." It was Savard who mastered "the spinnerama." Other teams tried to hire him by offering considerably more money than he was earning in Montreal, but Danny was content to stay put.

"We've been talking with Danny Gallivan about becoming our play-by-play man," St. Louis Blues executive Sid Salomon III told me one day in 1967. "I want this team to go into business with the best. What do you think?"

"Not a chance," he was told. "He won't go."

"Why not? We're offering him a heck of a deal," said Salomon.

"I'm sure you are, but I can't see Danny moving out of Montreal. He's the number-one guy in the business. He's with a winner. I really can't see him making a change."

"I think we can get him. We're going to give it a heck of a try," said Salomon.

Two weeks later, Salomon was on the telephone again. "Gallivan turned us down," he said. Did I know anybody who could do the play-by-play at the Arena?

"I'd go after Dan Kelly if I were you," Salomon was told. "He's done a lot of work in hockey, and he's itching to move out of Ottawa." Kelly was based in that city with the CBC.

Kelly did, in fact, join the Blues in St. Louis, where he became one of hockey's most highly-regarded voices.

Gallivan was, in many ways, a private person. He didn't like to show off or throw his weight around. While he spent more than thirty years behind a Canadiens microphone, Danny, to the best of my memory, probably visited the Canadiens' dressing room no more than a dozen times. I never asked him why and he never explained. After his retirement in 1984, he remained in close touch with the game, but most of his time was spent watching hockey on television or listening to radio play-by-play. He rarely visited the Forum.

Now and then, he would telephone seeking tickets for out-of-town friends or, perhaps, for tickets to games in Vancouver where his daughters resided. That's where it ended, though. He was always apologetic about it. "I really hate to bother you," he'd start, "but I've got this letter from the Maritimes asking for tickets. Do you think. . .?"

"No problem, Danny, but have you called the Forum?"

"Aw, I wouldn't want to bother anybody up there," he would say. "I don't even want to bother you, have you go out of your way."

Danny wasn't merely the voice who came into your home on Saturday nights. He sat at your table. He entertained you. The sound of his voice, his observations were with you in your office. Day in, day out, from September to April and beyond, he was part of your conversations. He was your friend.

He had an impish sense of humour which he often brought into his broadcasts.

"We want to try something a little different this year," the television people told me one day. "We want to give our viewers more information about injuries. Whenever you see a player going to the clinic, get down there as quickly as you can. When there's a break in the action, we'll have Danny bring you in with an injury report for fifteen seconds or so."

The formula worked well for several weeks. An injured player would head for the clinic. I'd join him there a couple of minutes later. No more than two or three minutes later, the viewers would be told about the injury and whether or not they could expect the player back on the ice that night.

On this night, Chicago Blackhawks forward Eric Nesterenko suffered a severe gash on his face. Danny accordingly threw the broadcast to me in the clinic.

"Eric needed seven stitches," I started, then stopped. The floor manager was waving his arms frantically. "Your mike's dead," he hissed.

Upstairs, Gallivan told his audience: "We're having a small problem with the audio. We'll get that report in a couple of minutes."

Two minutes later: "Now, let's go downstairs for that report on Nesterenko . . ."

New microphone in hand, I started again: "Eric needed seven stitches . . ."

More waving of hands from the floor manager. Again, there was no sound.

Danny had to go through the same routine upstairs. An apology for the problem. A promise to return once the problem was solved.

Another microphone was found. "No way this one won't work," the floor manager promised. No way it worked.

Upstairs: "We still can't get Red," said Danny. "Maybe he dropped out for a beer. And there's a shot by Cournoyer . . ."

The day Danny Gallivan died had begun with that early-morning telephone call. Among the others that followed in the next few hours was one from Ottawa at 2:27 that afternoon at the *Gazette*.

"I heard about Danny and I thought I'd call just to tell you how saddened I am," the caller said, his voice a rich, mellifluous baritone. "I know how much you thought of Danny. All of us did."

We talked about Danny for a few minutes. We talked about Doug Harvey. The caller also mentioned his great friendship with Joe Mac-Donald. "Danny was a great pal of our old pal," the caller said.

"Thanks for calling," I said.

"God bless," said Brian Mulroney.

23

Nobody Ever Said
It Would Be Easy

Dr. Milne was on the telephone that Wednesday afternoon in November 1962. He sounded worried.

"Where does the team go this weekend?" he asked me.

"Boston," I said.

"You going?"

"Of course."

"I don't think you should."

"Why not?"

"I want you in the hospital," he said.

Several days earlier, there had been a, well, small problem. I had passed some blood two or three times. Urine samples were taken and now Dr. Milne was saying: "I don't think it's serious, but it's something we've got to look at."

Other people everywhere hear these things every other day on the telephone, but it's never supposed to happen to you, right? I was thirty-six. Young, healthy guys aren't supposed to hear these things over the telephone. Young, healthy guys can't even be bothered to find the time for regular check-ups. I had been a pretty lucky guy up to that point. I didn't exercise as much as, well . . . as much as I do now. I ate the wrong foods at the wrong hours – an occupational hazard of this business. Some reporters and broadcasters I know can finish off a full table of Chinese food at 2:00 in the morning – and then be digging into a breakfast buffet only a few hours later. Still, up until Dr. Milne's directive, my only visit to a hospital went back to the time I had my tonsils removed. That was when I was four or five years old. Beyond that, nothing much. A cold now and then was usually as bad as it got.

Monday morning at the hospital, there were X-rays and blood tests. Dr. Moore, the urologist, didn't look worried when he dropped in to my room for a visit that evening.

"Find anything?" I asked.

"I see a small polyp on your bladder," he said.

"So what happens?"

"We remove your bladder," he laughed, then followed quickly with, "No, no . . . what we do is go up with this thing and snip off the polyp. It might be a little uncomfortable for a while, but I don't think it's serious."

"When?"

"Tomorrow morning," said Dr. Moore. "At eight. Have a good night's sleep."

He was back the next afternoon. "We got it," he said. "But I'll want you back here three months from now for another look."

"Why?"

"Nothing serious," he said, "but the tip of the polyp was inclined to malignancy."

Boom! Do you know what a clout to the ribs feels like? Suddenly, I wasn't feeling well at all. Dr. Moore noticed. "All I said was that it was inclined to malignancy," he said. "I want to keep an eye on it, that's all. It's important that we keep an eye on it."

Dr. Moore did keep kept an eye on it. Dr. Eric Reid called me in for annual check-ups for several years after that. They were good and caring men and I was lucky. There was some discomfort for several weeks after each examination, but that was the extent of it.

Athletes are always missing time with one ailment or another, but I always hated the idea of missing a game because of illness. Of course, that's a silly way to respect one's health. Is it ego? Is it because too many of us in the news business don't think anyone else can do the job? When I started to follow the Canadiens in the mid-1950s, there was no time off from the seventy-game schedule. All of the pre-season games were covered. If the Canadiens happened to be eliminated before the Stanley Cup final, I would be on the road until the end of the playoffs.

Back in the days of the six-team league, there were thirty-five road games to be covered during the regular schedule – and they were. At the same time, I was expected to be in the office each weekday at 6:30 a.m. whenever the Canadiens weren't out of town. It wasn't unusual to return from a game in Chicago at 2:00 a.m., catch three hours' sleep, and be in the office an hour or so later. Once, while on a Grey Cup assignment, I left Vancouver at 2:00 on a Sunday afternoon. The plane stopped at every major city across the country and didn't arrive in Montreal until 7:30 a.m., Monday. I went directly to the office.

"You look a little tired," I was told at 2:30 that afternoon. "Why don't you take the rest of the day off?"

Long days and nights came with the turf in the 1950s and '60s but, even now, too many among the reporting fraternity, myself included, are inclined to push themselves to the brink. It's not something I learned to do. It's what I wanted to do. Still is, I guess. The problem is that there's only so much the body can take – particularly in a job where the travelling is heavy and the hours are long. Sooner or later, there's a price to pay.

1985. May. It had been hot in Philadelphia for games three and four of the Flyers' Wales Conference final with the Quebec Nordiques. Very hot. Air conditioners in restaurants and hotel rooms were on maximum all day and night. By the time I stopped off in Montreal for a one-day break before game five in Quebec, I had a wracking cough deep in my chest. Breathing was difficult. I missed the next two games the Flyers needed to win the Wales. I also decided to miss my first Stanley Cup final in three decades.

The cough lingered for a while, then disappeared. The breathing problems didn't. I would sit there for a long time reaching for a deep breath. Finally, it would come. Still, there was a job to be done. Seventeen days had passed, the Edmonton Oilers had won the Stanley Cup – and now the annual June meetings of the NHL in Toronto awaited.

I managed to stay on my feet for twelve hours at the first day of the meetings, but there were complications. My appetite, for one.

"You look awful," Tillie said when I returned to our hotel.

I told her I had ordered a club sandwich earlier but hadn't been able to eat it.

"Why don't you get some rest?" she suggested.

"Can't. I haven't written a line for the paper yet."

"At least take a hot bath before you start writing," she said.

The next morning, I had an early breakfast meeting with Canadiens president Ronald Corey. He said that I looked tired. I said I wasn't sleeping well and not eating very much.

That night, after another full day at the meetings, there was a dinner date with Tom Watt, now director of professional development for the Maple Leafs, and his wife, Mabs. There was no problem with the food. The next night, however, my wife and I were in another restaurant that the Watts had recommended. Each of us had ordered filet of sole. When the meal arrived, I couldn't eat it. Minutes earlier, I'd been hungry. Now . . . nothing.

To this day, my wife remembers that night. "I still can't believe I ate both meals," she says.

We returned home the next day for the start of a long summer vacation. The breathing problem was still there. So was the absence of appetite. The anxiety grew.

"I can't find anything wrong," said the first doctor, who was a general practitioner. "I'll give you some antibiotics."

The second doctor was an ear, nose, and throat specialist. "There's nothing wrong," he said. "Forget about it."

"You handled that stress test pretty darn well," said the cardiologist a couple of weeks later. "Nothing wrong."

Did I mention two late-night visits to the emergency ward of St. Mary's Hospital in Montreal?

Nothing wrong, the doctors assured me.

What was terribly wrong was the effect it was having on my family, particularly my wife. We had been married thirty-seven years. Everything had always been upbeat among the Singer women. Don't worry, be happy. They made it work. Now, my wife and I found ourselves sitting on the living-room sofa for hours, arms entwined, and talking about my health problem. "You've got to stop thinking about it," she would say. "You've got to stop running to all those doctors. They've already told you there's nothing wrong with you. You've got to get on your feet and start doing things." Now and then, tears would flow.

"I know what you're saying," I would tell her, "but I'm the guy who's having a problem breathing. I'm the guy who doesn't have an appetite any more. I don't know how much more of this I can handle."

More tears.

Two months later, my wife and I were walking along Ste. Catherine Street in downtown Montreal when we met Joan MacDonald. Joan was a nurse who had married a doctor. Her father, Joe MacDonald, had been a good friend of mine and of Danny Gallivan. She recommended that I see a friend – Dr. Michael Spevack – at Montreal General.

Dr. Spevack was in charge of the hospital's behavioural clinic. His specialty was individuals with anxiety problems. He was certain he could help, but I wasn't so sure. "A couple of doctors I've seen told me it's all in my head," I said. "You seem to agree with them."

"Why don't we just work on this thing together," he suggested.

"Let's get together once a week. Let's see what happens."

We met for an hour each week just to talk. At home, I would listen to tapes he had made. The same message was delivered over and over again: relax. Be calm. Still, the problems continued for the first few weeks. Sleep didn't come easily. The luxury of a deep breath was hard to find. I would lie in bed for hours trying to reach for one. No luck. It wasn't much fun. Exercise helped, so there I'd be at 3:00 in the morning, doing deep knee bends. Anything for that deep breath.

The eating problems continued. Worse, another hockey season loomed. With no great improvement in my health, could I realistically continue to follow the Canadiens on the road?

"What is it you're afraid of?" asked Dr. Spevack at one of our early sessions. "Are you afraid of flying?"

"Flying has never been a problem. I don't see why it should bother me now," I said.

"So what is it then?" he asked. "Is it that you'll be away from home? You shouldn't be, you know. There are team doctors in every city you visit. If you need one, you're only a telephone call away. If you feel you need one . . ."

In September I found myself in Edmonton covering an exhibition game. "I feel rotten," I said to the team's doctor, Gordon Cameron, before the game.

He agreed I looked rather pale and wondered if I had eaten something that disagreed with me. When I told him I hadn't, he took my blood pressure. It was normal. "Tell you what," he said. "If you're not feeling well, why don't you lie down on the sofa in the directors' room for the first period? Come and see me after the game, and I'll take a closer look at you."

I didn't get to the press box until the second period. Somehow, I got through writing the eight hundred-or-so words expected from me, including a brief description of a punishing first-period fight I didn't see involving a Canadiens rookie named John Kordic and Edmonton's Kevin McClelland. Thirty minutes after the game, I was on my back in the Oilers' clinic.

"I'll get to you in a minute," said Dr. Cameron. "First, I've got to give Paul a tetanus shot."

Paul Coffey, the team's star defenceman, lay on a table a few feet away. Late in the game, he had become involved in an unfriendly exchange with Claude Lemieux, not one of hockey's great fighters then or now. Lemieux had bitten off more than he could chew in his altercation with Coffey, most of it being Coffey's thumb.

"That's why I'm getting a shot," Coffey sighed. "I'm not taking any chances with that guy."

"Geez, Paul, I've seen you take shots before, but this is ridiculous."

"Very funny," grunted Coffey.

Dr. Cameron, of course, couldn't find anything wrong with me. He recommended a visit to my doctor in Montreal upon my return.

"I think I've already seen most of the doctors in Montreal," I said to him. "I'm seeing one right now. We've met a half-dozen times. He says I've got to learn to be calm."

"Sounds like a good idea to me," said Dr. Cameron.

Looking back on it, I still don't understand how I was able to get through the 1985-86 season. Flying suddenly became a challenge, even though it had never bothered me before. I'd get around that by sitting on the team charter alongside players such as Ryan Walter, a born-again Christian who loved to talk but didn't push his views on people. If a guy wanted to discuss the subject, however, Ryan was quite happy to oblige. I owe him a lot.

The breathing and eating problems continued through the season. Over time, though, the loss of appetite began to show up only every second day.

My weekly meetings with Dr. Spevack continued, even though like many individuals receiving counselling, there were times when I wondered what I was doing there.

"We're not going to get this done in a matter of only a few visits," he said. "I'll know when I can't do anything more with you. More important, you'll know because you'll be feeling better. This thing takes time. It takes work."

What it took was a lot of talking about many subjects, including my work and the effect my illness was having on my wife and children. We talked about a lot of things – and then one day early in 1986, after some five months of visits, Dr. Spevack announced he didn't want to see me at Montreal General any more.

"You sure?" I asked.

"I'm sure," he said.

My breathing continued to improve. So did my appetite. I exercised vigorously. I made it through the season.

Nobody ever said it would be easy.

24

Looking Back, Moving Ahead

I was twenty-seven when I joined the *Montreal Star*. One year later, I was hand-delivered something young reporters would kill for. Well, almost.

"How'd you like to write a daily column?" Ken Edey, the *Star*'s managing editor, asked one spring day in 1955. I had written a few columns on an irregular basis, but Edey had something more consistent in mind. "Five a week," he said. "Interested?"

"I've always wanted to do the National Hockey League beat, Mr. Edey."

"You can do both," said Edey.

"The desk work, too?" I asked. What that involved was editing stories written by other reporters, writing headlines, and selecting photographs for the sports pages.

"The desk work, too," he grinned.

I carried a big stick with me into the column-writing business. I picked the biggest names I could find and came out swinging. The bigger, the better.

Edey was back the following week. "It's your column," he said. "If you want to go after big names for a good reason, that's fine. I don't have a problem with that. If you're doing it just to get attention, well, maybe you're the wrong guy for the job."

He was right, of course. I turned down the volume.

Those were exciting days. A daily column, the NHL beat, and desk work weren't a full plate: they were a banquet. A Swaps-Nashua horse race brought me to Arlington Park in Chicago, a Floyd Patterson–Archie Moore heavyweight championship fight to Chicago Stadium. It was a good fight, but what I remember most about it is that after filing the story and column, I decided to walk from the Stadium to the LaSalle Hotel in downtown Chicago. Chicago Stadium was located in one of the meanest areas of the city and I wasn't more than half a block away when a police car screeched to a halt.

The cop on the passenger side rolled down the window. "Where you goin', buddy?" he asked.

"The LaSalle Hotel."

"You stupid or somethin'? Get in the car," he ordered. "We'll drive you downtown. People don't walk in this area, bud. We keep our windows rolled up around here, know what I mean?"

That same year, the British Empire and Commonwealth Games were being held in Vancouver. Roger Bannister, of England, and John Landy, of Australia, would be meeting in the "Miracle Mile" on Saturday, August 4. Was I interested? Edey asked.

"Sounds good," I said.

"One problem," he said. "You've got to do the story off the television. We'll have about ten minutes from the start of the race to get it all into the late afternoon edition. We'll be carrying the story on the first page of the paper."

Bannister and Landy ran the Miracle Mile in Vancouver, both covering the distance in less than four minutes. I ran it in the *Star* office, with Edey and news editor Dermot Baker ripping sheets out of my typewriter paragraph by paragraph. It wasn't the best play-by-play of a race in newspaper history, but it was the fastest. A Miracle Mile, so to speak. When it was over, it was a toss-up who was breathing more heavily: Bannister, Landy, or me.

When I started travelling with the Canadiens, Western Union was the fastest, most secure, and, truth be told, the only way to file out-of-town stories to a newspaper office. Reporters who worked for an afternoon newspaper such as the *Star*, had more than enough time to get the job done. A game would end at, say, 10:30 p.m. The next thirty minutes, or longer if the extra time was needed, were spent visiting dressing rooms and talking with the coaches and players. This was followed by a leisurely ride back to the hotel. Once the story was finished, the three or four typewritten sheets would be delivered to the nearest Western Union office, where an operator would have it on its way in a matter of minutes. It was a foolproof system . . . almost.

There was a game in Detroit one night. Later, a story and column were delivered to the Western Union office. No sweat.

I flew back to Montreal the next morning. The game story was in the paper. There was no sign of the column.

I telephoned the overnight editor at his home. He told me he'd received the story of the Canadiens–Wings game in plenty of time. "I wasn't told you also had a column coming," he explained. "If I had, I would have telephoned you in Detroit."

A little later, the telephone rang in my home. A man who identified himself as the foreman of a machine shop in suburban St. Lambert was on the line. "I think I've got something that belongs to you," he said.

"You mean . . ."

"Yeah, your column. It's from Detroit. I guess the Western Union guy sent it to the wrong place."

"I guess," I said.

"What do I do with it?" asked the machine-shop foreman.

"I'll give you one guess," I said.

"It's that bad, eh?" he said.

Everything about the business of reporting has changed since then. Filing has become faster, easier, and as foolproof as eight hundred words being transmitted in less than one minute from a lightweight computer over a telephone line can be. Most of the time, that is, but not always.

Four years ago, the Canadiens were on a ten-day trip to Europe. First, six days in Stockholm, where the livin' was easy and so were the communications. Want a telephone line? No problem. One telephone number brings in the operator in Montreal. Piece of cake.

Leningrad, by contrast, was stale bread. There were thirty media persons on this hockey pilgrimage. Imagine our dismay when we learned that from 8:00 p.m. until the following morning, no telephone lines would be available. No lines out, none in. We were cut off from the rest of the world. A person in hiding in Kuwait could pick up a phone and be heard crying for help live on CNN, but Kuwait wasn't Leningrad.

"Sorry, the operator is sick. There are no lines," said the matron behind the hotel desk. "Be patient. There will be a line at 8 o'clock in the morning. In the morning, you will see."

"I can't wait until the morning," I said. "I must have a line into Montreal at midnight."

"There are no lines. Moscow," she said. "Everything is Moscow. There are no lines."

"We will pay the operator U.S. dollars."

"Tomorrow. Tomorrow you will be happy."

Mikhail Gorbachev was still in charge of a whole Soviet Union at the time, but cracks were starting to show. People were angry. There were demonstrations on the streets. It was at this point that Vladimir showed up at the hotel.

Wherever Soviet hockey teams would travel, Vladimir would be there. His name might be different from venue to venue, but he would look the same. He would describe himself as a team trainer, but it would be obvious that he had never, ever hefted a water bottle or taped a hockey stick. This particular Vlad was a big man, with a face as round and as soft as a Soviet meatball. His blond hair was coiffed, Western style. He wore a cream-coloured suit which hid his soft middle beautifully. Alligator shoes. He smiled a lot. So did his partner.

Vladimir said he understood the problem. He apologized. He was very sorry, really he was. Somebody else's fault. Moscow. He would try to see what he could do to solve the problem, but it would be very difficult. He would try.

Vladimir made a lot of calls. Or, at least, so it seemed. Trainers are gentle souls. They take orders. Vladimir gave them. It took hours, but things started to happen. As if by magic, a telephone line appeared out of the Leningrad sky. You could almost hear it falling into the media room – but only after some hard-nosed, Western negotiating.

"It is possible to get one line," Vladimir explained, "but it will be expensive. It will be a thousand dollars. There are people who must be paid. Not me. Important people."

"Rubles?"

"U.S.," said Vladimir.

Thirty media persons spent the best part of the night taking turns on one telephone line. It was not much fun dictating stories at 4:00 a.m., Leningrad time.

"There will not be any problems tomorrow," promised Vladimir. "Do not worry. Everything will be done that must be done. Tomorrow, lines for everybody. Only a thousand dollars," said Vladimir.

The next day, only one line was available. The price: five thousand dollars.

Riga, the Latvian capital, wasn't much better.

"It will take a little while for a telephone line," said the person behind the hotel desk, "but we will get you one, in time. You will not be able to transmit on your computer. The telephone lines, they are not so good for that. You will be expected to pay in rubles for the time you spend on the telephone."

"How much?"

"We will see."

259

"Okay."

Eventually, the word came down: twenty rubles per minute which, at the black market exchange, was a little more than a dollar U.S. Two stories: forty minutes. The *Gazette* could afford forty dollars U.S. No problem. The telephone line wasn't available until 2:00 a.m., Riga time. The stories were dictated to the *Gazette* office in roughly forty minutes.

"There is a telephone bill you must pay before you leave," the front-desk person said the next day.

"I'm aware of that. I was on for about forty minutes. At twenty rubles, well . . . here." I deposited eight hundred rubles on the desk.

"That will be in golden rubles," she said.

"What's a golden ruble?"

"Golden rubles, please."

"I do not know what a golden ruble looks like. I do not have any golden rubles."

"In that case," she said, "you will have to pay in U.S. dollars. That will be 548 dollars U.S."

The media circus travelling with the Canadiens in Europe was indicative of what has become the best and the worst about this business of reporting.

In the mid-1950s, only three print-media people travelled with the Canadiens during the regular season, even though at least a half-dozen dailies and at least that number of weeklies were publishing in the city. Shrinking newspaper circulation has kept the print media to three even today, but now at least five radio broadcast people are on most trips. Television brings in at least a half-dozen more. During the playoffs, the media family can swell to twenty-five.

Some days, the road isn't much fun, even when you're in the relatively comfortable confines of North America as opposed to Eastern Europe.

How old was he? Five? Maybe six? The Canadiens were meeting

the Maple Leafs in Toronto in a couple of hours. Time for a telephone call home before heading to the Gardens.

"Everything all right?" I asked my wife.

"Yes, I guess so . . ." Then her voice broke. "It's Ian. The doctor says it's scarlet fever."

You've probably gone through it. You hear the words and they're like a blow to the chest. It's hard to breathe. "I'll take the next plane home," I said.

Tillie said no, said there was nothing I could do even if I was in Montreal. I thought, my son is on fire more than three hundred miles away and you're not there because there's a hockey game less than two hours away.

Hell! Walk it off! That's it, walk! Back and forth . . . back and forth . . . and suddenly the hotel room is like a cage. All that's missing are the bars. Banging a fist against the wall doesn't help. Nothing helps – and then the tears come. They help.

The game was a blur that night. So was everything else for a couple of days until the fever broke and the kid managed a weak grin. "Where you been, Dad?" he said. "You look awful."

The road is one of the perks linked with covering a beat but, obviously, not always. Once in a while, it becomes part of office politics.

"We've got to talk," the Montreal Star's managing editor, Art Wood, said to me one day in the mid-1970s. "The union's in here now and you've got to make a decision."

I was head of the sports department at this time, overseeing a staff of nine. I was also covering the Canadiens at home and on the road.

"You won't be able to do it now that the union is looking over your shoulder," Wood explained. "You can't travel and be an administrator at the same time. It's one or the other."

"No problem," I said. "I'll travel."

Wood's proposed division of labour was hardly a surprise. I could see it coming. Several months earlier, while the Canadiens were on a lengthy road trip, he had invited the sports-department staff into his office for one-on-one meetings. Each was asked a simple question: Was Fisher too tough to work for? The answers were predictable. Those, like baseball writer Bob Dunn, who always put in a good day's work, had my full support. The clock-watchers had problems.

"If you want to keep on travelling and writing, I'll have to bring somebody else in to run the place," said Wood.

"Are you sure you want to do that?" I asked.

"You'll still be the boss," he promised, "but somebody else will have to do the day-to-day stuff."

I said I'd work with whomever Wood hired, but predicted that a "disaster" was in the offing.

Wood was as good as his word. Within a week, a news-desk person was brought in to handle the assignments and the small mountain of paperwork linked with running a department.

One morning, a week or so later, there was a memo on my desk from an overnight member of the staff. "Who's my boss?" the note read.

The reply I left in his mailbox was brief. "I am."

The next day, I was in Wood's office. He waved the note I had left. "You're not in charge," said Wood.

"That's not what you told me a week ago," I said. "What you said was that you were bringing somebody in to handle the assignments and paperwork, but I was still in charge."

Wood shrugged.

"If that's what you want, Art, here's what I'm going to do. I'm cleaning out my desk and from now on I'll do my work from home. You don't need me in here."

He shrugged again.

I left.

My decision was wrong, largely because it made life miserable for my wife. There was still all that travelling to do with the Canadiens, but now I was underfoot all of the days the Canadiens were at home – except for the few hours each morning I spent watching practices and gathering information for the next day's paper. It wasn't much fun for me, because I had too much free time on my hands, and no fun at all for my wife. Where I was dead right, though, was that the disaster I suspected would happen at the office, did happen. Three sports editors later, Wood was on the telephone. "You've got to come back and take over."

"What for?" I asked. "I'm having fun at home."

"We've had $55,000 in overtime for the sports department during the past year," he thundered. "That's got to stop."

"It shouldn't be too hard to cut out most of that overtime," I said. "But if you want me back to run the department, I still want to travel with the club."

"Do whatever you want," he said, "but I want you in here tomorrow. You've got to make some sense out of this overtime."

A year later, the department's overtime expenditure had been slashed to roughly $5,000. That, needless to say, left a few of the staff somewhat disgruntled. Wood, of course, was elated.

"I hope you understand that the biggest reason we saved about $50,000 was that I did a lot of the work myself," I told him. "I've put in a lot of extra time here this past year. I think I deserve a piece of the action."

"What have you got in mind?" he asked.

"What have *you* got in mind?" I asked.

"Tell you what . . . when are you going on holidays?" he asked.

"Pretty soon."

"Here's what I'll do: go on holidays, write a couple of travel pieces for us, and we'll pay for the holiday for you and your wife."

"It's not what I had in mind," I said, "but I'll talk to my wife about it."

"Where do you want to go for a holiday?" I asked her that night.

"Israel," she said. "Let's go to Israel for three weeks."

"It's all set," I told Wood the next morning. "We're going to Israel for three weeks."

"I've changed my mind," said Wood.

By now, you may suspect that in this business, you win a few and lose a few. Nothing is carved in stone.

When I joined the *Montreal Star*, the working week was six days and each day started at 6:30 a.m. On game nights, they didn't end until midnight, often later. The pay in March, 1954: $110 per week. On the other hand, Henri Richard earned only $7,000 with the Canadiens when he joined the team for the 1955-56 season.

In other words, sportswriting wasn't a get-rich-quick vocation. It still isn't, although newspaper salaries have greatly improved since the 1960s. What it is, is something I've wanted to do ever since I was a kid. It has gone through one upheaval after another, affecting both my professional and personal life. On the other hand, it's been everything I thought it would be. It's been everything I've wanted it to be.

What does it take? It helps if you happen to be a workaholic. I take no great pride in admitting I put the job first, but it won't work unless you're blessed with a perfect marriage partner, which Tillie has been since we were married on that Sunday in June in 1948. The uncommon amount of time I've spent travelling didn't exactly set me up as a father-of-the-year candidate, but Tillie has always been there for me, and still is. It takes a special person to understand and accept the idea of being alone roughly six months of the year while your husband is hundreds and, often, thousands of miles away doing his job.

"Don't you get tired of the travelling?" I've been asked that over and over again in recent years, and the answer is yes, of course. Wouldn't anyone? It's draining. It often hurts a marriage, although my wife of forty-six years insists to this day it has helped ours. Travelling comes with the job of being a beat-writer and/or columnist. Anyone who can't handle it should move on to something else.

There's more pressure on the job than there once was. Is this because there's a new breed of athlete out there, part-celebrity, part-entrepreneur, part-whatever? Is it because a new breed of media person emerged in the '80s and '90s? Whatever the cause, there's certainly more suspicion. More mistrust. Tempers are strained.

All-sports stations and radio hot-line shows contribute to a forest of rumours. Myths attain the status of truth, gossip takes on the aroma of fact.

Women sportswriters have been part of the changing face of sport – for the better. In many cases, much better. They're my kind of guy, so to speak. They work as hard as any of their male colleagues and harder than most. It's true that dressing rooms have been opened to them but, sadly, some coaches, players, and male sportswriters still haven't made women sportswriters wholly welcome or comfortable.

I was there the first time a woman reporter visited a team's dressing room. It happened in 1975. Robin Herman, a *New York Times* reporter, had been assigned to an All-Star Game at the Montreal Forum. After the game, I was talking with Phil Esposito. My back was to the dressing-room door. We had been talking for several minutes, when Phil's head suddenly jerked up. "Whoa! Wait a minute! Is that a broad?"

I turned. Ms. Herman was there. Entering the dressing room was a small step for Ms. Herman, a giant step for women sportswriters.

"Yeah, I guess so," I replied.

"Boy," said Esposito, "she's got balls!"

What makes sportswriting so fulfilling? For one thing, athletes keep a guy young. Games and ideas don't age: people do. Today's best athletes are younger, faster, stronger, and richer. They're also better. Has this, in turn, generated a new golden era of sports reportage?

I have met and read sportswriters in recent years who would have made my all-star reportage team, just as Wayne Gretzky would have easily made any All-Star Team in the six-team National Hockey League. I have also met sportswriters of the so-called modern era who are impostors. They beat the perks to death, but skate miles to avoid the perils.

As mentioned earlier, my favourite four-letter word almost from the moment I started in this business is "fair." There's nothing wrong with criticism as long as it's fair. The late Jimmy Cannon, who was a New York sportswriting icon, always used to offer this suggestion: "Don't complain when I knock you if you didn't say thanks when I applauded you." It's immensely important to be fair. The athletes I have known respect it. They're open with sportswriters they respect. They're tight-lipped with those they don't.

Sounds fair to me.

It's why I plan to keep on doing this until I get it right.

Index

267